GRIEVANCE PROCEDURES

Grievance procedures

A.W.J. THOMSON
Glasgow University
V.V. MURRAY
York University
Toronto

SAXON HOUSE | LEXINGTON BOOKS

Published by

SAXON HOUSE, D.C. Heath Ltd.
Westmead, Farnborough, Hants., England

Jointly with

LEXINGTON BOOKS, D.C. Heath & Co.
Lexington, Mass. USA

ISBN 0 347 01128 4

Library of Congress Catalog Card Number 75–44745
Printed in Great Britain by Robert MacLehose & Co. Ltd.
Printers to the University of Glasgow

iv

This book is to be returned on
or before the date stamped below

UNIVERSITY OF PLYMOUTH

PLYMOUTH LIBRARY

Tel: (01752) 232323

This book is subject to recall if required by another reader

Books may be renewed by phone

CHARGES WILL BE MADE FOR OVERDUE BOOKS

A book may be renewed by telephone or by personal visit
if it is not required by another reader.

CHARGES WILL BE MADE FOR OVERDUE BOOKS

Contents

List of tables

List of figures

Preface and acknowledgements

The desirability of an effective system of grievance handling is now taken for granted in modern industrial relations; indeed the obligation to have a procedure was written into the Industrial Relations Act of 1971. Yet there has always been uncertainty about the way in which grievances are actually handled at plant level, and even more uncertainty as to what constitutes a 'good' procedure in any given context – the Commission on Industrial Relations, whose terms of reference included the subject of procedures, was unfortunately wound up before its work was completed. It is to these issues, therefore, although hardly to their definitive resolution, that this study is directed, and thanks are due to the SSRC, the Canada Council, the Canada Department of Labour and the Bronfman Foundation for providing financial assistance.

A large number of individuals were interviewed during the fieldwork phase of the research. Without a single exception, all were unfailingly courteous and responsive, and many, indeed, went well beyond the bounds of the questionnaire in their answers, sometimes to the detriment of the time available for completing all the topics! For their very evident interest, and the obvious effort which they put into answering the questions as fully as possible, we are extremely grateful. Again, a considerable number of people had to be contacted to make organisational arrangements, and here we would like to give special thanks to Mr F.J. Lawton of the Food Manufacturers' Federation and the Hon. W.G.M. Spens of the Federation of British Carpet Manufacturers. Various academic colleagues have also given help in a number of ways: L.C. Hunter and S.R. Engleman in particular have given up a good deal of time in commenting at intervals on successive drafts. We alone, however, are responsible for any remaining deficiencies. Again, several secretaries have less than congenial memories of the typing required: most of the burden has been borne by Mrs E. Cousin and her successor, Miss M. Halliday. The last thanks are to our wives for their patience and encouragement, as well as sundry editorial services.

A.W.J. Thomson
V.V. Murray
January 1976

1 Introduction

> It would, moreover, be unjust to ask men to abide by procedures which, as everyone knows, cannot deal with some of the most important grievances, and which more often than not yield no result at all. It would be futile to expect men to be deterred from using the strike weapon if they know that its speedy use is the only means at their disposal to get speedy redress for their grievances.
>
> Those resorting to unconstitutional action should not be threatened with any disadvantages imposed by law until new procedures have been put into operation, procedures which are clear where the present procedures are vague, comprehensive where the present procedures are fragmentary, speedy where the present procedures are protracted, and effective where the present procedures are fruitless.[1]

This book examines the operation of grievance procedures at the level of the establishment, a subject which is close to the heart of the present concern about British industrial relations, a concern which was expressed (with impressive pungency for a Royal Commission report) in the quotation at the head of the page. For all the Donovan Commission's sense of urgency on this question, however, and for all that the 1971 Industrial Relations Act imposed an obligation on employers to provide a procedure for grievance resolution, few would assert that procedural reform has achieved the effective reduction of unconstitutional action which Donovan saw as its objective. To be sure, the Commission saw many other facets of the British industrial relations system as being in need of reform, and it is unfair to blame only deficiencies in the procedural area for the present difficulties of the system. Nevertheless, the grievance procedure is a subsystem of the larger collective bargaining process and represents perhaps the primary mechanism by which the industrial parties interact on a day-to-day basis. As such, it deserves more critical attention than it has received. In particular, we would argue that the structure of procedures contributes significantly to their effectiveness: indeed, we would further argue that while procedures cannot prevent the occurrence of 'primary' conflict resulting from the industrial relationship and its environment, inadequate procedures can be a source of 'secondary' conflict resulting from the inefficiency of the mode of resolution of the primary conflict. We therefore reject the view that the procedure itself is unimportant, as

1

expressed in the argument advanced by the Confederation of British Industry that 'Experience shows that without goodwill on both sides no procedure is effective in practice; on the other hand given goodwill many issues will be resolved informally and the actual form of the agreement becomes of relatively minor importance.'[2] At the same time, however, we would not go to the other extreme of arguing that 'procedures govern results'.[3]

The origins of the present study lay in the lack of knowledge about what happens within the establishment, as opposed to the more extended, although by no means comprehensive, surveys of dispute handling above the establishment through the traditional industry-wide channels.[4] Thus in his leading work on the subject of procedures in 1966 Marsh wrote:

> National procedure agreements seldom lay down in much detail the procedural position in the workshop; many do not lay it down at all. In some establishments written procedures have been drawn up. There is no ready means of determining the proportion of establishments in which such procedures exist; probably in a majority of *large* establishments and in a minority of *all* establishments in the country. But investigation shows that, even where procedures are written, they seldom operate strictly 'according to the book', partly because the issues to be dealt with are too varying and complex to make this easily practicable, and partly because most managements are too little concerned about the letter of procedures to administer them consistently or invariably.[5]

Even allowing for the increase in numbers of domestic procedures as a result of the urging of the Donovan Report and the obligations imposed by the Industrial Relations Act, we still do not know a great deal more about the operation of procedures than this account suggests. How far have similar patterns developed within any given category of situation, and what are the reasons for differences between categories; what is the balance between the formal and informal operation of procedures; what are the main issues and the roles of the different actors? Investigation of questions such as these can clearly contribute to the development of soundly based procedures.

But as well as surveying actual practice, it is desirable to do more in the way of constructing an analytical framework for relating the various factors to each other. It is arguably a legitimate criticism of previous work in this field that it has tended to adopt a historical and institutional approach.[6] There has been relatively little input from the behavioural and social sciences, although some attempts at building models of workplace

2

behaviour are now beginning to emerge.[7] In particular, it is surprising that little attention has been given to the workplace as a source of material for theories of conflict and conflict resolution. While the various recommendations which have been made about changes in the British system have for the most part been based on intimate practical knowledge, they have not incorporated any satisfactory system of differentiating one situation from another. Marsh and McCarthy used three criteria for evaluating procedures, namely whether they were 'acceptable', 'appropriate' and 'in the public interest',[8] but these criteria were applied on an *ex-post facto* basis with reference to industry-wide procedures and, while useful, it is far from certain that they can be easily applied on an *ex-ante* basis in the context of the individual plant seeking to improve its institutions. Dunlop, in his seminal work on industrial relations systems, pointed out that 'the web of rules' will vary according to market, technological and power factors, and that this will be true of procedural as well as substantive rules.[9] What is required, it can be argued, is some means of translating these into operational terms in the structure of procedures, without in any sense pretending that a universal model or prescription can be developed.[10] Before taking up these issues, however, we shall describe the historical background to the procedural situation described in the opening quotation, and secondly, the contents of this book, and in particular the nature of the fieldwork carried out for the study.

The development of procedures

One of the key aspects of the existing structure is that it has been the outcome of a long period of organic and separate development in the various different industries, interspersed with important incidents. Indeed the strength of the system lies in its traditions, to which have accrued a continuity and a significance not found anywhere else in the world. As Flanders commented with reference to unions: 'The normative and binding characteristics which traditions acquire is due to their having proved their worth as patterns of behaviour which have consistently succeeded in advancing the group's goals and values.'[11] So it has appeared with procedures. But this does not explain how the traditions grew up, and, in particular for our purposes, why institutions and procedures did not emerge at the level of the establishment, even though many unions originated as works clubs within particular establishments. It is therefore desirable to turn to the nineteenth-century origins of present-day institutions to see why this was so.

3

In considering the development of institutions, employers, motivated by a property ideology, could be expected to resist strongly any threat to their prerogative of control within their own establishments. Nor was there any law to force recognition on them. On the union side there was the general objective of 'the common rule', and also a suspicion of 'works' unionism, based on a feeling that it meant lack of independence and domination by the employer. Thus in Cole's words:

> In most occupations, therefore, no regret was felt as the works basis of Trade Union organisation was gradually superseded, and most Trade Unionists were not conscious of the need for it. The problem of the period was for them the successful establishment of standard or minimum district conditions: the insistence was all on the uniformity of conditions throughout the Trade, and not on diverse problems arising in particular trades.[12]

There were various more explicit reasons for this development. In the craft-based trades there was little interest in joint action with men of other trades in the place of work, who were seen as potential rivals for aspects of job ownership and control. Links were formed rather on a geographical basis, with fellow craftsmen in other establishments. In other industries, often with non-craft operatives but with a homogeneous product, the need was for a common wage rate to prevent wage competition, and, as writers such as Burgess have pointed out,[13] union leaders were happy to develop external structures and procedures because these gave them greater control over policies which might endanger the union organisation and funds, and thus their own positions.

The first joint dispute solving institutions developed in the homogeneous product industries in the form of boards of arbitration or conciliation, mainly to decide issues of pay. Coal, iron and steel, footwear, and the various textile trades were examples of industries where such boards grew up on a district basis in the 1860s and 1870s. But although the boards continued to grow in number,[14] the features of external arbitration which had been so significant in the early years declined in importance as industry-based disputes procedures grew up, such as the 1893 Brooklands agreement in cotton textiles, which brought the ultimate decision making back into the hands of representatives of the industry who became effectively collective bargaining bodies.

In the craft-based trades, especially engineering, boards developed less readily. This was primarily because the traditions of both employers and the craft unions did not easily accept decisions being made outside the control of the parties, given the detailed nature of negotiations, which tended to be much more complex than wage bargaining. Moreover, compromise was less easy than over wages and there was less room for external standards or equity. The key factor was that both sides wanted unilateral control over job regulation in the workplace. It was this question, especially in the area of machine manning, which led to the great strikes and lockouts in engineering in 1897–98. These battles were followed by the effective imposition by the employers of a procedure for avoiding disputes, creating the framework of works, local and national conferences which stood (with some modifications) until 1971. Essentially, it enabled the employers to stand together, to make issues of job regulations within the individual shop a 'federation' question. It was significant that the national procedure pre-dated a national bargaining structure.[15] A somewhat similar process of development occurred in construction. Thus for rather different reasons, the issue of formal workplace procedures did not really arise in either of the two main types of unionised occupation, although there was undoubtedly interaction of a limited kind, and checkweighmen in the coal industry and fathers of the chapel in printing were well established as workplace representatives before the end of the nineteenth century.

The period of the First World War brought three significant developments. One was the extension of district bargaining to national bargaining, largely as a result of the system of compulsory arbitration that was set up under the 1915 Industrial Arbitration Act. Another was the shop stewards' movement in the engineering industry, which, although often characterised as political in nature, was in the first instance primarily a battle for control over working conditions at shopfloor level in a period of great industrial pressure and change. Nevertheless, it went well beyond trying to set up some sort of procedural mechanism to reflect the workers' interests, seeking to assert workers' control in a more absolute form, although there were doubtless many establishments where the concentration was on the resolution of workshop issues. The unrest did however draw attention to the lack of adequate institutions, and resulted in the third major development, the setting up of the Whitley Committee. This recommended the extension of collective bargaining through a tripartite structure at industry and district levels and, through works committees, at the plant level. Although seventy-three JICs were established in between 1918 and 1921, the move to set up works committees was far less successful. As Charles has commented: 'Experience was to show that the problems of establishing this structure were very great; works committees required singularly favourable conditions. They were not considered seriously as part of the industrial relations structure in the majority of the JICs.'[16] One reason for this was that although Whitley decreed a number of functions which should be carried out below national level, including the development of disputes procedures, these were not supposed to interfere with 'questions such as rates of wages and hours of work, which should be settled by District or National agreement.' A further reason was that employers were still not prepared to compromise their managerial functions at plant level, and sought the assistance of their fellow employers on difficult issues arising at the workplace. The major battle over this question came in engineering, as might be expected, and in the 1922 lockout the employers were able to reinforce the 1898 disputes procedure with its emphasis on external grievance settlement, *ad hoc* decisions, and employer solidarity. After 1922, and particularly after the General Strike, the power of the shopfloor workforce to enforce joint regulation diminished, but as a goal it was never forgotten.

Soon after 1922 it could be said that the main outlines of the 'traditional' structure of industrial relations had come into existence. If we look at the structure of formal procedures as it existed roughly between the mid-1920s and the mid-1960s[17] we can see a spectrum across industries with an absence of any written agreement at all at one end, a broad framework leaving detailed arrangements for operation to be determined by custom or practice in the centre, and a considerable amount of detail at the other end. A few industries distinguished between disputes of various kinds and in some cases provided separate machinery. In all instances the attempt to settle within the plant was seen as being only a single stage. At the establishment level there was little or no discussion of the need for any formal structure, although at all times, even during the Depression, a good deal of informal negotiation and grievance resolution took place.

Associated with this system were certain characteristic values which can be subsumed under the concept of voluntarism, whose twin advantages Flanders saw as 'permitting flexibility' and 'encouraging responsibility'. Flexibility meant that 'the parties could leave themselves with a good deal of freedom to adjust the application of their agreed rules to the circumstances of individual cases [and] to suit changing conditions.' Responsibility involved the conception that 'difficult issues of conflict, whether over the terms of a new agreement or the application of an old one, could not easily be transferred to a third party', which in this sense meant one external to the industry.[18] It also meant that sanctions were social, not legal. Procedural rather than substantive rules were the key to the operation of voluntarism. As Marsh put it, there has been a 'tendency in the British system for the parties to rely for their relationship upon mere frameworks of substantive rules and to improvise their detailed joint regulation upon procedural handling of grievances.'[19] Alongside voluntarism lay the concept of pluralism or mutual survival, which meant a recognition by both sides of interdependence and a vested interest in each other's belief in the stability and integrity of the system. Each side must accept the legitimacy of the other's aspirations and be willing to temper demands so as not to threaten the other's survival. Even if some conflict were overt, compromise must be the essence of decision making.

This system has been argued by writers such as Kahn-Freund to be significantly different in its methods of conflict resolution from those of other developed countries.[20] Kahn-Freund, writing in 1954, differentiated between 'dynamic' and 'static' methods of formulating standards. The former, operating in Britain, determines standards through procedural institutions so as to permit continuous adaption according to changing circumstances, while the latter, covering most other countries, involves signing contracts laying down mutual obligations over a given range of issues and normally for some minimum period of time. In Britain the constitutional nature of the relationship has traditionally been contained solely within the procedural agreements between the parties, whereas in most other countries it is backed by legislation. The autonomy of the parties from the legal process is in fact a key to the dynamic system, since norms can continually be challenged and provide no basis for intervention by the law, whereas a static system both results from and contributes to control by law. Differentiation can be made in principle and, with somewhat more difficulty, in practice between issues of contract negotiation and interpretation. In the dynamic system, by contrast, 'there is no separation of powers: legislation, administration and adjudication all range into one', and the bodies concerned with the creation of the collective relationship are frequently the same as those responsible for enforcing and interpreting it. On the other hand, the social values of the dynamic system must be such as to permit the relationship to continue, since only social sanctions are available to enforce decisions and the methods of arriving at them. Hence voluntarism.

In explaining these differences, much has depended on the role of the state in developing the basic industrial relations structure. In most countries the labour movement was dependent on the state for setting up its basic rights of recognition and consequently had to accept as a *quid pro quo* some measure of legal control of the processes of collective bargaining. In many cases, indeed, the state felt the need to protect the individual more directly through a system of labour courts. In Britain, by contrast, while it was certainly true that the industrial and political parties accepted a minimal role for the state, the judiciary nevertheless tried to impose the common law

7

and was only prevented from doing so by a series of statutes culminating in the 1906 Trade Disputes Act. It would be wrong, therefore, to characterise voluntarism as something which evolved naturally and without interference. It was a measure of the strength of the labour movement that not only was it able to develop a strong bargaining relationship without state aid, but it was also able to take on, and defeat, one of the main constitutional branches of the state. No other labour movement can claim anything approaching this degree of control over its own development.

The highwater mark of the traditional system might be said to be the 1950s, when Kahn-Freund challenged anyone to say the system was not working well. In the years since then, however, the system has fallen from grace. Indeed, in spite of the stability which Kahn-Freund saw, it is now thought that both the structure and the spirit of procedures were being undermined by economic forces at both national and shopfloor level even before that.[21] On the one hand governments sought to influence (and later to determine) the macroeconomic levels of wage settlement, whilst on the other there was an increase in the power of workshop negotiations. These were Flanders' 'challenges from above and below',[22] which required different procedural and institutional mechanisms from those of the traditional industry-wide system. The challenge from above required some form of incomes policy, while that from below (according to the Donovan Commission) required a reconstitution of plant level relationships.

The reasons for the twin challenges are many and varied, but full employment was undoubtedly the single major factor. It meant less constraint on the actions of plant level negotiators, less power for union officials over their rank and file, and less credibility for employers' sanctions. In any case, employers could generally offset higher labour costs with higher prices, and they had to be prepared to compete for adequate supplies of labour. The result was a shift in the main focus of bargaining from industry to plant level, where the nebulous existing procedures frequently proved inadequate to the task of resolving the new level of conflict. Moreover, the values and structure of procedure had been created by national level bodies on both sides and it did not necessarily follow that these were equally acceptable at the lower levels to which power was now shifting. This is not to say that the existing industry level procedures did not continue to perform useful functions, indeed they were increasingly used in the 1960s. Nevertheless, they were to be strongly criticised by the Donovan Commission. Recognition of the developing difficulties of local institutions was first made by the TUC in its 1960 General Council Report. It made a strong defence of unions that were accused of breaching procedure, pointing out that these accusations were often onesided and manipulated for purposes of delay. But perhaps the key sentence was the assertion that: 'Recognition for wages alone is not enough',[23] since this showed that a wider range of issues were being included in the new grievances, and these were frequently not suited to the industry-wide system. When the Labour Party came to power in 1964 it handed the problem over to the Donovan Commission.

The evidence on which the Commission based its report was of two kinds: research which it commissioned itself, and views of interested bodies and individuals. The former was of far more value than the latter which tended to be defensive and unimaginative in nature.[24] Thus the CBI, in its evidence, was distinctly complacent about procedures:

> Employers attach the greatest importance to the voluntary machinery for the prevention and settlement of disputes . . . They consider that the comparatively good record of the British industrial relations system in preserving industrial peace is primarily due to the constant attention given by both employers and unions to the development and preservation of these procedures.[25]

The TUC was much more critical, essentially repeating its comments of 1960. Nevertheless, it did not seem able to conceive of the concomitant existence of national and domestic procedures:

> The reason why there is virtually no local negotiation of procedure agreements is that disputes may involve machinery external to a particular enterprise, such as joint national machinery . . . It is not easy to negotiate procedure agreements in such a way as to take account both of local characteristics and of the need for an orderly procedure for calling in parties to the national procedure agreement at a higher level.[26]

From such comments it can clearly be seen that there was little recognition by the leadership of the main industrial parties that the real problem lay within the enterprise, not between it and the industry level. In this respect Donovan performed a signal service. The Report, published in June 1968, took as its main theme the discrepancy between the formal and the informal system of industrial relations. It noted the great importance of workshop bargaining, which, in Flanders' words, was 'largely informal, largely fragmented, and largely autonomous.'[27] For its development and the failure to develop adequate institutions in changing circumstances, both management and unions were strongly criticised. The Report was also strongly critical of procedures, as noted in the opening quotation of this chapter. But whilst recognising the apparent advantages to the participants, the Report argued that the shortcomings outweighed any benefits and condemned 'the tendency of extreme decentralisation and self-government to degenerate into indecision and anarchy; the propensity to breed inefficiency; and the reluctance to change – all of them characteristics which become more damaging as they develop.' [28]

In paragraph 182 the Report set out what have come to be accepted as its major recommendations, namely the actions that should be taken in order to help bring into existence a more orderly system of industrial relations at plant level. All are significant, but the first two are worth quoting in full. The Report suggested that boards of directors should review industrial relations within their undertakings with the following objectives in mind:

1 To develop, together with trade unions representative of their employees, comprehensive and authoritative collective bargaining machinery to deal at company and/or factory level with the terms and conditions of employment which are settled at these levels.
2 To develop, together with the unions, procedures for the rapid and equitable settlement of grievances in a manner consistent with the relevant collective agreements.

The Report and its associated publications had attacked many aspects of the British system of industrial relations with procedures in the forefront. It was therefore to be expected that either the Report would be heavily criticised, or that re-evaluation and reform of the system would take place. In fact, the Report was only mildly criticised, from the political right for being insufficiently positive in imposing reform, and from the left for threatening the role of shop stewards and shopfloor bargaining. From the primary representative bodies, the CBI and the TUC, there was acceptance with reservations in a joint statement recognising the need for review in a number of fields, including plant level institutions.

But however much statements like these might express a general willingness to re-examine the whole bargaining structure, it was soon apparent that the message had not been entirely assimilated and that change would only be slow. Not only were the parties at establishment level unprepared for change but they were not at all sure how to go about it or what criteria to use. The Donovan Commission was not unaware of this problem, and recommended an agent of change, the Commission on Industrial Relations, which was duly set up by the Labour government early in 1969 to provide leadership through research and investigation. At the same time, a parallel body within the Department of Employment and Productivity – the

Manpower and Productivity Service – was instructed to monitor the procedure agreements of the largest companies. More will be said in later chapters about developments in voluntary reform, but it must be noted here that progress has been overshadowed by the attempts of both major political parties to hasten the pace of change by assuming legal powers in the industrial relations area. The Labour government's attempt to put certain elements of the White Paper 'In Place of Strife' onto the statute book ended abortively with the withdrawal of the Bill in June 1969, while the Conservative government's 1971 Industrial Relations Act produced a major political confrontation between the government and the legal system on the one hand and the unions on the other. However, the fieldwork for this study was carried out in 1971 when the latter legislation was passing through Parliament, and it is therefore appropriate to leave our review of the background history of British procedures at this point, and turn to a brief outline of the study itself.

An outline of the study

The book is based around a fieldwork study of grievance procedures in a sample of British industry but tries to put grievance procedures in a wider perspective than would be possible from fieldwork alone. Chapter 2 examines the behavioural theory bearing on the grievance process, and, in the absence of any substantial theory of procedures, puts forward some basic analytic concepts, hypotheses and assumptions about their role. Chapter 3 is the first chapter to deal directly with the fieldwork of the study, and portrays various dimensions of the procedures in our panel of plants. Chapter 4 then presents the research on the grievance process as we found it in the panel, and looks at the frequency and types of grievance, the roles of the participants and the deviations from the procedure, before trying to present a composite view of the process. Chapter 5 examines some of the attitudinal aspects surrounding the process, and then presents a contingency based approach to procedural structure. Chapter 6 tries to put this approach into practical form by examining the pros and cons of various components of procedure, and presenting various scenarios of procedural structures and their environmental correlates. Finally, Chapter 7 looks to various wider industrial relations models within which procedure may need to be fitted, together with the actual mechanics of possible procedural change for Britain in the future.

The fieldwork for our study consisted primarily of interviewing members of management in thirty-five plants in three broad industry categories, namely, food, chemicals and textiles. The fieldwork was carried out in the first six months of 1971, i.e., while the Industrial Relations Act was passing through Parliament. This had implications not only for cooperation in the study, but also for the views expressed and the nature of the system observed. For reasons of obtaining cooperation, little attempt could be made to structure the sample plants; however, a reasonable balance was achieved in geographical spread, with most areas of Britain being represented, and also in terms of plant size. Of the 35 plants, 13 had more than 1,000 employees, 9 had between 300 and 1,000, and 13 less than 300. The degree of autonomy of the plants in industrial relations matters differed considerably, ranging from dependence on industry-wide agreements through substantial control from company headquarters elsewhere to almost complete plant autonomy. All the plants except one dealt with unions, although the degree of union membership varied considerably. No attempt was made to obtain conflict prone situations. Of the plants in the panel, 13 had experienced at least one strike in the previous three years, a further 7 had experienced industrial action short of a strike, and the remaining 15 had experienced no industrial action. In general, therefore, the panel represented a cross-section of the 'middle' range of British industry along the dimensions mentioned, although clearly this is not intended in any statistical sense.

The actual interviews were conducted with four types of management: senior managers; personnel managers; departmental managers; and supervisors and foremen. In all, 268 individuals were interviewed in the thirty-five plants. On each visit three questionnaires were used: one dealing fairly comprehensively with structural and environmental factors concerning the plant, which was answered either by senior line or personnel management; a second, concerned with the grievance process, for answering by departmental managers; and a third, similar to the second but with rather fewer questions, for supervisors. The vast bulk of those interviewed were highly responsive and in very few cases did we get the impression that there was any holding back or any attempt to disguise the situation; indeed, the reverse was true. For this reason, the data in later chapters does not always cover all respondents, although we are convinced that the general patterns which emerge are representative of the panel of plants and respondents. The picture built up of each plant was surprisingly coherent, with answers at different levels and functions reflecting a considerable unanimity of perception.

At the same time it will be as well to acknowledge at this point the inherent and special limitations of this study.[29] We cannot pretend that either the methodology or the data meet the highest standards of scientific

rigour. We had little control over the selection of plants, or of the inter-
viewees within plants, except to request that those selected should all play
an active industrial relations role in dealing with blue collar employees.
The data themselves, whose limitations are more fully explained in
Chapter 4, can do no more than provide orders of magnitude, and as a
result we have not utilised any statistical techniques, which while they
might sharpen the interpretation of the results, could also convey a spurious
sense of accuracy. An even more important criticism is that the data are
based on interviews with management alone, although in approximately a
quarter of the plants we did talk with the senior shop steward or other
workplace representatives and these interviews provided valuable background information. In general, however, managements were reluctant to
let us talk to stewards, possibly because they felt that the study itself might
become a source of friction, while we were also warned that many stewards
would not participate without authority from higher levels within their
unions. Given the refusal of unions at that time to cooperate with
investigatory bodies such as the CIR, it was felt that administrative
problems and delays might jeopardise other aspects of the fieldwork. The
fact remains that the study is unquestionably weakened by the absence of
the union viewpoint, and further research is required to rectify this
omission.

On a broader basis, the operation of grievance procedures is not
independent of the technical, social, organisational and economic environment which surrounds it; indeed, this is the main thesis of this book. Yet
the identification and measurement of such variables is an extremely
difficult undertaking and detailed examinations of these areas were well
beyond the scope of the present study. Again, related institutional features
such as the scope of bargaining, the nature and negotiation of the collective
agreement, the operation of industry-wide procedures, the nature of custom
and practice, and numerous others equally affect grievance procedures, but
could only be given very limited attention in the project. Yet in spite of
these deficiencies, we feel that the study does provide a starting point in an
important area which has been neglected for too long, perhaps because of
the very problems to which we have just referred.

A final introductory point needs to be made about the values underlying
the study. Inevitably, value judgements will be made explicitly or implicitly,
and it may be as well to state our position now. We see procedures as a
means of channelling and institutionalising conflicting views in a pluralist
context. This involves some rough equality between the two sides and a
mutual recognition of each other's position and interests. This is, of course,
not a new idea, but rather the basic concept underlying voluntarism in the

British system. It does demand, however, that procedures should not be seen on the one hand as a mechanism for imposing a unitary conception of the firm, nor on the other as a mechanism for furthering class warfare. When we talk of procedures in normative terms we are therefore referring to procedures which help to bring about accommodation between the two sides in the context of divergent interests, not means by which one side or the other can impose its views alone. We would approve of a trend towards greater industrial democracy, but even in such a context we would argue the continued need for a pluralist representation of interests and grievance machinery for resolving the day-to-day issues which will still be part of any organisational structure.

Notes

[1] Royal Commission on Trade Unions and Employers' Associations (hereafter RCTUEA), Cmnd 3623, HMSO 1968, p. 136.

[2] Confederation of British Industry, *Disputes Procedures,* 1970, p. 15.

[3] B. Sherman, 'The role of procedure agreements', *Industrial Relations Review and Report,* no. 54, April 1973, p. 13.

[4] The most important surveys are: A.I. Marsh, *Disputes Procedures in British Industry,* and A.I. Marsh and W.E.J. McCarthy, *Disputes Procedures in Britain,* respectively Parts 1 and 2 of Research Paper No. 2 for the RCTUEA. Much other material comes from documents associated with the Royal Commission. The following also cover this topic: A.I. Marsh, *Industrial Relations in Engineering,* R. Hyman, *Disputes Procedures in Action,* both Heinemann, London 1972; and A.I. Marsh and R.S. Jones, 'Engineering procedure and central conference at York in 1959: a factual analysis', *British Journal of Industrial Relations,* July 1964.

[5] Marsh, *Disputes Procedures,* op. cit., p. 24.

[6] On the same lines, see J.R. Crossley, 'The Donovan Report: a case study in the poverty of historicism', *British Journal of Industrial Relations,* November 1968.

[7] E.g. S.R. Parker and M. Scott, 'Developing models of workplace industrial relations', *British Journal of Industrial Relations,* July 1971.

[8] Marsh and McCarthy, *Disputes Procedures in Britain,* op. cit., p. 3.

[9] J.T. Dunlop, *Industrial Relations Systems,* Southern Illinois University Press, Carbondale 1958, reprinted 1970.

[10] Relatively little written guidance is currently available. The termination of the Commission on Industrial Relations before its reference on procedures was finished meant that a major chance to provide guidance on

the construction of procedures was lost. The Advisory, Conciliation and Arbitration Service, which now incorporates the Manpower and Productivity Service and the role of the CIR, will give advice in any specific situation, but it has produced no written guidelines. The Code of Practice does give general advice, as does the TUC's 'Good Industrial Relations: A Guide for Negotiators' (1971), the CBI's 'Dispute Procedures' (1970), and, amongst bipartisan bodies, the Industrial Society's 'Model Procedural Agreements' (1969). More recent is a pamphlet by N. Singleton, *Industrial Relations Procedures*, DE Manpower Papers no. 14, HMSO 1975. Various other unions and employers' associations have also prepared guidance on the contents of procedures, but none have tried to link procedures in any systematic way to the particular environment of the plant. Even in the American literature there is little explicit guidance of this sort, but one book which does examine procedural structure is B.R. Crane and R.M. Hoffman, *Successful Handling of Labor Grievances*, Central Book Co., New York 1956.

[11] A. Flanders, *Trade Unions and the Force of Tradition*, Fawley Foundation Lecture, University of Southampton, 1970, p. 5.

[12] G.D.H. Cole, *Workshop Organization*, Clarendon Press, Oxford 1923, p. 7.

[13] K. Burgess, *The Origins of British Industrial Relations*, Croom Helm, London 1975, p. 309.

[14] According to Sharp there were 325 boards in 1913 (I.G. Sharp, *Industrial Conciliation and Arbitration in Great Britain*, Allen and Unwin, London 1950, p. 5).

[15] According to Wigham, the significance of the procedure was not apparent to the parties at the time; it was merely one of the terms of settlement (E. Wigham, *The Power to Manage: A History of the Engineering Employers' Federation*, Macmillan, London 1973, p. 66).

[16] R. Charles, *The Development of Industrial Relations in Britain, 1911–1939*, Hutchinson, London 1973, p. 104.

[17] The best sources for this structure are: Ministry of Labour, *Industrial Relations Handbook*, HMSO 1961; and, for industry disputes procedures, evidence given by the CBI to RCTUEA, *Selected Written Evidence*, pp. 311–25.

[18] A. Flanders, 'The Future of Voluntarism', Institute of Personnel Management National Conference, 1966, p. 4.

[19] Marsh, *Disputes Procedures*, op. cit., p. 17.

[20] O. Kahn-Freund, 'Intergroup conflicts and their settlement', *British Journal of Sociology*, 1954, pp. 193–227.

[21] A. Fox and A. Flanders, 'The reform of collective bargaining: from

Donovan to Durkheim', *British Journal of Industrial Relations,* July 1969, pp. 167–73.

[22] A. Flanders, 'What is Wrong with the System?', *Institute of Personnel Management,* 1965.

[23] TUC General Council Report, 1960, p. 127.

[24] Exception must be made for the contribution by Flanders, elsewhere published as 'Prescription for Change', which together with his 'What is Wrong with the System?' provided the theoretical underpinning for the Commission's Report.

[25] RCTUEA, *Selected Written Evidence,* p. 281.

[26] Ibid., p. 173.

[27] Quoted by RCTUEA Report, op. cit., p. 18.

[28] Ibid., p. 45.

[29] The problems of sampling, interpretation, and cross-comparison of responses in this field are well stated in the much larger statistical survey carried out by the Social Survey Division of the office of Population Censuses and Surveys, *Workplace Industrial Relations 1972,* HMSO 1974.

2 Theories of the grievance process and procedure

In order to better understand the results of our empirical study and the subsequent discussion of grievance procedures, it is necessary first to clarify conceptual issues surrounding the nature of grievances. This chapter therefore first presents a brief discussion of various dimensions of the grievance process, reviews the existing literature on what shapes this process, and then moves from the process as such to concentrate on the concept of grievance *procedures,* the particular focal point of our study.

Dimensions of the grievance process

What is a grievance?

An employee feels his weekly pay packet contains a little less than he thinks it ought to and asks his foreman about it. The foreman reminds him that he took half a day's leave earlier in the week and the employee goes back to work satisfied with the answer.

A group of piece-rate workers in a particular department suddenly encounter substandard raw material that causes them to produce less, make more errors and consequently earn less. Their shop steward points this out to the departmental manager who proposes that a 'special rate' be introduced which would bring earnings back to normal levels while the offstandard material is being processed. He also promises to find out why the poor material was sent to the department in the first place and make sure it does not happen again. The steward accepts these responses to his protest and persuades the workers to carry on.

A company, in response to falling sales, decides to abandon what had been 'regular' overtime for the production workers in a particular department. The workers, who had come to count on the overtime pay as part of their income, protest to stewards and union branch officials who take the matter up with the factory manager and get no concessions. The workers begin a work-to-rule slowdown; they eventually gain the support of the rest of the union members in the plant and they all strike for higher wages to 'compensate' for the lower incomes. The wage claim and the strike spreads to other factories in the industry. It is settled when a new wage rate is finally negotiated at industry level.

As the above examples illustrate, the kinds of issues which may be called an employee grievance are extremely varied in content and significance for the organisation concerned. At one extreme they may affect only a single individual, have nothing to do with union–management agreements and have no implications for general company policies. The whole process consists of no more than the raising of a question and the provision of a satisfactory answer. At the other extreme is the opposite of all these conditions: groups of workers, a challenge to the interpretation of a prior union agreement or management decision manifesting itself in a process which grows to include increasing numbers of people and results in highly disruptive actions before eventually being settled.

While all of the incidents just described could be called grievances there is a point along the scale of significance at which an issue becomes something more than a grievance and in general, if imprecise, parlance becomes a 'claim' or a 'major dispute'. The essence of the distinction between the two lies in the way they are initiated and in the degree of proposed change in the status quo. A grievance begins as an expression of dissatisfaction by an individual or group of employees, whereas claims typically originate higher in the union hierarchy in the name of large groups or all union members in the plant or beyond, as in the case of a claim for higher wages or shorter hours or improved pensions.

This basis for defining a grievance is reflected in the definition provided by the International Labour Organization in its major work on the subject:

> . . . in general a grievance may be submitted by a worker or workers concerned in respect of any measure or situation which directly affects or may affect the conditions of employment of one or several workers in the undertaking when that measure or situation appears contrary to the provisions of an applicable collective agreement or of an individual contract of employment, to work rules, to laws or regulations or to the custom or usage of the occupation or country. Where a grievance is transformed into a general claim at some stage of its examination, the claim falls outside the grievance procedure and normally comes within the area of collective bargaining.[1]

The general grievance process

While the term 'grievance' usually refers to a specific issue, it is important to remember that the occurrence and handling of a grievance is a *process* involving the attitudes, beliefs and actions of the parties involved. The

18

following is a depiction of the 'typical' grievance process based on a general framework developed by Pondy.[2]

1   All industrial situations contain conditions and events which can be potentially dissatisfying to employees (latent issues). A grievance begins with some sort of 'triggering event' in the form of a management action or other occurrence within or outside the plant which transforms a latent issue into a conscious one.

2   This event creates a 'cognitive' or psychological reaction in the mind of the employee affected. Two key questions are raised and tentative answers provided, although not usually consciously or explicitly: (a) if there is confusion or ambiguity over 'what's wrong', clarification of the dissatisfaction is sought along with a clearer idea of what it will take to correct the 'wrong'; and (b) initial conclusions are also reached regarding 'why' and 'who'. The reason for the dissatisfaction may be seen to have been caused by a variety of motives or events. If other people are seen as the source of the problem they must be given a social identity. Thus one may perceive the 'opponent' as a co-worker, a specific manager, a group of managers, the union or various forces beyond the enterprise.

3   Assuming one decides to act on the feelings of dissatisfaction, several choices are possible. One may seek out fellow employees to see if they have the same sense of grievance (potential allies). If they do, a process of building a sense of group cohesion around the grievance may begin. The other typical action is to confront someone who is seen as being able to correct the grievance. Usually this is a foreman but it may be another member of the management or a union representative. The latter will usually be seen as an agent who will act on one's behalf. It is at this point also that the first occasion arises in which the grievant must decide whether to follow the requirements of an official grievance procedure (given that there is one and he is aware of it) or deviate from it.

4   Once the grievance is made manifest the parties involved usually engage in mutual probing to establish how strongly the other feels about the issue; what the other 'really' wants and intends to do about it, etc. This position clarification stage may be as perfunctory as a single question or it may involve lengthy meetings or 'behind the scenes' investigation.

5   Once a management representative has received a grievance and obtained some clarification of the grievant's position on the matter he is the one who must now make several decisions. He can choose to ignore the matter; try to handle it himself; consult with colleagues; ask for a superior's advice; or turn the matter over to a superior for a decision.

6   Once a first decision on the grievance is reached and communicated a

'reaction phase' begins. Assuming the decision is unsatisfactory, the grievant can choose to live with the dissatisfying situation, to seek out allies or agents for support or to pursue the matter further on his own. If the grievant, either alone or with support, decides to pursue the matter it must be decided which management representative to approach. It must also be decided again whether or not to follow 'procedures'. The major action decisions open are those of persuasion, positive bargaining (offering some benefit in return for a concession), negative bargaining (the use of threats), actual punishing actions (e.g., strikes, slowdowns, resignation, etc.) or problem solving (seeking to discover a mutually beneficial solution to the issue).

7   The person on the management side who receives the grievant's reaction to the initial management response must go through the same cognitive process as in steps 4 and 5. The 'second step' decision precipitates in the grievants a repetition of the questions faced in step 6 and so on until finally at some point an agreement is reached between the parties.

8   The final outcome may involve a compromise, 'total victory' for one side or the other, or a solution in which both parties are better off than previously. The outcome also contains an aftermath: it will affect the attitudes of each side about the overall continuing relationship between them. The whole issue then rejoins the latent pool from which it originally arose.

Critical to the way the grievance develops in the process of being handled by the parties involved are two other key elements of the situation. One is the long term overall relationship between the parties in terms of their general level of trust and respect for one another and their perceptions of the power each has over the other. For example, the degree of trust can affect the way the grievant perceives the motives of his opponent in management. The perception of the relative power each party possesses to influence the other can strongly affect the choice of actions in pursuing the grievance.

The other element is the nature and extent of third parties to the grievance. Occasionally third parties may have an explicit identity as such, for example government conciliators, special appeals committees, etc. Usually, however, they play informal roles. Potential roles are those of 'ally' (e.g., co-workers seen as being willing to help a grievant to gain an end that both desire); 'agent' (e.g., a steward who is seen as being willing to represent a grievant in return for benefits not directly related to the conflict issue; 'mediator' (e.g., a union official or manager who is seen as seeking to end a conflict or certain manifestations of it without identifying with either of the opponents); and 'judge' (e.g., a top level executive who seeks to impose a solution in keeping with criteria which are independent of those of the two parties). These third party roles are among the more subtle and least discussed influences on all forms of conflict in organisations.[3]

The foregoing description of the typical grievance process provides an idea of the phenomenon we have sought to analyse and understand. The essential elements of this descriptive outline are summarised in Fig. 2.1. As can be seen, key attitudes, beliefs and perceptions regarding the issues of the grievance, the social identities of the parties and the overall relationship in which the grievance arises are the preconditions which determine the grievance manifestations or actions which in turn eventually result in a resolution which has an aftermath which feeds back to the attitudinal states.

Typical grievance handling patterns

Fig. 2.1 depicts the process that occurs for any specific individual grievance. It is also possible, however, to conceptualise stable, relatively long term normative patterns in grievance handling as they apply to a number of specific grievances arising within an overall relationship over time. These patterns are the result of the cumulative effect of individual grievance aftermaths coupled with other past events affecting the overall relationship and present environmental pressures.

That such relatively stable grievance patterns exist in labour relations is well documented by Kuhn, Whyte and Derber et al. in the United States and by many of the studies of companies carried out by the Commission on Industrial Relations in Britain.[4] Most of these concentrate on delineating patterns in the overall relationship of the union branch and management within the company rather than emphasising *grievance* handling patterns *per se*. However, in spite of this minor limitation the study of Derber et al. on plant labour relations in seventy-four firms in the mid-western US provides a particularly useful categorisation of relationships which can also be easily adapted to apply to grievance handling within the context of our conceptual framework of small scale social conflict.

Derber discerned five basic types of overall plant level union–management relationships.[5] This typology is based on configurations of three basic variables as follows. Firstly, perceptions of the issues and the degree of mutual regard in the overall relationship combine to form an overall measure of satisfaction with the relationship. In an unsatisfactory relationship, for example, many issues of difference arise, many are seen to be 'zero-sum' or 'us versus them' and there is low trust and respect between the parties. A second overall variable is that of the relative power of union

Fig. 2.1   Detailed conceptual framework of the key elements in the grievance process

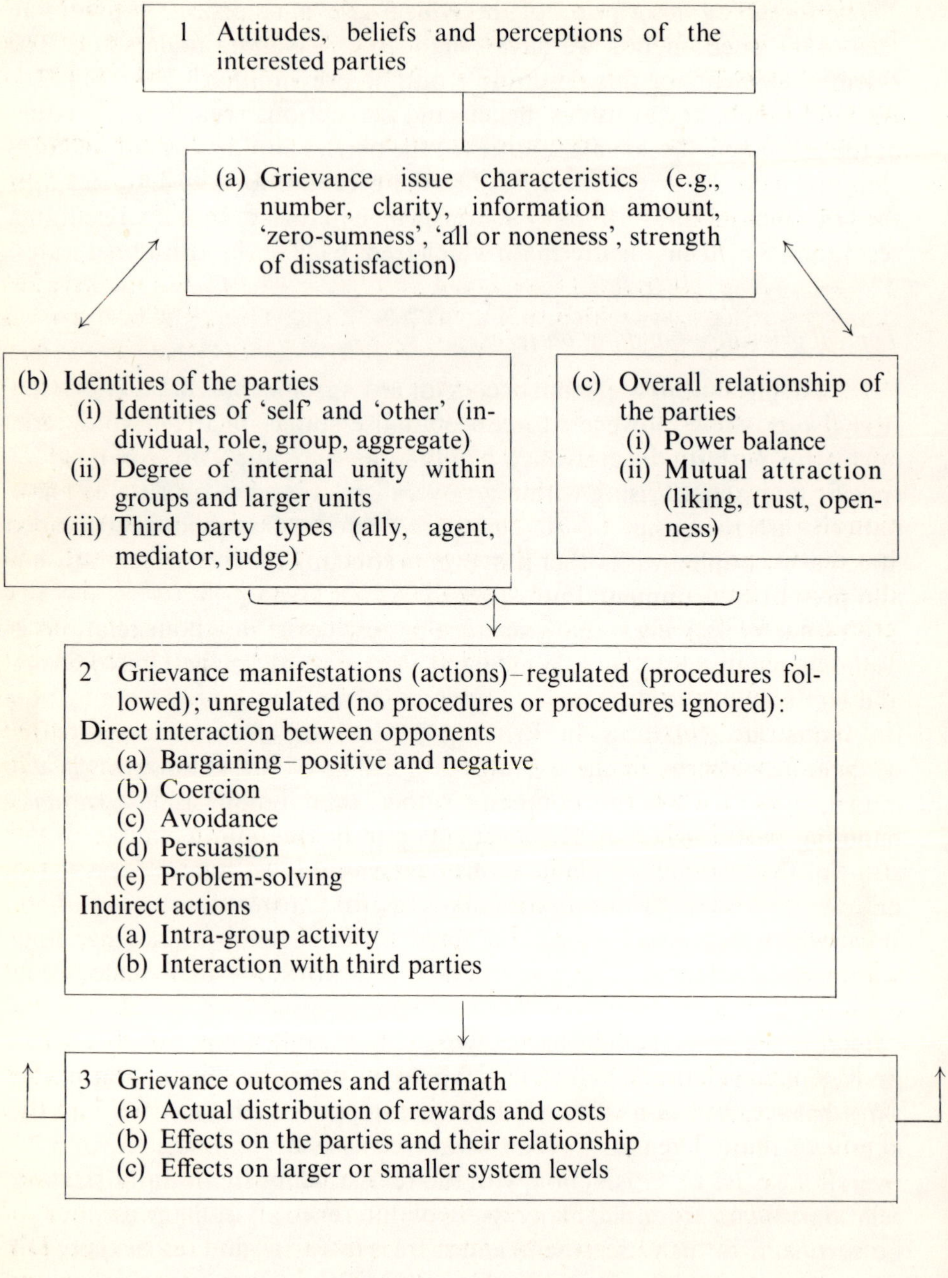

```
┌─────────────────────────────────────────────────┐
│  1   Attitudes, beliefs and perceptions of the   │
│      interested parties                          │
└─────────────────────────────────────────────────┘
              │
      ┌───────────────────────────────────────────────────┐
      │  (a) Grievance  issue  characteristics  (e.g.,    │
      │      number, clarity, information amount,          │
      │      'zero-sumness', 'all or noneness', strength   │
      │      of dissatisfaction)                          │
      └───────────────────────────────────────────────────┘
```

```
┌─────────────────────────────────────────┐   ┌─────────────────────────────────┐
│ (b)  Identities of the parties          │   │ (c)  Overall relationship of    │
│      (i) Identities of 'self' and       │   │      the parties                │
│          'other' (individual, role,     │   │      (i) Power balance          │
│          group, aggregate)              │   │     (ii) Mutual attraction      │
│      (ii) Degree of internal unity      │   │          (liking, trust, open-  │
│           within groups and larger      │   │          ness)                  │
│           units                         │   │                                 │
│      (iii) Third party types (ally,     │   │                                 │
│            agent, mediator, judge)      │   │                                 │
└─────────────────────────────────────────┘   └─────────────────────────────────┘
```

```
┌─────────────────────────────────────────────────────────────────┐
│  2   Grievance manifestations (actions)–regulated (procedures    │
│      followed); unregulated (no procedures or procedures          │
│      ignored):                                                    │
│  Direct interaction between opponents                             │
│      (a) Bargaining–positive and negative                         │
│      (b) Coercion                                                 │
│      (c) Avoidance                                                │
│      (d) Persuasion                                               │
│      (e) Problem-solving                                          │
│  Indirect actions                                                 │
│      (a) Intra-group activity                                     │
│      (b) Interaction with third parties                           │
└─────────────────────────────────────────────────────────────────┘
```

```
┌─────────────────────────────────────────────────────────────────┐
│  3   Grievance outcomes and aftermath                            │
│      (a) Actual distribution of rewards and costs                 │
│      (b) Effects on the parties and their relationship            │
│      (c) Effects on larger or smaller system levels               │
└─────────────────────────────────────────────────────────────────┘
```

and management, defined as the amount and scope of union influence in management decisions. This would be reflected in the perceptions of who controls which essential and exclusive resources needed by each side. The third descriptive dimension in the Derber typology is that of action. Three basic actions are considered: 'give and take' bargaining, problem solving mutual accommodation, and negative bargaining (threat) and the use of coercive force.

Drawing on these underlying variables it is possible to re-state Derber's typology with specific reference to grievance handling patterns as a continuum ranging from most to least severe.

1   *'Aggressive' pattern (Derber's type 'A')*   In this situation workers feel many dissatisfactions which they articulate as grievances and both parties see most of the issues as 'zero-sum'. Workers do not trust or respect management and vice versa. Grievants possess a good deal of influence which is expressed in the form of threats and the use of force. There is no attempt at meaningful joint consultation or problem solving activities.

2   *'Repressed hostility' pattern (Derber's type 'D')*   Workers in this situation also feel many dissatisfactions and believe them to be 'zero-sum' issues but do not articulate them as open grievances. Attitudes of mistrust and disrespect are dominant. The main difference from type 'A' is that the grievants feel they have no power to influence things in their favour: hence they engage in no actions of any kind (nor, of course, does management attempt genuine joint consultative activity).

3   *'Moderate' pattern (Derber's type 'X')*   Grievances in this situation arise with moderate frequency and some are seen as 'zero-sum' issues. On the other hand, workers and management basically accept and respect each other while still believing that each acts mostly for its own interests which are not always complementary. The grievants have moderate levels of power to influence matters in that they can affect issues of traditional direct concern to them (such as hours, some working conditions, some work allocation decisions). There is some prior consultation by management with workers or their representatives, again on relatively traditional and minor issues (e.g., holiday schedules or new shift rotas but not major technological changes). There is some use of problem solving approaches to grievances but also some 'positive' bargaining of the type 'we'll do this if you do that.' The use of threat and force is relatively rare.

4   *'Passive' pattern (Derber's type 'C')*   Attitudes are basically positive: few grievances are felt, few are articulated, there is little perception of 'zero-sum' issues and respect between the parties. Again (as in type 'D'), the workers have very little influence, there is little joint consultation and

little other action of any kind. Workers basically 'do what they are told' and do not mind it.

5   *'Cooperative' pattern (Derber's type 'B')*   In this situation attitudes are generally favourable: few grievances are felt or articulated, none are seen as 'zero-sum', a feeling of liking and trust exists between the parties. Worker influence is high and is expressed primarily through joint consultation activities prior to management decision making. When they arise grievances are handled solely by problem solving approaches. There is never any use of threat or force.

The grievance process and behavioural theory

The relevance of general approaches to the study of conflict

Having described the nature of grievance conflicts we now wish to review existing attempts to analyse why these kinds of problems arise and develop as they do. Many of the social sciences deal with the study of conflict in one form or another but there is as yet no easily definable body of systematic theory which is generally accepted. Rather there are large numbers of approaches, each of which reflects various dimensions of conflict and helps explain certain of its elements. Most of these approaches tend to be alternatives rather than complements and supplements to each other. Moreover, although most are useful in the discussion of grievances, few are designed to analyse grievances as a specific subject.

One way to summarise the general approaches taken to the analysis of social conflicts is shown in Fig. 2.2. The *dependent* variables which the themes seek to explain can be categorised as those referring to the subjective state of the parties – their attitudes and perceptions, the actions or conflict manifestations the parties engage in, and the results or outcomes of these actions. The *independent* variables used to explain conflict can be grouped under three headings, namely, process, contextual-structural and procedural variables. Process variables are those which describe the flow of thoughts, feelings and actions which comprise the phenomenon under study. Used in analysis, they seek to explain one aspect of the conflict process with other process variables – for example, explaining strike actions in terms of prior employee attitudes or as an employee's attitudes toward an issue in terms of his attitudes toward his superior. Contextual-structural variables deal with conditions which surround the conflict process – for example, explaining strike actions in terms of the state of the economy or the technology of work or explaining attitudes toward incentives in terms of the structure of the incentive scheme. Procedural variables

Fig. 2.2   A classification of general approaches to the analysis of social conflicts

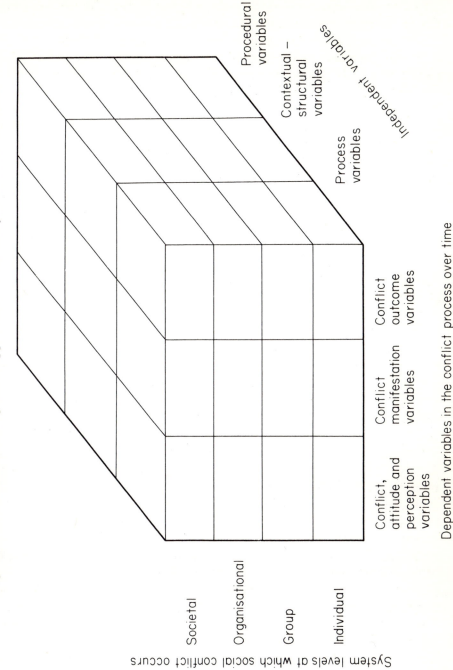

Independent variables

Procedural variables

Contextual – structural variables

Process variables

Conflict outcome variables

Conflict manifestation variables

Conflict, attitude and perception variables

Dependent variables in the conflict process over time

Societal

Organisational

Group

Individual

System levels at which social conflict occurs

are previously agreed upon rules designed to govern the behaviour of the parties in dispute–for example, explaining strikes in terms of the absence of a proper in-plant disputes procedure.

A third facet of the various conflict theories is the level of the social system at which conflict occurs. Some aim at explaining the conflicts between husband and wife, or worker and supervisor, i.e., individuals acting as such; others concentrate on the conflicts between groups of people acting together; for example, all employees in a given department or residents of a street or community. Still others examine the conflicts between formally constituted long lasting organisations such as businesses, unions or government institutions. Finally, there has always been much interest in explaining conflicts at the societal level or between nations or major subcultures within a society.

With the help of Fig. 2.2. we can begin to see the kinds of questions one can ask of the various theories of social conflict. Are they mainly interested in explaining conflict manifestations at the organisational level (for example, strikes), utilising primarily process variables? Or are they more concerned with attitudes in inter-individual conflicts (e.g., worker–foreman feelings) as affected by contextual conditions? Do they recognise that conflict at one system level may affect it at another?

In looking at the existing conflict literature of relevance to understanding employee grievance processes four broad categories can be discerned. There is first the works of what might be called general conflict theorists who seek to offer an explanation of all kinds of conflict, or at least major subclasses of it. The works of Marx, Dahrendorf, Simmel (and his latter day interpreter Coser) and modern games theorists are examples of this. [6]

Secondly, since grievances are conflicts which originate and develop largely within work organisations, one might reasonably turn to those who offer general theories of organisation which seek to explain the overall structure and climate of behaviour in all kinds of formal organisations. In this context one would look at how conflict is treated in the works of people such as Weber, Urwick, Follett, the various writers who comprise what has been termed the human relations school, the decision theory school and the socio-technical or contingency theory school. [7] Thirdly, grievances also form a part of the industrial relations system in society and consequently one would look at general theories such as those of Dunlop which seek to analyse and explain these total systems. [8] Finally, one would naturally consider those theories which explicitly set out to examine the specific subject of vertical conflict between superiors and subordinates in organisations which is the particular relationship within which grievances occur. [9]

Limitations of space prevent a thorough discussion of each of these categories of conflict theory. However, Fig. 2.3 briefly outlines the way a representative sample of theorists have approached the subject in terms of the questions raised by Fig. 2.1. A general review of this and other works on conflict unfortunately reveals little of *direct* applicability to the phenomenon of grievances, though much that is suggestive of what must be considered. It is particularly noteworthy that very little attention has been given to the role of procedures in the conflict process.

The approach that will be taken therefore will be to examine the relevant conflict literature in the context of two basic sets of questions that arise from our previous discussion of the grievance process. The first set of questions concerns the attitudinal or cognitive phase of the process: what creates the dissatisfaction that is the basis of grievance issues? What will feelings be about the 'opponent' (management)? Aside from attitudes and feelings, however, there is the entirely separate set of questions regarding what people intend to *do* about them: whether to turn the grievance from one involving an individual or small group to a major workforce dispute; whether to bargain, use industrial action, seek mutually beneficial new approaches, follow or disregard procedures.

Attitudes and perceptions in grievance conflicts

Causes of worker dissatisfaction In examining differences between different situations, one category of explanations has looked at the sense of deprivation or unfairness in treatment that may be felt by workers. Thus Smith posits that dissatisfaction is the difference between what one feels one deserves and what one actually receives.[10] If current psychological or material rewards decrease or if expectations and realistic aspirations increase, dissatisfaction grows. The standard of what one deserves is usually set by comparison with past rewards and those of other individuals and groups. Such others are seen as being as deserving, less deserving or more deserving than oneself. Insofar as the individual or group is made aware of a number of these comparative reference groups and sees the rewards received by them as changing, personal sense of satisfaction will also change. Smith was writing from the perspective of social psychology, but a similar concept has been put forward by writers in other disciplines. Runciman, from the viewpoint of sociology, argued that relative rather than absolute deprivation is the key to dissatisfaction,[11] while many British writers in the industrial relations field have emphasised the importance of comparability and precedent in the triggering of disputes.[12] Finally, the concept has also been influential in economics, with

Fig. 2.3 Summary of some major theoretical approaches to conflict

	Elements of conflict 'explained' by theory: 1 conflict emergence (feelings of conflict) 2 conflict manifestations 3 conflict outcome	System levels addressed by theory: 1 interpersonal 2 intergroup 3 inter-organisational 4 societal	Types of explanatory variables utilised		
			Process (e.g., issue characteristics, power, attitude of parties, outcome of past actions)	Contextual (e.g., external environment technology, structure of organisation)	Procedural (rules, laws)
I 'General' theories Marx	(1) Conflict emergence is inevitable between classes. (2) Manifestations assumed to be in form of violent class warfare. (3) Outcome assumed to be only one – total victory for the proletariat.	(4) Societal (inter-class conflict).	No detailed analysis of the conflict process in terms of how conflict manifestations will be chosen, sequence of events, etc.	Ownership of the means of production. Economic exploitation of workers by owners in situation in which societal 'superstructure' supports owning class.	No detailed discussion of effects of procedure (laws, etc.). Assumption that all formal procedures support power of bourgeoisie.
Simmel/Coser	(1) Conflict is inevitable and may be beneficial. (2) Feelings of group members about each other and group as a whole during conflict may vary depending on nature of group and type of conflict.	(1, 2) Interpersonal and intergroup conflicts of all kinds.	External threat increases group unity given that issues do not cause division on key values and group possesses good initial cohesion.	No discussion of effects of context.	Little discussion of procedural effects.
'Negotiation models' (e.g. Cross, Pen, Siegal and Fouraker)	(3) Conflict outcomes the nature of bargained settlements. Models assume conflict is inevitable and bargaining will be only manifestation of it.	(1) Interpersonal (with untested inferences made to larger system levels).	Models use such variables as amount of information provided, power of the parties, concession rate. Many assumptions and constraints placed on variables to achieve theoretical and methodological rigour.	No discussion of context.	No discussion of procedures.
'Influence' theories (e.g. Porsholt, Rapoport and Chammah, Richardson)	(2) Conflict manifestations such as use of threat, war, strikes, problem solving. Models assume conflict inevitable and are not concerned about nature of outcome.	(1) Interpersonal (with untested inferences made to larger system levels).	'Cognitive', 'learning' and 'reaction process' theories used to explain action choices.	No discussion of context.	No discussion of procedures.
II Organisational theories Weber	A general organisational theory containing ideas (1, 2, 3) on the apparent absence of conflict feelings and actions within bureaucracies. Assumes conflict not inevitable.	(1, 2) Behaviour within organisations at all levels.	No analysis of conflict process.	Bureaucratic structure of authority eliminates need for interpersonal or intergroup conflict. No recognition of union movement as a significant contextual force.	Effects of rules is to control potential disputes. Disagreements settled by appeal to precedent, rules or higher authority.
Urwick	(1, 2, 3) A general management theory containing normative prescriptions on how to avoid conflict arousal and handle manifestations. Assumes conflict not inevitable.	(1, 2) Behaviour within organisations at all levels.	No analysis of the conflict process.	'Correct' division of labour, departmentalisation and structure of authority reduces conflicts and provides clear means for resolving them. No recognition of union movement.	Unresolvable disputes to be referred to next highest superior for settlement.
Follett	(1, 2, 3) A general management theory which assumes conflict inevitable but resolvable through certain manifestations.	(1, 2) Behaviour within organisations at all levels.	Conflicts will not become destructive if the parties follow 'law of the situation' by gathering all facts and trying to be rational, i.e. all inter-organisational conflicts are potentially non-zero sum.	No analysis of structural or procedural influences on conflict process. No discussion of unions.	

Theory / Theorists	Conflict emergence	Levels	Process / manifestation	Conditions / effects	Procedures
Mayo. Argyris. McGregor. Likert	emergence of conflict inevitable. Believes that which does emerge can be settled amicably with solutions of joint benefit.	in organisations at all levels.	festation determined by quality of informal group relations and leadership style.	...analysis of structure or procedure other than implication that formal authority systems which are highly centralised will increase probability of conflict emergence. Unions seen as symptoms of faulty human relations at plant level; implication is that they will wither away when managers create proper interpersonal relations (Mayo).	No discussion of procedural regulation.
The decision theorists Simon and March. Cyert and March	(1) Conflict posited as being inevitable but controllable. Manifestations and outcomes not discussed at length.	(1.2) Behaviour within in organisations mostly among managers.	Relationships among elements of the process not discussed.	Organisational slack, compartmentalisation of subgoals as a result of economic conditions and design of organisational structure will prevent conflict emergence.	Decision rules which emphasise 'satisficing' and sequential attention to goals which prevents emergence of major issues and destructive manifestations. Specific conflict related procedures not discussed.
Socio-technical and contingency theorists Woodward. Burns and Stalker. Crozier, Trist and Bamforth, Sayles. Lawrence and Lorsch	(1.2) Conflict emergence within and between all segments of the organisation is seen as inevitable.	(1.2) Behaviour within in organisations at all levels.	Little detailed analysis of relationships among the elements of the process.	Technology and environment affect job design and organisational structure, which in turn affect number and type of conflict issues and relative power of the parties.	No discussion of procedures.
III General theories of industrial relations Dunlop	(2) Primarily attempts to explain the institutional structure of union-management relations and collective bargaining conflict.	Recognises all system levels.	Relatively little emphasis on process characteristics other than general effects of historical events on present conditions.	Major emphasis placed on effects of political and economic conditions.	External procedures in the form of state regulations of labour relations given considerable emphasis. Little consideration of effects of intra-organisational procedures.
IV Specific theories of organisational conflict Schmidt and Tannenbaum	(1) Conflict emergence seen as inevitable: conflict manifestation described in terms of five phases of development. Implicit belief that most conflicts can be resolved to everyone's satisfaction. No specific concern with conflicts involving unions and independent organisations.	(1) Primarily discusses interpersonal conflicts (one to one) within organisations.	Presents normative directions on how to prevent destructive manifestations but no analysis of what determines the use of these.	Notes that faulty information systems and role definitions can precipitate conflict.	No discussion of procedures.
Blake, Shepard and Mouton	(1) Conflict emergence treated as inevitable but determinants of its origin not discussed. No explicit discussion of conflicts involving union representation. (2) Theory mainly deals with how conflict process affects the parties and their subsequent actions. (3) Determinants of substantive outcomes not discussed but attitudes toward them are.	(1, 2) Primarily discusses interpersonal and intergroup conflicts within organisations.	Attitudes toward inevitability and resolvability of issue, importance of issue ('stakes') and degree of interdependence of the parties.	Contextual conditions affecting process or outcomes not discussed.	No discussion of procedural effects on conflict.
Robbins, Filley	(1 and 2) Conflict seen as inevitable. Emergence and manifestation of major concern; actual outcomes not considered. Primary emphasis on lateral conflicts with little on worker–management conflict involving union representation.	(1, 2) Interpersonal and intergroup levels are the only ones considered.	Process factors considered as the most critical in explaining conflict manifestation.	Recognition of the significance of contextual influences on conflict issue creation but little on conflict manifestation.	Limited discussion of procedural approaches to conflict management.

29

the Ross–Dunlop debate on the theory of wage determination centering on the relative importance of the 'political' forces of comparability and the 'economic' forces of the labour market.[13]

Closely related to this approach is the attempt to analyse individual 'needs' as the basis of aspirations. The major writer here is Maslow with his hierarchy of needs, such as security, affection, esteem, and self-actualisation, which come to be identified with specific aspects of the work setting.[14] Stagner and Rosen, stressing the importance of individual motivation, note that while the employing organisation allows the worker to achieve some of his goals, it frustrates others, with the consequent creation of dissatisfaction.[15] Argyris has posited that many of the conditions of modern work run counter to basic human needs that manifest themselves in the desire to do interesting and varied work, to have control over one's work methods and pace, and to be able to associate freely with others on one's own terms.[16]

A further source of dissatisfaction is the distribution of power within an organisation. Marxist analysis has been centered on the power of capital to exploit and thus to alienate the worker and to create class antagonisms. From a very different ideological standpoint the human relations movement has given a lot of attention to the style of supervision and leadership. If employees feel that a superior does not deserve the authority he has over them or if that authority is exercised in an unacceptable way the grievance arising may well be over the power distribution itself rather than the specific conditions or actions of the superior. Moreover, in an organisational context it has been pointed out by Blau and Scott,[17] amongst others, that low levels of interaction and poor communications between superiors and subordinates increase the probability of mutual mistrust arising over matters of mutual concern. Many writers have stressed the need for trust in an authority relationship. In particular, Fox has described at length the implications for dissatisfaction of a low trust syndrome.[18]

Another group of explanations have concentrated on the *context* in which conflict is manifested. At its most immediate level this deals with the working environment. The Donovan Report and many British writers have seen the source of conflict as inadequate wage structures, low management efficiency, poor procedures, inequitable overtime distribution, and many other aspects of the day-to-day operation of a factory which could, with better planning, be put right. Turner, Clack, and Roberts' work on the British car industry is a classic example of this and Clack's own monograph on his experience as a participant observer lends immediacy to his analysis.[19]

A more recent and very influential context-based school has been the socio-technical group, stressing technology as a determinant of social inter-action and potential conflict. The socio-technical theorists see the nature of the tasks being performed as the critical source of feelings of satisfaction. Blauner, for example, compared feelings of alienation among workers in printing, oil refining, automobiles and textiles.[20] These industries varied according to the extent to which their technologies required work which was routine, repetitive, low skilled, mechanically paced, and permitted little interaction with fellow workers. In general, the more technology mani-fested these qualities, the more alienated were the workers, although Blauner did note the mitigating effect of community social structure in the case of a textile factory in a small rural location. Sayles[21] carried out a more detailed study of the impact of technology on small work groups to which we shall refer later in connection with the role of the group in power relationships. An aspect similar to technology which has been seen by Cleland and others[22] as a potential factor in conflict is size of unit, the argument being that large units involve a social and structural complexity which makes close relationships difficult. Ingham,[23] however, found that the expectations of workers in large plants, which also tended to pay more, were more instrumental and economic in nature than those in smaller plants, which tended to prefer close social relations. This finding, while not denying the importance of plant size, suggests that a more important factor is the workers' backgrounds and objectives.

This finding is in line with that of Goldthorpe et al. Arguing against this technological determinism,[24] they represent that group of researchers who believe that the past experience and background characteristics of the workers has more to do with how satisfied they will be with a given work situation. Those who have known nothing better by virtue of having been occupationally and geographically immobile will be more likely to accept current conditions. Those who are at a point in their life cycle where the need for money and family responsibilities dominate will take an instru-mental view and care little about the nature of the work so long as it is well paid. Conversely, older workers whose families are grown up and whose job mobility is reduced by age may care more about current physical–psychological conditions and less about money. Such differences in life interests would clearly affect the kind and number of issues likely to arise as shop floor grievances.

A final approach to worker dissatisfaction is concerned with change. Terryberry[25] has argued that the more frequent and complex the changes in technology, markets, and other institutional features, the higher the probability that large numbers of issues of dispute will arise between various groups of workers and management. The rapidity and number of changes can create a climate where resolution becomes difficult, possibly leading to a negative attitude towards management's right to make the changes it does. Perrow[26] has also suggested that where work technology is highly constraining, small changes in methods and equipment can provoke a much greater outcry than where the nature of the work provides for more worker flexibility or autonomy. This approach is also linked to the work of Burns and Stalker[27] in positing organisational flexibility along a 'mechanistic'–'organic' continuum in accordance with the needs of technology and markets, and consequentially different modes of decision making and conflict resolution.

Feelings of power An important aspect of a latent conflict situation is what the parties feel they can do about it, and this provides a second category of factors underlying conflict. One frequently noted factor is membership of a group. Kerr and Siegal, Sayles, and Blake, Shepard and Mouton have all pointed out that being part of a group can intensify feelings in either positive or negative directions.[28] The realisation that 'others feel as I do' lends a sense of justification and conviction to one's beliefs. A shared grievance is thus more strongly felt than an individual one. Coser[29] has also argued that membership of a close-knit cohesive group having relatively few dealings with others makes it more likely that 'outsiders' will be seen as untrustworthy; conflict with them will therefore be more likely. Kerr and Siegal have put forward as a major factor in strike frequency the 'isolated mass' of workers in occupations separated from other groups.[30] Moreover, conflict with outsiders (who can include management) can add to feelings of group solidarity and outsiders can thus become scapegoats where group cohesion is threatened. Again, the power of a group as opposed to an individual is enhanced when the group develops its own unofficial leadership. This can serve to sharpen and clarify the issues, identify the opponents, and maintain the internal dynamics of the group so that dissent is minimised and social needs are met.

Group membership thus greatly adds to a sense of power felt and thereby increases the possibility of conflict. In addition, as Thibaut and Kelly have pointed out,[31] the greater the feeling of power, the higher expectations and a sense of desiring more are likely to be. On the same basis, success in previous activities is likely to heighten both the feeling of power and aspirations. McCarthy and Kuhn[32] have both noted that the past success of militant tactics is likely to lead to their repeated use.

The converse of these findings is likely to be true for the individual who is not a member of a group and who has had a long experience of frustration and failure. He will tolerate more because he feels sure there is little chance of being successful and he may be unwilling even to initiate grievances. It is this sense of individual impotence which is, of course, one of the basic reasons for wishing to join a union.

The grievant's attitude towards the power relationship in a given situation will also be affected by what Thomas[33] has called the 'concerns' which he perceives both sides to have. More specifically, the strength of the grievant's desire to satisfy his own concern can be expressed as the degree of assertiveness with which the grievance will be pursued, while the grievant's willingness to satisfy what he perceives to be the opponent's concern can be expressed as the degree of cooperativeness which can range from full cooperation to total non-cooperation. Fig. 2.4 illustrates these conflict handling orientations.

Fig. 2.4   Conflict handling orientations

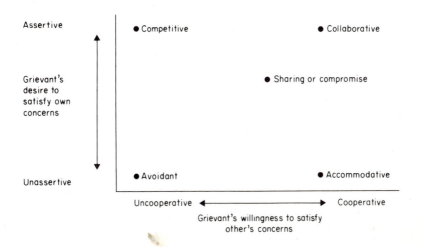

Thus when a grievant feels a strong desire to win his grievance and feels no empathy for management's viewpoint, a competitive orientation can be said to exist, while low assertiveness and a cooperative view of management's position will lead to an accommodative stance. Cases in which employees feel a strong desire to assert their own interests but also feel a willingness to satisfy others' concerns are perhaps the most constructive combinations to be found. They yield a collaborative orientation in which new approaches are sought which satisfy both parties.[34]

The nature of the issue   We have already pointed out that grievances have varying significance for the parties. The reasons for this are partly self-evident: some issues are more about money than others; some set precedents, others do not; some involve a single individual, others the union. In more general terms, the closer an issue comes to an individual's most fundamental needs or values or a group's most cherished normative beliefs, the more it will be seen as a matter of principle and the stronger the reaction to it will be.

The nature of the issue can affect the mode of its resolution. Most issues can, of course, be approached attitudinally in a number of different ways (cf. Thomas), but some, such as union recognition, are almost always seen as 'zero-sum' in the sense that what one party gets, the other party loses. Monetary issues, by contrast, are potentially possible to resolve so that both sides can achieve some of their objectives. The parties are less likely to adopt a collaborative problem solving approach where the issue is zero-sum, because they have less to gain by cooperation.

It is, of course, true that although a single issue may be or may appear to be zero-sum, a number of issues considered simultaneously can create a non-zero sum situation by permitting trade-offs between parties, or what Walton and McKersie[35] call 'utility swapping'. These package deals generally involve a union and may require that one individual's grievance be traded off for that of another in the interests of the group as a whole. This is, however, relatively rare in Britain, where grievances tend to be considered on an individual and 'on their merits' basis.

Another approach to the nature of the grievance issues has been provided by Gouldner's[36] categorisation of work rules according to the degree of legitimation which they receive from each side. In his study of labour relations in a US gypsum plant he noted a situation where both workers and managers tacitly ignored externally imposed rules (from head office) and had few disputes. He then traced the evolution of labour strikes as the rules were unilaterally enforced by management, ending in compromise and peace with a situation of more or less equal influence between union and management.

 Societal level factors shaping attitudes A final set of attitude creating factors can be seen as having a primary impact at the societal level. The Marxist analysis, which has already been mentioned, falls into this classification. Works concerned with changes in the larger society as an explanation of conflict include the recent report of the US Department of Health, Education, and Welfare, Wesley and Wesley, and Shepherd and Herrick.[37] Among the hypotheses put forward are: (a) increased education levels raise expectation levels amongst workers, who feel they deserve more interesting, challenging and better rewarded work than is available;

34

(b) the increasing pervasiveness of the mass media and the increasing geographical mobility of the population serve to make them more aware of comparative reference groups; (c) modern technology and greater organisational size bring about increasing rationalisation, fractionalisation and depersonalisation of work; (d) conditions of economic growth and concomitant increasing affluence lead people to feel they deserve more than the actual rate of increase in rewards; (e) the growth of the union movement serves as a focus for dissatisfaction, an enhancement of sense of power, and a mechanism for engaging in conflict.

The way in which norms and aspirations change and manifest themselves in challenges to existing norms and institutions has been brilliantly and evocatively described by Fox and Flanders[38] in relation to Britain in the post-war period. In part this works through its impact on procedural structures through 'the fragmentation of normative regulation', but the impact on attitudes creates a situation of anomie in which, following the authors in quoting Durkheim: 'The limits are unknown between the possible and the impossible, what is just and what is unjust, legitimate claims and hopes and those which are immoderate. Consequently there is no restraint upon aspirations.' Effects at one level can spill over at another and the dangers are social and political as well as economic, as is borne out by the history of British industrial relations since the article was written. Fox and Flanders have written apocalyptically about the spread of conflict between situations and system levels, but others, such as Whyte and Derber,[39] have also pointed out the influence on attitudes to resolving relatively minor grievance issues which the handling of relations at industry and national level can have.

Explanations of actions in the grievance process

The actions taken by grievants represent the culmination of the process that begins with their awareness of issues, attitudes toward the issues and the parties involved and feelings of power. It will be recalled that the actions possible are those of following procedural regulations or not, and, among specific actions, choosing to engage in information exchange, persuasion or problem solving; entering into bargaining; using direct punitive or rewarding actions or appealing to third parties. Unfortunately, theory and research which examines the choice among these kinds of actions in industrial disputes at the plant level is very limited.

Insofar as grievance actions are restricted to bargaining (an admittedly limited view of reality), one may gain some insight from what is known as 'games theory'. As Hyman[40] has noted, however, much of the games theory approach is both highly abstract and too complex to be useful within the limiting assumptions which are made. A more pragmatic, behaviourally oriented application of this approach is to be found in the masterly synthesis of Walton and McKersie.[41]

Labour negotiations, according to these authors, are comprised of four systems of activity, each with its own function for the interacting parties, its own internal logic and its own identifiable set of instrumental acts or tactics. The first subsystem, distributive bargaining, refers to zero-sum issues where one party's gain is the other party's loss. The second activity, integrative bargaining, occurs when the objectives of the two sides are not in direct conflict; instead there is an area of conflict in which 'the nature of [the] problem permits solutions which benefit both sides, or at least where the gains of one party do not represent equal sacrifices by the other.' The third subprocess is attitudinal structuring, which is 'the system of activities instrumental to the attainment of desired relationship patterns between the parties.' As such, it is not connected with the resolution of specific issues, but rather with the nature of the overall relationship. The last subprocess, intra-organisational bargaining, is, as its name implies, designed to achieve consensus within rather than between the parties, and particularly the bringing of 'the expectations of principals into alignment with those of the chief negotiator.'

Each subsystem contains its own process of resolution and, equally importantly, its own range of tactics which the parties can utilise. Thus, to take an example of the tactics of distributive bargaining, Walton and McKersie suggest two main categories of tactical behaviour. The first is manipulating utility parameters, by which the authors mean influencing the way in which the other side views and values the issue, including actions that either side might take in pursuit of it. Control of information is a key factor in this activity. The second is commitment tactics, which involves taking a position 'with some implicit or explicit pledge regarding a future course of action.' The objective is for the bargainer to reduce 'the range of indeterminateness down to the point most favourable to himself' by committing himself irrevocably to a position near the opponent's 'resistance point', i.e., the point beyond which the opponent will not accept a bargained settlement.

While Walton and McKersie's work contains numerous interesting hypotheses concerning the operation of the various activity components of bargaining, there has as yet been little systematic empirical research to test them, owing primarily to the difficulties of operationalising the variables and gaining access to suitable sites. The applicability of these hypotheses to the action phase of the grievance process is even more difficult because

36

they do not cover the transition of a grievance from individual to group identities, nor the many non-bargaining responses to it, including 'do nothing', withdrawal, and use of third parties. Among the few empirical studies available, those of McCarthy and Brown[42] examine the tactics used in grievance bargaining in Britain but, again, neither undertakes a detailed analysis of determinants of the choice of tactics.

Sayles[43] has argued that different types of work groups will manifest different patterns of grievance activity. 'Apathetic' groups produce relatively few grievances; 'erratic' groups are likely on occasion to erupt without warning in defiance of procedures but on other occasions give little support for important grievances; 'strategic' groups utilise planned and sustained pressure tactics in a cohesive way; while 'conservative' groups, although powerful, are more likely to pursue their objectives according to the rules of procedure. The reasons for these different behaviour patterns are largely, but not entirely, due to the cohesiveness and power of the group, which in turn is shaped by the technology of the work performed.

Perhaps the major studies directed explicitly at grievance actions at plant level in the United States are those of Kuhn, and Peach and Livernash.[44] Kuhn's particular interest is in the nature and extent of work group bargaining over grievances (which he called fractional bargaining) in the rubber and electrical industries. In his analysis he, like Sayles, saw the degree of this type of bargaining primarily as a function of the power of work groups, the number of issues created, and the strength of the group's attitudes toward the issues and management. Unofficial bargaining would not take place unless the work group felt itself to be frequently and seriously aggrieved and in possession of strong power *vis-à-vis* management (indicated by a high sense of its own uniqueness and autonomy and exclusive control of essential resources). These process characteristics he felt to be most strongly shaped by the technology of the work group:

> The technology most conducive to fractional bargaining has four characteristics: First, it subjects a large portion of the workers to continued changes in work methods, standards or materials as they work at individually paced jobs. Second, it allows workers a considerable degree of interaction with others in their task group as they work at their distinctive and specialized semi-skilled jobs. Third, it groups most of the work force into several nearly equal-sized task departments. And fourth, it requires continuous, rigidly sequential processing of materials into one major type of product.

The first and second of these above characteristics stimulates willingness of members of the work group to engage in fractional bargaining. The third tends to weaken the political authority of the local union over the work group and the fourth enables the work group to disrupt the plant's total production at a cost to itself which is small in relation to the cost it inflicts upon management.[45]

Peach and Livernash report a study of departments with high and low rates of written grievances in each of five plants in the US steel industry. In attempting to analyse the causes for the differing grievance rates both within and between plants they consider factors associated with the departmental and plant environments, union influences and management influences. The results of this study are well summarised in the following outline of characteristics which combine to give rise to a high grievance rate.

1   Environmental influences
1.A   Task organisation and work environment
1.A.1   High individual worker responsibility for quality and quantity of product
      2   Close attention to work required
      3   Satisfactory quality standards difficult to achieve requiring close supervision
      4   Frequent routine product and process changes, creating many non-routine problems and an unstable task situation
      5   A work environment that makes informal problem resolution difficult
      6   An incentive system with many non-standardised tasks and with many earnings and effort inequities
      7   A difficult-to-manage task environment with various possible additional unfavourable characteristics
1.B   Technological change
1.B.1   Frequent non-routine product and process changes induced by technological change creating job, employment, and wage-rate insecurity
1.C   Socio-economic conditions
1.C.1   Location in a large city environment with frequent union–management conflict and social unrest
      2   A large plant with impersonal relations and long lines of communication
      3   A plant history of union–management conflict
      4   Departmental civil rights issue
2   Union influences
2.A   Union leadership

2.A.1   Militant leadership of the radical, politician, or advocate type at both departmental and third-step levels
2.B   Union organisation
2.B.1   A union organisational structure placing minimal constraints on individual leadership behaviour
2.C   Union policies
2.C.1   Some special policies carrying all grievances of certain types at least to step 3
3   Management influences
3.A   Management leadership
3.A.1   Line management of an inactive or advocate type, inducing or requiring formal grievance and resolution at step 3 or above; little informal problem resolution
    2   Inactive foremen
3.B   Management organisation
3.B.1   Labour relations staff not active below step 3, again necessitating formal grievances and appeal to step 3 to reach the locus of staff decision making power
    2   Labour relations staff swamped by large numbers of formal grievances
3.C   Management policy
3.C.1   An incentive system with many inequities in earnings and effort aggravated by pressure tactics
    2   A weak and ineffective system of discipline
    3   Substantially no consultation with the union in advance of management action
    4   Other inconsistencies in management action, indicating an inadequate policy framework [46]

While the above two studies are among the few empirical works which deal explicitly with actions in grievance handling, it is nevertheless possible to hypothesise a few other influences on action choice by drawing on more general ideas from the study of the conflict process.

For example, it is probable that the greater the number of issues of complaint which arise in a work situation, the more likely it will be that procedures for regulating grievances will be insufficient for handling them and that some form of trading off, bargaining or direct action will result. One of the reasons this takes place is the tendency for many issues to be subsumed into one embodying the 'right' of the other party to control the outcome of the issue. Once the issue of such rights arises a zero-sum perception is quickly created.

39

The extent to which issues are viewed as zero-sum or the 'opponent' seen as untrustworthy is likely to move the action away from both regulated procedural paths and the use of persuasion and information exchange as the basis of action. Given the existence of a set of attitudes toward the issues and the parties, the net balance of power between the parties can also modify the actions they take. As Derber[47] has suggested, low net power on the part of union members will inhibit *any* action irrespective of the attitudes involved. High net worker power will result in *some* action, the particular choice being a function of the attitudes toward the issues and the opponent.

Although virtually no research has been carried out on the matter, the *bases* of sources of power as identified by French and Raven[48] may affect the kinds of actions used in grievance disputes. Where, for example, the power of workers is based strictly on their *number* rather than their specific skills or knowledge, it is more likely that the only action likely to be chosen in the course of bargaining over a grievance conflict is that of collectively withholding or threatening to withhold their labour. The group existence as a group becomes the main basis of power; it is also true that calm, thorough information exchange is more difficult when a number of people are involved on each side than when it is a case of two individuals who can act as such.

Perhaps the greatest determinant of the choice of actions in grievances or any other conflict at a given point of time is the outcome of immediate preceding actions. As Rapoport, and Pilisuk et al.[49] have pointed out, the strongest influence on the choice between cooperative and non-cooperative behaviour in the conflict simulation exercise known as the 'prisoner's dilemma game' was the 'tone' set in the first few encounters between the parties. Cooperative behaviour tends to elicit and perpetuate cooperative responses while the use of threats and punishment evokes like responses.

There are two contextual factors which are undoubtedly of considerable influence on the action choices of employees in small scale social conflicts over grievances within the plant. One of these is the effect of conflicts at 'higher' or 'larger' system levels and the other is the effect of third party intervention (other than as allies). The problem is that both questions have been so drastically under-researched that there is little to go on but pure speculation.

It seems obvious, for example, that where industrial relations at the level of the industry or the nation are in a state of high disruption with frequent conflicts, low levels of trust, considerable use of industrial action, etc., this will somehow be reflected on the shop floor in terms of a large number of difficult grievances from individuals and small groups. However obvious this may seem, though, it is not at all well established in fact. It may be that higher level conflict over money issues spurs the occurrence of money related grievances, e.g., over piece rates, special allowances, overtime, holiday pay, etc., but has little or no effect on non-monetary grievances over discipline, work allocation, physical conditions, etc.

Very little is known either in the matter of the effects of third party intervention on grievance related action where the third parties play the roles of agents, mediators or 'judges', e.g., arbitration. Some evidence from experimental conflict studies[50] indicates that people who view themselves as agents or representatives of the main opponents in a conflict are less willing to engage in coercive actions, possibly because they are not as emotionally bound up with the issue. Their behaviour seems to depend most strongly, however, on the nature of their relationship with their 'client'. Where an agent such as a union steward needs the 'client' employee(s) more than the latter needs him (for instance, when their votes are important), he is more likely to try not to do anything which would be displeasing. Thus grievances will sometimes be actively 'pushed' no matter how unjustifiable they may be. In the reverse situation the steward/agent may act with impunity in his dealings with the client, telling him his case is not justified or agreeing on a settlement without his approval.

The evidence of the effects of mediators and arbitrators in labour relations conflict is as skimpy as that on agents, if not more so. Most work on the mediation process has been on conflicts between managers[51] with only anecdotal discussions regarding the determinants of their effectiveness in labour relations situations. Regarding the process of arbitration, be it binding or not, there is general agreement though little definitive research on the qualifications of good arbitrators in US literature.[52] There is less agreement, however, on how they should play their role. Some feel they should behave strictly as judges, hearing the two sides to the dispute and deciding on legalistic grounds, while others favour a heavy use of mediating activity to try to bring the two sides as close as possible to an understanding before judgement is passed.

This concludes our examination of the main process and context based factors affecting the grievance process as they have been seen by previous writers in the field. The range of approaches is too numerous and too fragmented to provide any comprehensive model for the explanation of plant level conflict. However, insofar as we have been consciously influenced in our own analysis, the socio-technical school has probably provided the most direct assistance. We now turn our attention to the other independent variable, the nature of the grievance procedure itself, prior to analysing our own fieldwork on this subject

The nature of procedures and their role in grievance conflict theory

Most long lasting human relationships result in the evolution of a stable set of expectations regarding how the parties in the relationship should behave. These are usually referred to as norms and roles. When a set of relationships expands and becomes formalised into an organisation or institution it is common for the unspoken roles and norms to be written down as rules. Procedures are rules governing how actions should progress and in their industrial relations context they govern the establishment and administration of substantive rules dealing with the employment relationship.[53] Procedural rules of a formal or informal nature are generally more necessary for the successful operation of any organisation in the various aspects of its functioning well beyond the industrial relations sphere. Yet at the same time, as Pugh et al.[54] have pointed out, procedures contain many pitfalls and problems if they become too numerous or are of the wrong type. It is also true that once power is differentiated and concentrated in the hands of the 'top people' in an organisation the rules promulgated may deviate completely from the norms and role expectations held by those not in power: thus procedures may or may not be followed. Conversely, 'standard practices' may exist that are never codified as procedures yet which exert normative pressure on all those who know of them. The following section considers the particular case of grievance procedures and their potential impact.

The potential impact of procedures

Let us begin by pointing out some of the ways in which grievance procedures may *potentially* have an impact on the process by which single grievances are treated as described in the previous section. When it is operating under optimal conditions the procedure may help first in identifying the persons to whom the grievance should be put both initially and subsequently and in identifying persons on the union side who may be approached for assistance (i.e., it plays a social identity and role specification function). Secondly, the procedure may help to clarify the issue insofar as it may require that the complaint be written down or that advisers such as stewards be provided who can help the grievant articulate his problem. Thirdly, it may assist in obtaining appropriate

42

information insofar as it may require the keeping of precedent records or may direct that certain experts be consulted for specific kinds of issues, e.g., job evaluation committees, time study engineers, etc. Fourthly, it may speed up the decision process on management's side insofar as it specifies time limits for the various stages and ensures that only those with the requisite knowledge and authority are involved. Fifthly, it may ensure that decisions reached are communicated fully and quickly insofar as it specifies such requisites for management. Finally, by requiring that records of settlements be kept, the implementation stage can be facilitated and dependence on ambiguous custom and practice be reduced.

In addition to its potential impact on the handling of specific single grievances, procedures can also play a significant role in influencing the *overall relationship* between employees, union and management. These overall relationship functions are as follows:

1 Constitutional or recognition function: particularly at the industry-wide level, but also at the plant level, the disputes procedure is the means by which the two sides accept each other's legitimacy and by which they can interact. Clearly, where there is no union, a grievance procedure could not play this role.

2 Legislative or rule making: insofar as a procedure provides a mechanism for employees to *legitimately influence* and participate in decisions made by management, it is giving them a potential part of the legislative function of the firm.

3 Executive or administrative function: the procedure can be used to clarify and expand on management decisions by raising issues which create uncertainty. In this sense, the procedure is amplifying the executive function.

4 The judicial function: this is the main function in the organisation theory approach to procedures. The procedure provides a 'due process of law' by which higher level authorities review the appeals of employees against the decisions of lower level managers.

5 Power distribution: by specifying what can and cannot be done in the conflict resolution process, the procedure can give a tactical advantage to one side or the other and hence distribute power.

6 Communications: a procedure can help management become aware of grievances and, conversely, can help disseminate management policy.

From this it can be seen that the *potential* of procedures to influence the actual process in grievance handling is great. It should be emphasised again, however, that procedures can play these roles *only* if they have a normative character in the eyes of all parties to the dispute or if all parties are 'made' to accept the rules by some external force. Thus, for example, if one party can effectively sustain a belief that grievance procedures do not guarantee any 'constitutional' protection from certain actions; do not ensure rights to participate in certain decisions; do not provide for genuine judicial 'due process' review of past decisions; and only act as power levers for gaining better settlements out of bargaining, then this is the only function they will in fact have for that party.

One way to facilitate the development of a supportive normative climate for procedures is to ensure that the 'right' procedure is created for the specific context in which it will exist. The following section begins to identify this context by pointing out the many other procedures in an organisation which surround and relate to the grievance procedure. Next we identify the various component parts of procedures in order to better see how they can either cause problems or facilitate their solution. The importance of the way procedures are perceived by the participants is stressed next before reviewing existing literature on the determinants of procedural effectiveness.

Other types of procedures in the worker–management relationship

In the study of industrial relations, reference to 'procedure' almost always means the grievance or disputes procedure, depending on the system level at which one is looking, but in fact, as the Industrial Relations Act of 1971 pointed out, there exists several sets of functionally different procedures aimed at different facets of the worker–manager relationship.

1   Work performance procedures, often called collectively the 'works rules' and incorporated into a rulebook, are regulations, frequently set unilaterally by management, which govern the behaviour of employees on the job. Examples of these rules are stopping and starting times, dress and deportment, job allocation and transfer procedures, etc. They also include procedures for the setting of piece rates, the evaluation of jobs and other changes of considerable concern to employees, and are one of the most frequent sources of grievance issues.

2   Consultative procedures are mechanisms created for consulting with workers or their representatives prior to or even after decisions on changes in various work related matters. No issues of 'dispute' are implied.

3   Specialised procedures covering specific issues or particular groups may also be differentiated from, although remaining part of, the grievance procedure. The purpose behind this is often to bring in management specialists who would have no role in the general grievance procedure. Examples of these might cover job evaluation, redundancy, safety and

various types of welfare arrangements such as canteens, leisure activities, parking, etc. Disciplinary and dismissal actions represent another somewhat unique case of special procedures.

4 Negotiating or 'claims' procedures are frequently not differentiated from grievance procedures in British industry, the two being lumped together as disputes procedures. It is nevertheless feasible to define claims procedures as those governing the process by which union leaders petition for substantial departures from the status quo on behalf of many or all of their members in a given plant, firm, or industry. One of the dominant recommendations in much of the recent literature advocating plant level industrial relations has been the need to create specific plant and company level negotiating procedures and committees in order to develop comprehensive collective agreements at this level.

5 Industry-wide disputes procedures, for a long time the only formal procedures in most parts of British industry, have rarely specified in detail how a grievance was to be handled at the plant level. However, the first stage of the industry-wide procedures was usually held physically within the plant with the attendance of union and employer association officials, and could thus be considered the last stage of the internal procedure.

6 Recognition procedures may be embodied in the disputes procedure; as Marsh[55] has pointed out, one of the primary functions of the disputes procedure is to confer recognition on the parties to it. But there can also be a separate recognition procedure incorporating, for instance, some element of union security such that new employees will be encouraged to or must join the union. Other elements of procedure, supportive of the basic mutual recognition, can also be included in this category. Dues check-off procedures, shop steward facilities and payment for union work are examples of procedures which can enhance union legitimacy.

7 Management functions and status quo agreements are procedures which help to determine the scope of the relationship. Thus a management functions clause may reserve certain decisions for management alone whether or not the workers and their representatives approve. Status quo agreements are those in which management is pledged to hold up implementation of any change which has been protested from the workers' side until the procedures have been exhausted. Such statements are of great importance in distributing power through procedures.

8 The final category of procedural type is that of intra-party procedures. These can be of great importance in affecting the internal structure of power and authority as well as the representatives of each side who must deal with each other over grievances. Most intra-party procedures are those common and necessary within organisations, providing for upwards and

downwards information flows, the appointment or election of individuals to deal with various functions, and so on. Occasionally the other side may have some influence in these procedures, such as management insistence that shop steward candidates must have a given period of service behind them. Of potentially great significance are cases where several unions are represented on the worker side and it becomes necessary to have joint inter-union bodies to deal with questions of 'sphere of influence' and demarcation conflicts.

The foregoing typology may be a little misleading in that it appears to assign fairly specific functions to different procedures. It is, of course, unlikely that all the above procedures would exist in any one enterprise and there is in any case likely to be more overlapping and less clarity than has been indicated. It might, for instance, be very difficult to tell whether a particular grievance should be processed through a specialised procedure or not; it might be unclear whether a grievance should be considered and negotiated directly as a claim; consultation may be an ambivalent term in the context of a particular issue. Nevertheless, the conceptual differentiation of procedural types is analytically useful in the way it reminds one to look beyond the conventional grievance procedure in examining procedural effectiveness.

Attitudes and perceptions towards grievance procedures

A further facet of importance is how the grievance procedures are *perceived* by the parties involved: employees, union officials of various levels, foremen, department heads, top management. The structure of procedures may be seen by the various parties as having various advantages and disadvantages which in turn can have a considerable impact on the way in which they are actually used.

For example, in the case of the senior management of the firm or plant procedures may represent excellent means for achieving consistency in policy formulation and application. Insofar as the procedure filters out matters of purely local interest and funnels upward those issues with major implication for costs and performance, it both saves them time and gives them better control and coordination of the organisation. It is also true that procedures which place them at the apex of the appeal system serve to confirm and support the existing social order and power structure, whereas in unregulated conflict this legitimising support is missing.

From the point of view of shop stewards there are at least two possible sets of expectations from procedures. Among those who take an active role, the objective of procedures may be to provide answers to grievances with the greatest possible speed. (Top management's desire for consistency and policy improvement may go against this, however.) They may also be seen as guaranteeing a greater amount of participation in decision making (which again may go against top management's desire for closer control). Among those who view their roles more passively (certain reluctant shop stewards, for example) the procedures may be seen as a handy 'crutch' of rules which specify the actions to be undertaken and thus remove the need to take initiatives about the matter. To follow procedures and report back the answers is simple and sufficient compared to a totally informal situation. Such a view does *not,* of course, seriously clash with top management's feelings about procedures.

The workers for their part probably wish to see procedures as yielding, first and foremost, greater speed and equity – a quick decision that ends a real or imagined sense of injustice. Again, speed is not always consistent with considered attempts to assess policy implications of decisions in accord with top management's desires. Workers may also see procedures as a guarantee against victimisation – a form of legal protection of the right to protest against management decisions. Similarly, they are expected to provide an official appeal function which ensures that complaints will go 'over the heads' of those who may have created the undesirable situation and be considered afresh by someone who was not involved. Both these expectations, while not in theory contrary to management's wishes, may nevertheless in practice be viewed by them as a threat to their authority and the desire to preserve a 'united front' of management personnel from all levels against the workers. This, of course, is a potential problem in any situation, whether or not procedures exist.

It is perhaps in the case of lower level managers that procedures present the greatest source of ambivalence and potential contradictions. On the one hand, they desire to obtain or retain the greatest amount of autonomy and flexibility in the running of their sections or departments and in this respect the appeals system presented by procedures and management's desire to use them for coordination and control runs counter to these wishes. On the other hand, there is also commonly found a desire for support and backing up by superiors which is just what workers do not want when appealing against a foreman's decision. When issues do arise which have broad policy implications many lower level managers would prefer to be able to pass them up rather than take the risk of making such decisions as procedures legitimately entitle them to do, yet it is also true that they would prefer to be involved in the making of such policy decisions if they are to be held responsible for implementing them and making them work. Since some procedures deliberately leave them out of these higher level decisions while equally deliberately including union representatives, a feeling of resentment is easily generated amongst the lower managers.

As well as these four main groups of participants, there are others who might have separate perceptions and feelings about procedures. Staff managers are one such group, especially those concerned with the personnel function. Their concerns are likely to relate to the division of authority between line and staff management, and also to their somewhat more detached perspective of the worker–manager relationship. Being less directly concerned with the immediacy of production, they may be able to take a rather longer term view of grievances. Again, full-time union officials may have distinct views about procedure. They will want most grievances to be settled at plant level, but they may not want stewards to have complete responsibility for issues that might affect union policy, nor will they want to lose influence within the plant. Employer association officials may have parallel views to those of union officials, although they are likely to be of less importance in setting plant level procedures. It is the fact that different groups have different interests in the various elements of procedure, and that procedures are also likely to vary according to technological, economic and organisational circumstances which has made it so difficult to develop acceptable criteria for evaluating procedural effectiveness.

Effects of procedures on the conflict process: existing research

The basic question is: what evidence is there that procedures facilitate, have no effect on or even exacerbate the settlement of grievances? As has already been intimated, there have been a great number of untested assumptions made about the value of procedures but very little development of a theory of procedures which integrates with theories of conflict and even less empirical research which systematically examines their impact on the conflict process. Most research to date in Great Britain has concentrated on industry-wide procedures rather than those at plant level.

While such works as the Donovan Report have urged the introduction of more and 'better' procedures at plant level, the basis for this emphasis on procedures has largely been on research which revealed numerous plant level conflict situations but did not prove that the absence of 'proper' procedure had caused them or would correct them.

Subsequent 'case studies' of specific companies by the CIR and other bodies have been much more careful in documenting the numerous other structural and contextual causes of poor plant level relations and have tended to recommend procedural reform in conjunction with numerous other changes in work arrangements, organisation structure and management style.[56] Based only on 'samples of one' there is, of course, no statistical generalisation possible from these studies.

Studies using more sophisticated methodology have tended to be of the survey type which investigates *attitudes* toward procedures on the part of stewards, foremen, etc., but does not dissect the actual content of procedures nor relate either attitudes or content to measures of procedural effectiveness.[57] Nor, of course, do we have any real idea of what constitutes a reasonable amount of conflict, taking account of a multitude of external factors. To this extent there is no criterion against which to measure the efficiency of procedures.

On the other hand, studies of plant level labour relations and grievances in the United States (such as those already referred to by Kuhn, Peach and Livernash, and Derber) have largely taken grievance procedures as given while concentrating on other factors creating the grievances. With the almost universal system of grievance procedures limiting grievances to contract administration and requiring compulsory arbitration, no thought appears to have been given to alternative approaches and their possible effects.

With few exceptions, US studies which are empirical in nature and include explicit references to the grievance procedure do not relate it to the grievance process while empirical and theoretical studies of the process tend to ignore the role of procedures.[58] For example, Lawshe and Guion[59] surveyed some 400 management and labour oriented individuals to assess similarities and differences in their attitudes toward grievance procedures. Ash,[60] in a study similar to that of Peach and Livernash, attempted to discover the correlates of high and low grievance rates, as did Sulkin and Pranis.[61] Both concentrated on the personality differences of individuals who were frequent and infrequent submitters of grievances. In neither case were procedures examined as such. Textbooks such as those of Chamberlain and Kuhn[62] and the research of Slichter, Healy and Livernash[63] point out that grievance procedures may be systematically subverted for tactical purposes by both union and management in the interests of their larger scale conflicts. They also discuss the pros and cons of 'clinical' versus legalistic approaches to grievance handling at the various stages, especially that of arbitration. They do not systematically relate the two discussions, however.

One of the few American studies which does explicitly link procedures and process is that of Ross.[64] In examining a number of plants suffering from what he calls 'distressed grievance procedures' (where grievance handling is over-mechanical, overloaded with issues and relies unduly on arbitration), a number of essentially procedural remedies are suggested:

less legalism, creation of special review boards within the union and other more minor changes in procedural structure. McKersie and Shropshire[65] deal with a particular case of distressed grievance procedure at the International Harvester Co. in the 1950s, crediting a change in the procedure from one emphasising the writing of grievances at all stages to one emphasising a much less formal treatment in the early stages. From a situation in which 48,000 grievances were appealed to arbitration between 1954 and 1958, the number of written grievances fell to almost nil in the early 1960s. Thomson also cites the case of the US steel industry in which greater emphasis on informality and a non-legalistic approach at the arbitration level coupled with greater emphasis on a problem solving approach at the earlier levels has similarly reduced 'distressed procedures'.[66]

This chapter has attempted to provide a conceptual framework for the analysis of grievance based in-plant conflicts and the particular influence on them of grievance procedures. From the admittedly brief review of existing theory and research on these questions it was concluded that conflict theory in general has been strikingly neglectful of the particular case of grievances involving individuals and small groups of workers while studies of procedures as such have largely failed to relate to the conflict process. In the next chapter we turn to the data from our own empirical study of grievance procedures in Britain after which we return again to suggest some tentative answers to the theoretical questions raised here.

Notes

[1] International Labour Conference Report 7 (1), *Examination of Grievances and Communications Within the Undertaking,* International Labour Office, Geneva 1965, pp. 7–9.

[2] L.R. Pondy, 'Organizational conflict: concepts and models', *Administrative Science Quarterly,* vol. 12, 1967, pp. 296–320.

[3] V.V. Murray, 'Some unanswered questions on organizational conflict', *Organization and Administrative Science,* Winter 1974–75, pp. 35–53.

[4] See James W. Kuhn, *Bargaining in Grievance Settlement,* Columbia University Press, New York 1961; Milton Derber et al., *Plant Union–Management Relations: From Practice to Theory,* University of Illinois, Urbana 1965; and W.F. Whyte, *Pattern for Industrial Peace,* Harper, New York 1951. See also the published case reports of the British Commission on Industrial Relations.

[5] Derber et al., *Plant Union–Management Relations,* op. cit., pp. 43–8.

[6] See Karl Marx, *Capital, The Communist Manifesto and Other*

Writings, edited by M. Eastman, The Modern Library, New York 1932; Ralf Dahrendorf, *Class and Class Conflict in Industrial Society,* Stanford University Press, Stanford 1959; George Simmel, *Conflict and the Web of Intergroup Affiliations,* Free Press, Glencoe 1955; Lewis Coser, *The Functions of Social Conflict,* Free Press, Glencoe 1956.

Martin Patchen has conveniently grouped modern games theorists under two main headings: 'negotiation model' theorists who seek to explain the settlement in bilateral bargaining and 'influence model' theorists who seek general explanations of the actions used by parties in conflict (strikes, wars, etc.). See Martin Patchen, 'Models of cooperation and conflict: a critical review', *Journal of Conflict Resolution,* vol. 14, September 1970, pp. 389–406.

[7] See Max Weber, *The Theory of Social and Economic Organizations,* Oxford University Press, New York 1947; Lyndal Urwick, *The Elements of Administration,* Pitman, London 1947; Mary Parker Follett, 'Constructive conflict' in H.C. Metcalf and L. Urwick (eds), *Dynamic Administration,* Harper, New York 1942.

It is, of course, impossible to find full agreement as to who the main figures are in any particular school of thought in the social sciences. It is also true that there are usually significant differences among those who comprise a 'school' in spite of the commonalities that bring them together. Such comments hold for the human relations school of organisation theory. There is fair agreement, however, that writers such as Mayo, Likert, McGregor and Argyris are strongly representative of it.

The two key works representative of the 'decision theory' school of organisation theory are those of James March and Herbert Simon.

The designations 'socio-technical' and 'contingency' theory are perhaps even less well-accepted than some of the others mentioned so far, yet they are commonly used in textbooks and reviews on the subject. Among the more frequently mentioned names in this group are those of Joan Woodward, L.R. Sayles, Tom Burns and G.M. Stalker, Michel Crozier, and Paul R. Lawrence and Jay W. Lorsch.

[8] J.T. Dunlop, *Industrial Relations Systems,* Southern Illinois University Press, Carbondale, 1958.

[9] For example, Warren H. Schmidt and R. Tannenbaum, 'The management of differences', *Harvard Business Review,* vol. 38, 1960, pp. 107–15; Robert R. Blake, H.A. Shepard and J.S. Mouton, *Managing Intergroup Conflict in Industry,* Gulf Publishing, Houston 1964; Alan C. Filley, *Interpersonal Conflict Resolution,* Scott, Foresman, Glenview 1975; S.P. Robbins, *Managing Organizational Conflict,* Prentice-Hall, Englewood Cliffs 1974.

[10] P.C. Smith, 'The development of a method of measuring job satisfaction' in E.A. Fleishman (ed.), *Studies in Personnel and Industrial Psychology,* Dorsey Press, Homewood, Ill. 1967.

[11] W.G. Runciman, *Relative Deprivation and Social Justice,* Penguin, London 1972.

[12] For example, W. Brown, 'A consideration of custom and practice', *British Journal of Industrial Relations,* March 1972.

[13] J.T. Dunlop, *Wage Determination Under Trade Unions,* Augustus Kelly, New York 1950; and A.M. Ross, *Trade Union Wage Policy,* University of California Press, Berkeley 1950.

[14] A. Maslow, *Motivation and Personality,* Harper, New York 1954.

[15] Ross Stagner and H. Rosen, *The Psychology of Union Management Relations,* Tavistock, London 1965.

[16] Chris Argyris, *Personality and Organization,* op. cit.

[17] Peter Blau and W.R. Scott, *Formal Organizations,* Chandler, San Francisco 1962.

[18] Alan Fox, *Beyond Contract: Work Power and Trust Relations,* Faber, London 1974.

[19] See H.A. Turner, G. Clack and G. Roberts, *Labour Relations in the Motor Industry,* Allen and Unwin, London 1967; and G. Clack, *Industrial Relations in a British Car Factory,* Cambridge University Press, Cambridge 1967.

[20] Robert Blauner, *Alienation and Freedom: The Factory Worker and His Industry,* University of Chicago Press, Chicago 1964.

[21] Leonard Sayles, *The Behavior of Industrial Work Groups,* op. cit.

[22] P. Cleland, *The Influence of Plant Size on Industrial Relations,* Princeton University Press, Princeton 1955.

[23] G.K. Ingham, *Size of Industrial Organization and Worker Behaviour,* Cambridge University Press, Cambridge 1970.

[24] J.H. Goldthorpe et al., *The Affluent Worker: Industrial Attitudes and Behaviour,* Cambridge University Press, Cambridge 1969.

[25] Shirley Terryberry, 'The evolution of organizational environments', *Administrative Science Quarterly,* vol. 12, 1968, pp. 590–613.

[26] Charles Perrow, *Organizational Analysis: A Sociological View,* Wadsworth, Belmont, Cal. 1970.

[27] Tom Burns and G.M. Stalker, *The Management of Innovation,* op. cit.

[28] Clark Kerr and A. Siegal, 'The inter-industry propensity to strike: An international comparison' in Arthur Kornhauser, R. Dubin and A. Ross (eds), *Industrial Conflict,* McGraw-Hill, New York 1954, pp. 189–212; Sayles, *Behavior of Industrial Work Groups, op. cit.*; Blake, Shepard and Mouton, *Managing Intergroup Conflict in Industry,* op. cit.

[29] Coser, *The Functions of Social Conflict,* op. cit.

[30] Kerr and Siegal, 'The inter-industry propensity to strike', op. cit.

[31] J.W. Thibaut and H.H. Kelly, *The Social Psychology of Groups,* Wiley, New York 1959.

[32] W.E.J. McCarthy, *The Role of Shop Stewards in British Industrial Relations,* RCTUEA Research Paper, 1968; Kuhn, *Bargaining in Grievance Settlement,* op. cit.

[33] Kenneth W. Thomas, 'Conflict and conflict management' in Marvin D. Dunnette (ed.), *The Handbook of Industrial and Organizational Psychology,* Rand McNally, Chicago, in press.

[34] Thomas, ibid.

[35] Richard E. Walton and Robert B. McKersie, *A Behavioral Theory of Labor Relations,* McGraw-Hill, New York 1965.

[36] Alvin Gouldner, *Patterns of Industrial Bureaucracy,* Free Press, Glencoe, Ill. 1954.

[37] United States Department of Health, Education and Welfare, *Work in America,* MIT Press, Cambridge, Mass. 1973; W.A. Wesley and M.W. Wesley, *The Emerging Worker,* McGill–Queen's University Press, Montreal 1971; H.L. Shepherd and Neal Herrick, *Where Have All the Robots Gone?,* The Free Press, New York 1972.

[38] A. Fox and A. Flanders, 'The reform of collective bargaining: From Donovan to Durkheim', *British Journal of Industrial Relations,* July 1969, pp. 151–80.

[39] Whyte, *A Pattern for Industrial Peace,* op. cit.; and Derber et al., *Plant–Union Management Relations,* op. cit.

[40] R. Hyman, *Disputes Procedures in Action,* Heinemann, London 1973.

[41] Walton and McKersie, op. cit.

[42] See McCarthy, *The Role of Shop Stewards in British Industrial Relations,* op. cit.; W. Brown, 'Piecework wage determination in Coventry', *Scottish Journal of Industrial Relations,* February 1971, and 'A consideration of custom and practice', *British Journal of Industrial Relations,* March 1972.

[43] Sayles, *The Behavior of Industrial Work Groups,* op. cit.

[44] Kuhn, *Bargaining in Grievance Settlement,* op. cit.; D. Peach and E.R. Livernash, *Grievance Initiation and Resolution: A Study in Basic Steel,* Graduate School of Business Administration, Harvard University 1974.

[45] Kuhn, op. cit., p. 148.

[46] Peach and Livernash, op. cit., pp. 137–9. It should be noted that Peach and Livernash emphasise that this outline is necessarily exaggerated for the purposes of summarising and it is not meant to imply that all causal factors must be present to cause a high grievance situation.

[47] Derber et al., op. cit.

[48] John R.P. French and Bertram Raven, 'The bases of social power' in Dorwin Cartwright (ed.), *Studies in Social Power,* University of Michigan, Ann Arbor 1959, pp. 150–67.

[49] A. Rapoport, 'Experiments in dyadic conflict and cooperation', *Bulletin of the Menninger Clinic,* vol. 30, 1966, pp. 284–91; M. Pilisuk et al., 'War hawks and peace doves: Alternative resolutions of experimental conflicts', *Journal of Conflict Resolution,* vol. 9, December 1965, pp. 491–508.

[50] Neil Vidman and J.E. McGrath, 'Forces affecting success in negotiation groups', *Behavioural Science,* vol. 15, 1970, pp. 154–63.

[51] For example, see Robbins, op. cit.; Filley, op. cit.; and Edgar F. Huse, *Organization Development and Change,* West Publishing, St Paul 1975.

[52] Sumner H. Slichter, James H. Healy and E. Robert Livernash, *The Impact of Collective Bargaining on Management,* Brookings Institution, Washington DC 1960.

[53] Dunlop, *Industrial Relations Systems,* op. cit., pp. 13–16.

[54] D.S. Pugh, D.J. Hickson, C.R. Hinings and C. Turner, 'Dimensions of organizational structure', *Administrative Science Quarterly,* vol. 13, 1968, pp. 65–105.

[55] A. Marsh, *Disputes Procedures in British Industry,* RCTUEA Research Paper, HMSO 1966.

[56] Many of these cases are discussed in chapter 6.

[57] See, for example, W.E.J. McCarthy, *The Role of Shop Stewards in British Industrial Relations,* op. cit.

[58] For a review of the American literature see A.W.J. Thomson, *The Grievance Procedure in the Private Sector,* New York State School of Industrial and Labor Relations, Cornell University 1974.

[59] C.H. Lawshe and R.M. Guion, 'A comparison of management labor attitudes towards grievance procedures', *Personnel Psychology,* vol. 4, 1951, pp. 3–17.

[60] Philip Ash, 'The parties to the grievance', *Personnel Psychology,* vol. 23, 1970, pp. 13–38.

[61] Howard A. Sulkin and Robert W. Pranis, 'Comparison of grievants and non-grievants in a heavy machinery company', *Personnel Psychology,* vol. 20, 1967, pp. 111–20.

[62] Neil W. Chamberlain and James W. Kuhn, *Collective Bargaining,* 2nd ed., McGraw-Hill, New York 1965.

[63] Slichter, Healy and Livernash, op. cit.

[64] Arthur M. Ross, *Distressed Grievance Procedures and Their*

Rehabilitation, reprint, Institute of Industrial Relations, University of California, Berkeley 1963.

[65] Robert B. McKersie and William W. Shropshire Jr, 'Avoiding written grievances: A successful program', *Journal of Business of the University of Chicago,* vol. 35, 1962, pp. 135–52.

[66] Thomson, *The Grievance Procedure,* op. cit., pp. 29–30.

3 Grievance procedures in the plants surveyed

Having provided a brief historical and theoretical introduction to the phenomenon of plant level grievances and the role of procedures in the conflict process, we now turn to the data obtained from our survey of grievance handling in thirty-five British factories. We begin by describing the number and kind of formal procedures and standard practices prescribed, i.e., the official way in which grievances were 'supposed' to be treated. Subsequent chapters reveal how they were handled in practice. Basic overall structural characteristics of the procedures are presented first, followed by a review of their content and the varying degrees of formality embodied in them. In addition, several procedural elements of the industrial relations structure in the plant *other* than that surrounding grievances are briefly described.

The structure of grievance procedures

Plants possessing written internal grievance procedures

Overall, 22 of the plants out of the total of 35 visited had some form of written intra-plant procedure to cover grievances (see Table 3.1). Usually, no differentiation was made between grievances and major disputes, the whole normally being referred to as a disputes procedure. However, it was clear that in all cases except one grievances were the form of dispute intended since the procedure began with reference to 'the' employee with a question or complaint.

From Table 3.1 it can be seen that of the 7 carpet manufacturing plants visited, 3 had some form of written grievance procedure. Only 4 of the 12 chemical plants had a written procedure while, conversely, 14 out of the 16 plants manufacturing food products were able to show us a written procedure. The size of the plants visited ranged from 80 to 7,000 employees. In general it appears that larger size (over 1,000 employees) is related to the existence of procedures since 11 of the 14 respondents of this size had procedures while only just over half of the 21 plants with less than 1,000 employees did.

Table 3.1

Factories with formal grievance procedures by size and type of industry

	Number of employees						Total by industry		
	1,000 +		300–1,000		Under 300				
	P	NP	P	NP	P	NP	P	NP	Total
Carpets	2	3	1	1	–	–	3 (43%)	4	7
Chemicals	1	–	–	4	3	4	4 (33%)	8	12
Food	8	–	1	1	6	–	15 (94%)	1	16
Total by size	11 (78%)	3	2 (33%)	6	9 (69%)	4	22 (63%)	13	35

P = procedure
NP = no procedure

Perhaps of greater influence on the existence of procedures than either size or type of industry was whether the plant was part of a large multi-plant firm in which the head office exerted relatively strong centralised control over personnel policies. Multi-plant firms appeared to be of two types. There were those which operated in a highly decentralised fashion in which financial performance indicators were the main source of control by the head office. These were firms usually constructed through relatively recent mergers among similarly sized previously independent companies. The second type was the multi-plant firm which established a number of standard operating procedures to be followed by all plants. Such firms comprised plants made up of 'old' mergers or simply expanded operations. While we did not obtain extensive systematic detail on the nature of head office control in the multi-plant firms studied, we did find out for most firms the extent to which head office was involved in designing the formal disputes procedures used.

Of the 16 factories surveyed in the food industry, 15 were members of multi-plant firms. All had formal procedures. Of these, it was clear that head office had been instrumental in setting up the procedures in 14 of them. Either they had simply imposed them on the plants or else they had 'assisted' the plants in developing their own procedural terms. On the other hand, 8 of the 12 factories in the chemical industry were members of multi-plant organisations and of these only 3 had formal disputes procedures. In all but one of those without procedures the amount of head office control of the factories was very low on all fronts. Their interest was primarily financial. Finally, in the case of the 7 plants in the carpet industry, 3 were part of multi-plant firms with very loose control over their branches. None were part of high control firms. The remaining four had all their manufacturing operations in one geographical site. Of these, one of the single plant and two of the multi-plant firms had formal grievance procedures.

Thus all of the sixteen factories which were part of multi-plant firms with a high level of head office influence had written formal grievance procedures. In factories which were part of multi-plant firms with low head office influence on operations 4 out of 10 had formal grievance procedures, while in 11 'single plant' firms studied, 2 had formal grievance procedures (see Table 3.2). Why this should be so is not certain; however, it is likely that: (a) large size is related to being able to afford the hiring of expensive and sophisticated personnel management staff aware of the current professional and academic literature emphasising the value of formal procedures; and (b) a feature of centralised control is written rules, of which grievance procedures are one form.

Table 3.2

Factories with formal grievance procedures by industry and nature of ownership and control

	Multi-plant with high head office control		Multi-plant with low head office control		Single plant		Total		
	P	NP	P	NP	P	NP	P	NP	Total
Carpets	–	–	2	1	1	3	3	4	7
Chemicals	1	–	1	5	1	3	4	8	12
Food	14	–	1	–	–	1	15	1	16
Total	15 (100%)	–	4 (40%)	6	2 (22%)	7	22 (63%)	13	35

As a final note on the number of formal disputes procedures at factory level, it should be noted that of the 22 factories possessing them, the vast majority were developed within three years prior to our interviews, i.e., from 1969 onwards. This presumably reflects in part the early effects of the Donovan Report's recommendations.

Plants with 'standard practices' for handling grievances

We have defined 'standard practices' to mean more or less habitual, officially accepted (though not formally promulgated) patterns for the handling of grievances. They are, in effect, like formal procedures in that they represent understandings about what *should* happen rather than what does, yet they are not 'official' procedures in that the understanding is tacit rather than explicit.

As may be imagined, the factual existence of such things as standard practices is difficult to distinguish empirically from actual processes. In addition to obtaining copies of formal procedures we asked top and middle management respondents what the 'usual' practice was for handling grievances. If several respondents tended to give the same or highly similar answers we assumed that a standard practice existed. If managers said there were no 'usual' ways of handling things or if we obtained highly varied responses as to what was usual we assumed no standard practices existed. As with the formal written procedures, however, these general statements of the 'usual' were not necessarily the *actual* process by which grievances were handled. This we inferred from asking people to describe the handling of specific types of grievances and their actual roles in dealing with particular complaints and disputes.

Using the above means for estimating, it appeared that in all but three of our thirty-five factories top and middle management respondents perceived the existence of some kind of accepted standard practice to be followed in the handling of complaints and disputes. As we will see later, these 'understandings' were often quite vague and general and carried little in the way of normative sanctions for deviation, yet they did exist. Unfortunately, it was not clear from our interview data whether this understanding simply evolved informally out of the manager 'learning' on a case-by-case basis what should be done; or whether the 'standards' were presented orally by higher level management as 'good general guidelines on what to do in the case of a grievance'.

Of the 3 factories which did not give any evidence of possessing a 'standard practice', 2 were in chemicals and 1 in carpets. One had only recently been unionised and was in the process of learning to adapt to this. The other two appeared to be managed in a highly decentralised fashion down to the middle management level within the factory so that each middle manager felt no obligation to handle disputes in a uniform way.

Content of procedures

When one looks beyond the mere fact of existence or non-existence of procedures in our sample of factories to their content, one is struck by their extreme simplicity. They are little more than statements of steps in the hierarchy through which any complaint or dispute must be taken. We will therefore now consider the content in terms of the number of levels of the procedures and the content of each level with specific emphasis on the terminal stage.

Number of stages in internal grievance procedures Of the 22 written procedures found in factories under study, 5 contained four stages, 5 contained five stages, 4 contained six stages, 5 contained seven stages; one contained eight stages and one did not specify stages but left the matter to the discretion of the grievant and his representatives. In terms of industrial grouping, all three of the carpet factories had procedures specifying only four stages; of the 4 chemical factories with formal procedures, 3 had five-stage procedures and one, the largest, had six. Among the 15 food factories with written procedures, 10 contained six or more stages (3 with six; 5 with seven; 2 with eight stages).

Why these inter-industry differences should exist, however, is not clear. In general, food industry plants were part of large companies; however, large (over 1,000) firms in carpets and chemicals had fewer stages than the large food companies. Another explanation may be in the control structure of the factories identified earlier in connection with the differences in the mere presence or absence of procedures. Of the 5 plants with only four levels, 4 of them belonged to either single plant firms or, in one case, a multi-plant firm with little or no influence exerted by head office. Conversely, where the number of levels exceeded six, all factories in this category belonged to multi-plant firms in which it appeared to us that there was considerable head office influence. The way this involvement of head office leads to more numerous stages is discussed below.

Content of procedural stages The first three stages of most written grievance procedures tended to be much the same from factory to factory. The typical first stage states that the employee must consult his foreman when he has a grievance. The main variation in this stage in our sample was whether or not the union steward was to be allowed in at the initial stage. The tendency was to keep him out—only 5 of the 22 procedures either required or allowed the steward to represent the grievant in the first stage. In one case, where the procedure was primarily written for group as opposed to individual grievances, the first stage involved informal bi-weekly departmental meeting of stewards, foremen and manager.

In the second stage, the typical procedural requirement was to take the grievance to the foreman's immediate superior. Such people have varying titles depending on the structure of the firm–supervisor, superintendent, assistant department manager, shift superintendent, etc. At this point the procedure usually allowed or required the presence of the grievant's union steward. Though this was the norm in our sample, there was much more variation than in the case of the first stage. In five cases, for example, the steward on entering the procedure had to go back to the foreman to whom the employee had initially spoken before he could take the case higher. In another seven or so cases (it was not always possible to obtain perfectly accurate organisational charts, hence our figures can only be approximate) the steward in this second stage could or had to leapfrog the level of management, often referred to as superintendent or supervisor, and go to the next level, typically referred to as department manager.

In the third stage, one typically found a split between those procedures which move only to the level of departmental manager and those which go higher. This was also the point at which some procedures allowed the entry of union officials higher than steward level. Twelve of our factories specified the department manager as being equivalent as the third stage and of these 9 left the steward as the chief spokesman for the employee and only 3 allowed the entry of a chief steward or union convenor at this point. Eight allowed the grievance to move beyond the department manager to the second in command of the factory (variously titled production manager, deputy manager, etc.) and with this action higher levels of union official invariably entered.

By the time the fourth stage of the procedure was reached diversity was quite widespread. Among procedures which *end* at the fourth stage, four specified a meeting between the top union branch official and/or a representative of the national union and the top factory manager (managing director, general manager, factory director, etc.). In another case, the fourth and last stage was a meeting of steward, branch secretary, assistant manager and factory manager. The factory whose procedure is for group-type grievances only typically ends at the fourth stage with a 'works meeting' at which all unionised employees vote by secret ballot on the management's last offer for settlement on the issue.

Among those procedures that did not end at the fourth stage, this fourth stage also tended to represent a top level in-factory meeting. The remaining stages then became statements on what to do beyond the factory level if no agreement was reached. In a large chemical factory for example, the fourth stage brought together the union's district officer and a committee of managers from different factories on the same site. A fifth stage referred the grievance to a 'regional conference' of union and management officials and the final stage was a head office conference among national union leaders and corporate directors.

In one large food factory the last stages varied. In an agreement with white collar workers the fourth stage put top branch officials in a meeting with top factory management; then, if no agreement was reached, it specified voluntary arbitration as a fifth stage if both parties were willing to accept this. In an agreement with maintenance engineers 'general issues', i.e., department-wide disputes, went to a negotiating committee of three union officials and the factory personnel director, while individual and small group grievances went up the hierarchy of management in typical fashion to a final meeting between chief steward and top management.

In another seven food factories the fourth stage involved the top factory manager and chief steward or branch convenor. Of these 7, 4 interposed a fifth stage meeting of factory management and full time union official. After this, in all seven cases, the scene shifted to head office for meetings between national union representatives and corporate management.

The longest procedure was an eight-stage one specified by one food firm in which we visited two factories. Up to the fourth stage the steward carried the grievance to the factory manager through lower management echelons. In the fifth stage the district secretary of the union would meet with the factory manager. In the sixth stage the same person would meet with the site manager or site industrial relations manager (since there are several factories on the same site). In the seventh stage the dispute would go to representatives of the national union and the head office board of directors and the last stage specified referral to a Department of Employment appointed arbitration board.

Content of the terminal stage   The last stage of written factory procedures is perhaps the most interesting since it can potentially specify what final actions are required, permitted or prohibited when all the in-factory talking between union and management is finished. Specifically, it may state when strike action can be taken and whether arbitration by third parties is possible.

In our sample (see Table 3.3.), 7 of the 22 written procedures ended not with a bang but with a whimper. They said *nothing* about what should or may happen after the final discussions between top union and factory representatives. It may be inferred that industrial action or some form of reference to industry disputes procedures were the most likely terminal steps, but these were not specified.

Seven of the 22 procedures specified arbitration and of these 5 allowed

62

Table 3.3

Terminal stages of formal disputes procedures

Required actions		Prohibited actions	
Action	Number	Action	Number
Meeting of top officials from company and union	7	No strikes or lockouts while procedure being followed	6
Reference of dispute to industry procedures	2	No strike without specified period of advance notice	1
Voluntary arbitration	5	No strike over inter-union disputes	4
Required arbitration	2	Refusal by management to bargain during strike	1
'Conciliation' by non-involved parties	5	'Status quo' clause	3
Vote by union membership on last company offer	1	'Status quo' clause plus no strike during procedure	1
		No prohibited actions of any type	6

voluntary arbitration only – the parties must jointly agree at the time whether the specific issue of dispute is to be arbitrated. Two factories concluded their procedure with *required* arbitration by a DE appointed tripartite board. Four factories concluded with reference of the grievance to a specially created 'conciliation board' appointed equally by union and management with a 'neutral' mutually agreed on chairman. This board was to attempt to decide the issue and if it could not, it could allow the chairman to act as arbitrator. If it chose not to do this, the board could report no decision and the procedure ended. One other factory made use of DE conciliators as its last stage while another put the last company offer to a vote of union members.

It was probably implicit in all factories where formal procedures existed that there should be no strikes while a grievance or claim was 'going through procedures'; however, this expectation was not always spelled out. Table 3.3 shows the types of prohibited actions which were specified in 16 of the 22 firms. Only eight of the factory procedures contained general constraining provisions on the use of strikes. One approached the matter obliquely by stating that management refused to bargain while a strike was in progress; four contained a provision guaranteeing immunity from strikes over the specific issue of inter-union disputes and three did not constrain the actions of workers but rather constrained *management's* actions through a 'status quo' provision in which management guaranteed not to implement disputed changes while the procedure was being followed.

'Standard practices'   Where a written procedure existed, the standard expectation was usually that it should be followed. Only a few exceptions to this were found. For example, a few procedures began with the steward and employee discussing a grievance with the foreman. The standard practice in such cases was that before the employee involved his steward he should discuss his complaint alone with the foreman.

Conversely, where most formal procedures did not specify any constraints on the use of industrial action, the clear cut expectation in most firms was that any such action (strikes, overtime bans, work to rule, etc.) should be avoided until the specified procedure had run its course. Similarly, where procedures said nothing about time off with pay for stewards on union business the standard practice was frequently to allow such time off. For that matter, most top management personnel also willingly admitted that they recognised the union as the exclusive bargaining agent even though there was no such written agreement on the matter.

Where standard practices were the sole guideline to management action in the handling of grievances the pattern was very simple. What was expected was simply that the employee(s) with a grievance should carry it up the hierarchy using union representatives only after the first stage. With regard to details such as who exactly should be involved on the way up from foreman to factory managing director the expectations were less clear and more diverse, as was the understanding on the part of managers as to who had what authority on various common grievance issues.

One common finding with regard to standard practices, however, was that grievances or claims involving large groups (whole sections, units or departments) were expected to short-circuit early stages of the process and to have higher union officials carry them directly to departmental or factory management or to special joint negotiating bodies.

With regard to terminal stages, standard practice expectations were quite vague beyond the belief in no industrial action while 'procedure' was being followed through. The only other relatively clear feeling was that referral to industry-wide procedures was scarcely to be considered except under the most extreme and unusual circumstances. (In fact we found virtually no instances in our sample of firms making use of their respective JIC procedures within the past five years.)

Participants in the procedure   From the foregoing it can be seen that the majority of the written procedures were quite general as to who could do what in handling grievances. At best they tended to specify who entered the process at which level. Thus stewards usually came in at the second stage but, once the matter got beyond department heads, senior stewards or convenors took over. Full time officials only were specified as having an official role in two cases and then they were restricted to being part of the union 'team' in the last stages of procedure. Staff advisers or managers other than line superiors of grievants were not specified as having any kind of role in formal procedures in any of the plants surveyed. This is all the more striking in view of the significant role they played in practice as will be seen in the next chapter. Similarly, there was only one plant in which grievances were referred to officially specified committees or joint bodies of any type, yet again we discovered in practice that these played a role in a variety of ways in a number of plants.[1]

Procedural differentiation

In our theoretical discussion of the conflict process and factors affecting it, the fact was noted that the differing characteristics of issues and the identity of the parties can have a major impact on the way conflict is manifested. Procedures, aiming as they do at controlling the behaviour of parties with disagreements, should therefore concern themselves with such questions as whether the same procedure should be used for all types of issues and all types of grievants. Procedures should ensure that problems are communicated as quickly and as accurately as possible to the person with the most knowledge of the matter and the greatest authority to handle it. Since all issues are not usually best handled by the same person it is understandable that procedures should become differentiated. What in fact was the case in our sample of twenty-two factories which possessed some form of formal written grievance procedures?

Differentiation of procedures by issue

Only 6 of the 22 procedures made some distinction regarding the handling of different types of issues. Five of the six are part of large firms which exert considerable head office influence on personnel policies. The main issue which was associated with separate procedures was that of discipline. Five out of the six factories had special procedures for special issues. This was even the case in one chemical company which otherwise had no formal grievance procedure at all.

One large firm in the food industry specified a certain procedure for discipline and another for demarcation disputes between unions. It was the only one to have a specific plant level procedure for this latter problem. Another (smaller) factory of the same firm had a special written procedure for disputes over the fairness of work standards. This involved the calling in of union stewards specially trained in work study technique to check the disputed standard.

A number of companies in recent years have gone into formal job evaluation studies to help clarify over-complex and confused job grading systems. In our sample seven factories (three in chemicals and four in foods) had created a special written procedure for the handling of complaints from employees who felt that their jobs had been wrongly graded by the job evaluation study. In all cases both the original decision making body on job evaluation and the appeal body were one and the same and included representatives of management, the union and, usually, an employee representative from the department or section being studied. In five of the seven cases there was no other grievance procedure of any kind.

Another way in which it is possible to differentiate among procedures is on the basis of whether the issue is a 'claim' or a grievance. In North America, for example, this differentiation is very common since a grievance is only an appeal against one's 'rights' under a formal substantive agreement and follows a specified grievance procedure. A claim, or 'contract demand' as it is called, is negotiated at the top of the organisation only when the contract period expires. In Britain, where the same formal distinction between 'rights' and 'interest' disputes is lacking, there has never been any procedural difference regarding claims and grievances at any level. Even so, however, people have implicit understandings about distinctions between issues raised by top union officials which are meant to apply to substantial segments of the unionised labour force and 'minor' issues or grievances raised by individuals or small groups of employees. (Such has been our own working definition of claims and grievances.)

In 10 of our 22 factories with written procedures there was some official recognition of a difference between 'large' and 'small' issues. In six cases negotiating committees of top union and management officials in the factory existed. These bodies were often the last step in the grievance procedure but also the main forum where general concern over wages, hours and conditions applying to the whole union membership in the plant or firm could be raised without there being any ritualistic carrying of the claim through lower levels of management as though they were grievances. In the remaining four cases there was no explicit body for handling claims but the disputes procedure formally specified that it could be short-circuited for issues which were plant-wide or 'of national significance'. In such cases it was specified that a top union official would directly approach the top factory management without first going through the lower levels. Presumably the bulk of such matters had to do with what most would agree to be claims rather than grievances.

Interestingly enough, it appeared to be mainly the large firms in the food industry that had adapted to the grievance–claims distinction by means of negotiating committees (none existed in the chemical or carpet plants surveyed); the official short-circuit method of handling major issues was favoured equally by both food and chemical industries and in plants of varying size. None of the carpet industry plants made any distinction in procedures on the basis of differences in the type of issue involved.

Differentiation by grievant

A complaint can be raised by individual workers, their union representatives, groups of workers or the entire work force acting through union officers. The procedure may differ according to the body wishing to raise the complaint. The rationale for such a differentiation is that group- and factory-wide involvement in a grievance is potentially more likely to lead to costly manifestations or outcomes; hence it should be treated more quickly or at higher levels of management than individual grievances.

Individual–group differences Six of the 22 factories with written procedures made a distinction between individual and group grievances. Of these all six were part of large multi-plant firms: 4 of the 6 experienced considerable head office influence over personnel policies; 4 of the 6 were also factories which in themselves contained more than 1,000 employees.

One of the factories, a carpet manufacturer, provided a written procedure for group grievances only while leaving individual complaints to be handled according to standard practices. The procedure involved a series of regular informal and formal departmental meetings between stewards, foremen and departmental management, and a senior joint negotiating council comprising plant-wide management and union representatives. In two food factories the form of procedural differentiation between individual and group grievances was by means of special short-circuiting

67

provisions for groups. Stages involving the foremen or supervisors were dropped allowing direct and immediate access to top department management. In a chemical factory, union representatives with group grievances could choose which level of hierarchy they would take them to, while individual complaints had to follow a multi-stage ladder beginning with the foreman.

Another of the food factories added extra stages for group grievances involving units of departmental size or larger by specifying that issues unsettled at the level of top factory management were to be taken up at head office between management officials and national level union representatives.

Occupational and other group differences   It is quite common for formal procedures to vary according to union membership. In most firms there is at least a distinction between a dominant union representing non-craft production workers (such as USDAW, GMWU) and a number of unions representing the craftsmen on the maintenance side of production. Where there is a formal procedure at all, it tends to apply to only one unionised group in the plant, e.g., to engineers but not production workers or vice versa. In no case did the same procedure apply across all unions represented and in only three cases were there two separate and different formal procedures between members of craft and production workers' unions in the same plant.

In one chemical plant the basis of different procedures was between day and non-day shift workers. In the case of the latter, procedure dropped the second stage (grievant to supervisor) and changed the third stage of appeal from department manager (who is only available between 9 a.m. and 5 p.m.) to shift superintendent. Considering the number of firms, especially in chemicals, which mentioned the problem of unnecessary delays occasioned because grievances could not be settled at night when departmental managers were unavailable, it is surprising that more companies had not made special provision for accommodating shift workers.

Formality of grievance procedures

As discussed in the previous chapter, the major aspect of grievance procedures identified in the literature has been their overall formality. The effectiveness of procedures in reducing unnecessary conflict has been thought by some to depend on increased formality, while others have argued that the essence of successful labour relations in Britain has lain in its informality. This issue will be discussed further in later chapters. The purpose here is simply to describe the degree of formality found in the plants of our sample of British industry.

The problem, of course, lies in the fact that there is no accepted operational definition of the concept of formality. Instead several empirical measures have been used explicitly or implicitly as indicators of the degree of procedural formality. Perhaps the simplest are those that consider formality as being revealed by the extent to which things are written down and/or communicated as official policies to a large number of people. Thus in this context one could look at: (a) the number of written procedural agreements; (b) the extent to which grievances are required to be written down; (c) the extent to which eventual settlements of grievances are recorded in writing; (d) the extent of the distribution of procedural agreements and written grievance settlements; and (e) the extent to which other labour relations agreements are written and collated in comprehensive form so that they approximate something like the American labour contract.

Even though there may be much that is written down (hence 'formalised') in the handling of grievances this is not a fully satisfactory operational definition because that which is written down may be very brief and worded in only the vaguest and most general manner. Written agreements which cover very little and specify few details have much less chance of 'formalising' or controlling grievance handling behaviour than the opposite type. Hence another way formality might be measured is by some indicators of the scope and specificity of existing agreements. Problems in carrying out this kind of measurement are discussed below.

Regarding the indicators of written and communicated official policies we already know that 63 per cent of our sample had reached the point of developing a written official grievance procedure, most of them within the previous three to five years. Beyond this point all the indicators show rather low formality. Thus there was only one plant in which it was official policy to write down grievances at any stage and this was a recent introduction and not used in practice. With regard to setting down eventual settlements of grievances in writing none of our plants made it an official part of the procedure that final decisions in *all* grievances should be written down although, of course, those few grievances that developed into issues involving major changes applicable to large groups of employees were subject to 'memoranda of agreement' in the usual manner.

Regarding the distribution of the written procedures, only two of our plants distributed copies to all employees and none distributed written grievance settlements beyond a few relevant top officials. Finally, in the matter of collated 'American style' written substantive agreements on other aspects of labour relations, none of the plants had reached the stage of presenting the bulk of their agreements in a single package. Negotiated agreements at factory level were on an issue by issue basis, not collated and not comprehensive in scope. Some movement toward this 'ideal' could be discerned, however, in the fact that 12 out of our total of 35 factories had concluded some form of productivity agreements which were in written form and usually covered a wide spectrum of issues. A further five plants had collated some of their collective agreements without the stimulus of productivity as a *raison d'être*. This makes a total of seventeen or just under half of our sample which had at least embarked along the road of 'formalisation' recommended by the Donovan Commission.

When it comes to measuring formality as indicated by the scope and specificity of the content of written agreements, the problem is one of having a suitable benchmark against which to make comparisons. Though no such benchmark exists, one possible basis for comparison is the guidelines on procedure represented by the government's *Industrial Relations Code of Practice*.[2] Several sections of the Code list what are felt by the Department of Employment to be desirable procedural provisions in collective procedural agreements. Altogether some thirteen suggestions are made which are of relevance to grievance procedures. They are listed here in Table 3.4 along with the extent to which such statements were actually found amongst our sample.[3]

Recognising that the Code recommendations are meant to go somewhat beyond the handling of grievances in the relatively narrow way in which we have defined them, it is nevertheless apparent from Table 3.4 that procedural scope and specificity is rather low in the written agreements from our sample of factories. The median number of procedural elements in our sample was two out of the possible thirteen and over two-thirds of the total sample had four or fewer of the recommended content areas. Clearly, by this indicator formality was low.

Table 3.4 also reveals that, while the general picture is one of low formality by this measure, the food industry was again the leader in producing agreements both broader in scope and more specific in detail than those of both the chemical and carpet industries. This could be due to its generally larger size, the influence of more sophisticated, up-to-date top management and personnel specialists from head office or to other factors of which we are not aware.

Since it is well recognised in Britain that the recommendations of the Code were well ahead of current practice in industry at that time it is perhaps not entirely fair to judge formality of procedural scope and specificity in our sample on that basis alone. Another approach is to

70

consider the relative degrees of formality within the sample itself. In this approach there is even less in the way of benchmarks than there is when one uses the Code; nevertheless it was remarkable at least to us how we were able to form strong overall impressions of the degree of overall formality in the plants visited. In effect, these impressions are based on a combination first of the extent to which we found procedures written, disseminated and understood and, secondly, their scope and specificity. Table 3.5 presents our conclusions regarding the *relative* procedural formality in the thirty-five plants sampled when they are compared to each

Table 3.4

Specificity and scope of grievance procedures by industry
(based on the government's *Industrial Relations Code of Practice*)

	Carpets	Chemicals	Food	Total
Constitution and scope of joint negotiating bodies*	1	0	1	2
Constitution and scope of subsidiary negotiating bodies*	1	3	4	8
Recognition of unions	0	0	6	6
Qualifications, status and functions of stewards	1	0	8	9
Matters covered by bargaining or other procedures	1	1	0	2
Level at which bargaining to take place	1	0	9	10
Procedures for 'collective disputes'	0	2	9	11
Procedures for 'individual disputes' and/or disputes in general	3	4	15	22
Facilities for unions	0	1	8	9
Procedures for redundancy	0	0	0	0
Procedures for discipline	1	2	3	6
Procedures for dismissal	1	1	4	6
Constitution and scope of joint consultative bodies*	0	1	2	3

* Though negotiating and/or joint consultative bodies have been created in a number of factories, their duties and the authority to which they are responsible have not been specified in written form except as indicated. For example, most of the eight 'subsidiary negotiating bodies' in our sample were job evaluation committees with joint rights to decide on employee appeals.

Table 3.5

Degree of relative formality in grievance handling within sample studied (authors' impressions)

	Formality		
	High	Moderate	Low
Carpets (7)	1 (14%)	4 (57%)	2 (29%)
Chemicals (12)	4 (33%)	4 (33%)	4 (33%)
Food (16)	6 (37%)	3 (19%)	7 (44%)
Total (35)	11 (31%)	11 (31%)	13 (38%)

other. It will be seen that, although in general the most common conditions are those of low formality, there still exists a relatively large number of plants which are high in formality, especially in the food and chemical industries. Carpets fell predominantly into the 'moderate' category with few widely disseminated written procedures but a clear understanding of what is expected (reflecting their highly traditional and stable context relative to the other two industries).

Formal procedures other than those for grievances

So far, with the exception of collated substantive agreements, we have been talking solely about grievance procedures. There are, however, other elements of labour relations which have considerable relevance to the way grievances are handled and which themselves can be subjected to greater or lesser amounts of regulation through their own kinds of formal procedures. It will be seen in the next chapter, for example, that various kinds of joint consultative bodies play a major role in both the raising and settling of grievances, though they are rarely mentioned in grievance procedures. While their actual behaviour is crucial in determining their relevance to grievances, the formal procedures surrounding them are also of interest.

Similarly, there are a number of formal agreements that relate to the long term relationship of the union and management other than those surrounding their negotiating and grievance settling arrangements. Finally, there are the potential procedures which may govern the internal relationships *within* the union and management groups that occur when each side must deal with actions. Lack of space prevents a detailed discussion of these non-grievance procedural matters; however, a few brief points can be made.

Procedural controls over joint consultation

Twenty-seven out of our thirty-five factories had one or more officially recognised and active joint consultative bodies. Twenty-five had at least one 'joint consultative council' (JCC) which met regularly to exchange information on the state of trade, employee concerns and pending developments. Two had abandoned this traditional British form of joint activity in favour of 'pure' union–management negotiating committees. Most JCCs formally or informally prohibit discussion of employee claims or negotiation of disputes, yet this in fact is what many of them drift into. The negotiating committees were a recognition of this situation.

Seventeen of our factories had more than one JCC. In addition to the basic plant-wide council there were such bodies as negotiating committees, job evaluation committees, productivity committees, safety and canteen committees, discipline committees plus, in the larger plants, departmental level JCCs.

In our sample there was virtually nothing to be found in the way of written constitutions or any other formal written agreements on the terms of reference of joint bodies. Twenty-two of the 27 plants had no formal statements of any kind, while 6 had only the vaguest and most general kinds of written statements, usually with the *caveat* that they would not be allowed to discuss matters normally subject to collective agreements such as wages and conditions.

Procedures affecting the overall union–management relationship

The review of conflict theory in chapter 2 noted that the way a conflict is manifested is partly a function of the characteristics of power balance and mutual respect which exist in the overall relationship between the two parties. This is particularly so in the case of employee grievances. How any given grievance is manifested is bound to be affected by the general climate of relations between union and management. In Britain this relationship had traditionally been and still is a non-formal one with little in the way of formal agreements to constrain it. The existence of formal agreements tends to reflect a direction recommended by the Donovan Commission, the Department of Employment and other official bodies. What was the situation in our sample?

Only 6 of our 35 factories had any kind of written statements of union recognition and these were only of the most general type, though, of course, verbal and non-verbal recognition was quite common. Ten of the plants had formal agreements regarding the 'checking-off' of union subscriptions from employee pay cheques. Eight were able to show written statements guaranteeing the provision of facilities of some sort for union officials such as an office, phone, filing cabinet or secretarial assistance (though, again, some firms provided minimal facilities on a non-formal basis). With regard to allowing union officials time off from their regular jobs to attend to union business, the norm was to allow this on an unofficial basis, although six of the plants embodied this in written agreements. A further seven had formal agreements to pay for or actually operate special training courses for union stewards.

Altogether, therefore, it can be seen that the 'formalisation' of the overall union–management relationship had not progressed very far at the time of our study.

Intra-party procedures of relevance to the grievance process

Intra-union procedures   Unfortunately we did not systematically interview union officials regarding procedural controls with their unions; hence we can say little about this beyond our general impression that formal procedural regulation appears to be quite slight within most union branches. In two cases we found inter-union coordinating committees for discussing joint concerns and dealing with jurisdictional disputes. In three factories agreements with management specified minimum qualifications for steward positions and a further factory had negotiated a code of conduct for stewards enjoining them from exhorting men to strike or break an agreement without prior approval of union branch officials.

Intra-management procedures   Within the ranks of management we could discover no formal controls detailing how managers were to relate to one another in the course of handling employee grievances or claims. All such behaviour was learned by experience rather than through the study of detailed written job descriptions or internal operating manuals.

From this review of the formal and written side of the grievance handling process in British industry it is clear that procedures of all kinds were rather few in number and at low levels of scope and specificity, though this was less the case in the food industry than in the other two studied. In general the plants had a long way to go to reach the nature and extent of procedural regulation recommended by leading government bodies and neutral advisory groups.

Notes

[1] As noted later, a number of plants distinguished between grievances and large scale claims as major changes in the status quo. The latter were more often directed to some form of negotiating committee.

[2] *Industrial Relations Code of Practice*, HMSO 1972.

[3] The thirteen items listed are taken from various parts of the Code. It should also be emphasised that to say the procedures in our sample contained 'statements' on the various matters suggested by the Code does not mean that their content is ideal or even ideal for that particular factory. Indeed, they may do no more than barely mention the subject.

4 The operation of the grievance process

The second aspect of our fieldwork was to investigate how the grievance process operated. Here we look first at grievance frequency and types, later correlating these with certain environmental variables. Secondly, we examine the roles of the participants and deviations from the formal structure. Finally, we shall attempt to draw some conclusions about the nature of the process, again linking differences to environmental variables.

Grievance frequency and type

In order to obtain information on the number and types of grievances occurring, we asked respondents an open question about the grievances they dealt with and then followed this up by providing a checklist and requesting them to indicate the frequency of different types of grievance, using any time period which seemed relevant. There are obvious drawbacks to this method of obtaining data: for example, people have different memories and different concepts of a grievance; those interviewed may not have been representative of the plant experience as a whole; some grievances may have by-passed the categories of people we interviewed, etc. Nevertheless, in the general absence of any records at any level,[1] direct questioning was the only means of obtaining even approximate data.

Having obtained estimates from the 133 supervisors and eighty-nine departmental managers whose responses formed the basis of the analysis, we then collated these into estimates for the plant in terms of orders of magnitude, which we designated as common, occasional, and rare. 'Common' means approximately one grievance per week of a particular type *per respondent*. The term therefore by no means implies that a plant was inundated with this particular type of grievance, but is merely used relative to the other terms. 'Occasional' was defined as more than four per year per respondent but less than four per month, and 'rare' as less than four times per year per respondent. It should be emphasised that individuals were requested to give estimates of absolute numbers in a given period, not to categorise their answers according to our classification, and it is therefore possible for the estimates of one or more individuals to bias the results for the whole plant. As Ash has shown,[2] it is certainly possible for individual members of management to have very different grievance loads, but our categories were wide enough to take most normal differences into account, and we are satisfied that no major errors have been made.

The results of the grievance frequency estimates are given in Table 4.1. A very crude approximation of average grievances per respondent was somewhat over three per week, but this figure is only quoted as an indication of the order of magnitude involved.[3] In only one plant were grievances recorded covering all the grievance types; most plants had grievances in half or fewer of the categories. There were some understandable reasons for this. Two of the categories we had created, technical change of more than a minor nature and personal problems, were hardly found at all. Some plants had recognised machinery for dealing with issues such as safety or welfare, so that grievances would not come through the lower ranks of management. In others with a time-based system of payment work delays would make no difference to pay and thus resulted in few grievances. Job grading grievances were in some respects an alternative to grievances over piecework or bonus systems. Other plants had virtually no overtime.

Other than those grievances listed in Table 4.1, the only important types spontaneously mentioned by respondents were technical grievances, complaints about machines, tools, etc., arising less out of the employment relationship than the needs of production. A secondary question, only put to senior managers, concerned the grievants themselves in terms of who originated the most numerous and difficult issues.[4] There was a wide range of answers regarding the most difficult department or occupation, with non-production departments such as maintenance, engineering, transport and warehouse frequently cited. Management attributed trouble in a particular department either to personalities, e.g., an inexperienced foreman or a militant shop steward, or alternatively advanced a more general reason such as the difficult working conditions of a particular group or their dissatisfaction with their status. Information on individual grievants was even less clear than that about departments, other than the general observation that women are more passive than men and hence generate fewer grievances. There was also a feeling that new workers (i.e., those who had not been 'socialised' to the ways of the plant) caused more difficulty than longer established ones,[5] although at least one personnel manager stated that the reverse held. One differentiation which was certainly recognised by our respondents was that between grievances originating from individuals and those originating from groups or shop stewards on behalf of individuals. There was no question but that the latter

Table 4.1
Grievance frequency by plant

Plant number	Pay error	Loss of pay	Minor pay changes	Job grading/ work standards	Major technical changes	Work allocation	Overtime	Other time issues	Working conditions	Discipline	Personal problems	Welfare
1		C	C			O		O	C	R		
2	C	C	C			O/C	C		O/C			O
3	C	C	C		R	C	O		O	O/C		O
4	O	C				C		R	O			R
5		C	C			C			O	C		R
6			C			O		C	C	O		R
7		C	R			O			O			
8	C			O		C	C	C/O	O	O		R
9	C	C		O		C	O		O			C
10	O					R	R		O	R		O
11	C		O				O	O	O	O		O
12	C		O			O		O/C	C	R		C
13	C		O	C		O	R		O			O/C
14	C	O	O	O		O/C	C/O	O/C	O			
15	C			C		C	C	C	O			O/C
16	C	O/C	C	O/C			R		C			R
17	C	O/C	O			O	O	R	C			
18						O/C	O	O	C/O	R		
19						C		C	C	O		C
20		C	C			C			O			O
21		C	C			C			O			O
22		C	C			C	O		O			O
23		C	O			C	O		O			O
24	C		C			C	O		C	R		
25	C			R/O		R	O	R	O		O	C
26	C					O	O/C	C	C			C
27	C	C	O	C	R	O	O	R	O	R	R	R
28					R				O	O		
29						O		O	O	R	R	
30	O					R	O	R	R	R	R	R
31			C/O	O/C		C	R	R	O/C	O/C		
32		R	R	R		O	O		O	O		
33	C					C	O/C	R		R		O
34	C	C	O			C						
35		O	C			C	O					

C = common   O = occasional   R = rare

Notes on grievance categories in Table 4.1

Pay errors   These were cases where the grievant was not challenging the pay structure, but rather whether he had been correctly paid under it.

Loss of pay   Instances where pay rates were again accepted, but unavoidable delays, downtime, poor material or some other factor resulted in a potential pay loss. These grievances arose almost entirely in conjunction with some sort of payments by results system.

Minor pay changes   Small changes in piecework or bonus arrangements or special allowances for duty or uncomfortable jobs and the like. This was the area most associated with fractional bargaining and precedent setting, although in the plants studied it was generally resolved on well-established criteria.

Job grading/work standards   This covers areas of job evaluation and specification. Also potentially liable to fractional bargaining: as one manager noted: 'We look on job evaluation as controlled negotiation rather than being pseudo-scientific. It also gives the stewards a role in decision making.'

Major technical change   Virtually no grievances in this category, perhaps because conflict would have been resolved at the planning stage and hence not emerge as grievances.

Work allocation and transfers   Second only to working conditions in its applicability, with two main types of issue: a general dislike of being transferred; and the pay appropriate for transfers to a different grade, which was often controlled by eligibility criteria.

Overtime   In spite of general awareness in companies of the potential problems of this subject and the common use of a rota system, grievances were still fairly frequent in this category.

Other time issues   This covered complaints about holidays, shiftwork, breaks, washing-up time, etc.

Working conditions   By far the most frequently quoted of all the grievance categories. The most common complaint was excessive heat or cold and, far from being a trivial issue, this had caused several strikes. A wide range of other issues regarding physical arrangements were also included here.

Discipline   Plants appeared to be divided between those where stewards grieved against discipline as a matter of course and those where they accepted it passively.

Personal problems   Intended to cover complaints against fellow workers or supervisors or personal problems as they related to the company.

Welfare   Partly overlapping with working conditions, this category covered issues such as toilets, protective clothing, canteen, parking, and availability of public transport. Although some of these issues were outside the authority of the respondents, a fair number of grievances on such issues were nevertheless reported to them.

were treated much more seriously to the extent that some foremen felt themselves unable to deal with anything involving the union – such issues immediately became a matter for higher management.

As was pointed out in chapter 2, there are many possible explanations for grievances and a very sophisticated regression analysis, for which our data are not suitable, would be necessary to provide anything like a complete answer. We have taken two independent variables, industry and size of plant, for which we reproduce detailed patterns of grievance frequency, and five others – extent of unionisation, formality of procedure, sex ratios of the labour force, type of wage payment system, and rural or urban setting of the plant – for which we give totals. Many of these variables are, of course, interconnected and some collinearity is to be expected. Other possible variables which come to mind are the range of attitudes towards the relationship by both labour and management, the technology of the plant, the distribution of authority and the organisational structure of management, and the pattern of union organisation, but these did not lend themselves to easy categorisation or measurement.

Table 4.2 shows grievance frequency according to the variables mentioned. The figures used are those from Table 4.1 expressed as a percentage of the total number of plants reporting the occurrence of the 'common' category of grievance. We have used the ratio of 'common' types of grievance per plant since the 'occasional' and 'rare' classifications make only a small contribution to the total number of grievances.

Perhaps more interesting than the overall scores are the types of grievance which appear to be most common in each industry. The carpet industry had a high number of grievances concerning monetary issues, due almost certainly to its decentralised system of piecework-based wage determination and a technology which was subject to breakdowns in machines, material availability, or yarn breakage. The chemical industry, with a more centralised structure and little technological capacity for individual piecework due to process nature, had relatively fewer grievances in the pay area, excepting the ubiquitous pay errors. It did, however, appear to have more grievances than the other two industries in three areas: grading (due to the frequency of job evaluation or similar schemes as a basis for pay); working conditions (resulting from the environmental and safety problems of working with chemicals); and welfare (probably for similar reasons). Overtime and other time issues, especially shiftwork, also seemed to be more of a problem than in the other industries as a result of the continuous process nature of the chemical industry and the need to keep all positions manned.

The food industry had the highest proportionate number of grievances

Table 4.2

Grievance frequency by independent variables

	Industry			Size of plant		
	Carpets (7)	Chemicals (12)	Food (16)	1,000+ (13)	300– 1,000 (9)	−300 (13)
Pay errors	0·29	0·75	0·37	0·54	0·56	0·46
Loss of pay	0·86	0·17	0·37	0·69	0·11	0·38
Minor pay changes	0·71	0·08	0·34	0·50	0·33	0·23
Grading/work standards	–	0·21	0·09	0·12	0·22	0·04
Major technical change	–	–	–	–	–	–
Work allocation	0·50	0·42	0·56	0·65	0·45	0·54
Overtime	0·14	0·21	0·06	0·15	0·17	0·08
Other time issues	0·14	0·25	0·06	–	0·28	0·19
Working conditions	0·50	0·42	0·16	0·31	0·22	0·38
Discipline	0·07	–	0·03	0·08	–	0·04
Personal problems	–	–	–	–	–	–
Welfare	–	0·33	0·12	0·08	0·22	0·23
Average number per plant	3·2	2·8	2·2	3·1	2·6	2·6

The figures below refer to the average per plant:
Formality of procedure: high (11 plants) 3·0; moderate (11) 2·6; low (13) 2·3.
Extent of unionisation: 100% (12 plants) 3·0; 75–100% (13) 2·5; less than 75% (10) 2·3.
Proportion of females: 0–33% (14 plants) 2·4; 33–66% (14) 3·0; 66–100% (7) 2·8.
Plant location: rural (7 plants) 1·7; urban light industry (12) 3·0; urban mixed industry (16) 2·8.
Main type of payment system: piecework (9 plants) 3·4; time rates with bonus (12) 2·5; straight time rates (14) 2·2.

in the area of work allocation and transfers. Since the industry employs a high proportion of unskilled women, many of them on a part-time basis, and also has a relatively high level of absenteeism, it may be that the possibility of and need for flexibility on the part of the workforce produces a reaction in the form of grievances of this type. It is also noteworthy that the food industry has a high proportion of occasional grievances in the time issues category, possibly due to the often quoted problem of fixing holidays, particularly for women wanting to fit in with their husbands' holiday periods.

The second variable selected was size of plant, since it is frequently argued that the problems of control and interaction multiply as size of plant increases.[6] Table 4.2, however, shows that the correlation is not as clearcut as this assumption would suggest. There is a higher ratio of common grievances in the larger plants, but the difference is not overwhelming. In part this is due to intercorrelation with other variables, especially the fact that the chemical industry tended to have more small plants than the food industry but a higher overall level of grievances. Indeed, there was a considerable difference in plant size between the three industries: carpets averaged 2,300, with a median of 1,500; food averaged 1,090, with a median of 725; chemicals averaged 370, with a median of 210. However, one feature which does stand out is that the large plants have a high proportion of grievances in the pay areas, although this again is correlated with the high average size of the carpet industry plants.

Finally, we dealt with five further variables in rather less detail, namely, formality of procedure, extent of unionisation, sex ratios within the plant, the geographical environment of the plant, and the main type of payments system. As with the previous two variables examined, certain trends might be hypothesised for these variables. Thus on the basis of commonly held impressions one might expect to find more grievances the higher the degree of unionisation, where the ratio of male to female workers is high, in an urban environment where heavy industry is present, and where a payments by results system is used rather than a straight time rate. Although the patterns are by no means clearcut, a look at the comparative figures for the 'common' category indicates that these hypotheses are borne out except for the male–female split. The wage system variable in particular produced a clearcut difference between plants with a piecework system and the rest, with the former having considerably more 'common' grievances of all types, while the rural variable in plant location produced the lowest proportion of 'common' grievances of any category of variable. The one variable not mentioned in the above explanation–formality of procedure–deserves special mention because it is perhaps less easy to stipulate an expected hypothesis here. Certainly, one of the arguments in the Donovan Report is that the absence of formal procedures at plant level is itself responsible for the occurrence of conflict, but this may be too simple a view; it is not so much whether the formal procedures exist as whether they are followed, and in any case the function of procedures is not to prevent grievances from arising, but to channel them towards a successful resolution. However, the setting up of a formal procedure may itself be a reflection of the number of grievances arising. In practice there was some tendency for plants with formal procedures to score higher in the 'common' categories of grievance than the others.

In summary, the data presented so far show that there are considerable differences between plants in terms of the number and types of grievances occurring, although we can say nothing about the relative importance of different types of grievance.[7] It should be emphasised, however, that relative to British factories in some other industries, it is highly likely that our sample was biased in the direction of generally low levels of grievance frequency. On the other hand, the evidence is also that there are few plants, at least within the size category that we visited, which do not have sufficient grievances to warrant taking them seriously as a recurrent phenomenon of plant life and consequently formulating a policy to deal with them. Grievance handling is a significant if not necessarily important part of the management function and needs to be treated as such.

Activities in the grievance process

We now seek to examine, within the limitations of our data, the way the grievance process actually works. We should like to be able to gauge the extent to which the process actually corresponds with procedure and the extent to which it does not; whether there are consistent patterns in grievance resolution, or merely random paths to settlement; and the impact of deviations on the ultimate decision. However, a definitive answer to these issues would require a degree of statistical information and continuous observation which was quite impossible, given the scale of the present study. But if we cannot trace the path of any one grievance from origin to solution, nor state accurately the level at which grievances of a particular type are settled, we can nevertheless infer certain things on the basis of the roles of the various participants as related to us during the course of the interviews, and also from the deviations from procedure of which we were told. We shall therefore now proceed to examine these particular facets.

One point about the analysis which follows needs to be made clear beforehand. We have perhaps been implicitly suggesting thus far that there is something innately desirable about following 'the' procedure. Such is certainly the impression given in public statements and newspaper accounts of disputes, and it is a theme which runs through much of the published literature on industrial relations. It is our conclusion, however, based on the views put to us, that following the procedure is a matter of very secondary importance compared with settling the grievance as smoothly and efficiently as possible.

As a result of these views, it is very difficult indeed to draw a line between legitimate and illegitimate means of grievance handling. Most respondents at all levels stressed the desirability of some informality in the procedure, and not only tolerated it, but actively encouraged or participated in it. We must differentiate, however, between consistency in the use of procedure and consistency in the answers given to grievances. All the senior managers we talked to were concerned and worried about the problem of coordination, realising only too well the difficulties that could be caused by setting precedents in one department that could be used elsewhere to justify demands for comparable treatment. But while there is a point at which procedural aberrations can lead to differences in substantive answers, it is also quite possible to have procedural abnormalities which nevertheless provide consistent answers to similar questions, essentially because the issues go to the same person. There is thus sufficient flexibility to allow the most appropriate person to respond to each issue, and sufficient consistency in the answers to ensure that the flexibility is not abused. It is such a situation which makes informality so attractive, and which in our judgement existed in most of our sample plants. As a result of this general attitude towards informality, our use of the term deviation from procedure is not imbued with any pejorative connotation.[8]

The roles of the participants

We shall now proceed to examine the roles played by the different levels of management in the grievance procedure, and also management's view of the role of union representatives from the shop steward upwards. (A further perspective of roles, that of the attitudes of our respondents, will be examined in the next chapter.) In looking at management, we are dealing almost exclusively at this stage with line management, since in the great majority of formal procedures line management was responsible for grievance handling and indeed saw itself as responsible in practice, although, as we shall see, staff management frequently played a much more significant role than line management admitted. The staff participation facet of grievance procedure operation will therefore be dealt with as a category of deviation.

The written procedure in our plants frequently did not identify levels of management to be approached above supervision, and on no occasion specified the scope of authority of managers or supervisors. The latter category was of course the principal determinant of levels of decision making on grievances. Although we asked respondents to define the scope of their authority, it proved to be too difficult a question within the limits of the interview.[9] Their capacity to answer grievances also depended on factors other than the general scope of their authority, e.g., the efficiency of the communications within management and the extent to which policy was clearly defined in any particular area. These latter factors are necessary contributions to what might be called effective authority and, as we shall see in chapter 5, a significant proportion of our respondents felt that they were limited in one or more of these dimensions.

The role of management

(1) *Foremen* As might be expected, the role of foremen in grievance handling tended to have definite limitations, partly through by-passing (which will be examined later) and partly through the inability of the foremen to answer issues coming to them. We asked foremen what proportion of grievances they estimated they solved without any upwards reference: the results are given in Table 4.3 and show a wide spread of answers, although in 22 of the 35 plants under study foremen handle over 75 per cent of the grievances.[10] It should be noted, however, that due to by-passing of the lowest level the table is very likely to be subject to error, since the foreman does not always know the total number of grievances going through his section.

Table 4.3

Percentage of grievances handled by foremen

	90–100%	75–90%	Under 75%
Industry			
Carpets (7)	1	3	3
Chemicals (12)	1	6	5
Food (16)	7	4	5
Size of plant			
Large (13)	6	3	4
Medium (9)	0	5	4
Small (13)	3	5	5
Total (35)	9	13	13

One point which does stand out from the table is that the food industry tends to have foremen who can solve grievances rather more easily than their counterparts in the other two industries. This is perhaps not unexpected if the predominant types of grievances in that industry are recalled, namely those dealing with questions of work allocation. There are no very clear trends with regard to the other independent variables we looked at in Table 4.2, although there is some tendency for foremen in highly unionised plants to solve a low proportion of grievances and those in less organised plants to resolve a higher proportion, a not unexpected result. But perhaps the more general lack of correlation is because there are factors which cut both ways. One example of this was a large plant with a high level of conflict in which a determined effort had been made to decentralise grievance handling, and where for that purpose specially trained foremen had been instituted at departmental level to handle labour issues, reporting to personnel as well as to line management.

Another dimension by which the foreman's role can be judged is the amount of time spent in handling grievances. From the answers to this question we created three categories, the figures for which are given in Table 4.4 below. A majority of supervisors spent less than two hours per week handling grievances, but there are definite signs that those in the carpet industry and, even more so, those in large plants spent considerably more time on this than other supervisors. This latter result is indeed one of the most clearcut findings in the whole study. Even though most of the carpet plants were large ones, this does not account for the imbalance by

Table 4.4

Time spent handling grievances by foremen

	Under 2 hours		2–4 hours		Over 4 hours	
	No.	%	No.	%	No.	%
Industry						
Carpets	16	3	13	31	13	31
Chemicals	27	75	4	11	5	14
Food	37	67	13	24	5	9
Size of plant						
Large	25	37	22	33	20	30
Medium	25	81	4	12	2	7
Small	30	86	4	11	1	3
Total	80	60	30	23	23	17

size of plant; those in large plants in the other two industries also spent a good deal more time on this than supervisors in other plants in their industries.

Taking the figures as a whole, it is of interest that these amounts of time are significantly higher than the figures reported in the government 1966 investigation.[11] According to that survey no less than 76 per cent of foremen had spent no time at all on grievances and claims the previous week, 5 per cent had spent less than one hour, 7 per cent 1–2 hours, 8 per cent 2–4 hours, and 4 per cent over 4 hours.

What type of grievances do foremen handle? This obviously varies from plant to plant and according to the particular issue within any type. One very definite impression that we obtained was that there was a major distinction between individual grievances on the one hand and grievances which are originated by a group or taken up by a shop steward on the other. One foreman noted: 'I can't really handle anything but individual issues,' and another: 'If the union becomes involved, I generally pass it up.' Beyond that, the main issues seemed to be pay errors, minor working conditions, overtime, short-run transfers, special allowances, downtime payments, time issues, and minor discipline. It was obvious that some foremen would prefer not to get involved in tricky issues which are not 'cut and dried' and which might affect their relations with their workforce. It appeared, in fact, that at least some of the foremen did not really conceive of the procedure as commencing at their level, but rather saw it as being concerned with the more important issues which they could not resolve. Thus one foreman said: 'If it involves everyone then we go through procedure, but most grievances are solved by me before going to procedure.' However, this sort of view, disassociating what happens at foreman level from the procedure, does not seem to us to reflect the reality of the grievance situation. We would place a high premium on the role of the foreman and his position in the grievance procedure. Even if the issues he solves are relatively insignificant, their solution is a major contribution to that relationship with the shopfloor which is an important determinant of the amount of latent conflict. Without the solution of minor problems, the resultant cumulation of dissatisfaction could easily generate major issues.

The picture which emerges from higher managers regarding the grievance handling of their foremen is in many cases one of dissatisfaction and does not altogether synchronise with the views of the foremen. Thus one factory manager said: 'I would expect foremen to settle 80 per cent but they only settle 50 per cent.' At the same time such managers generally do not accept that their own policies might be at fault by providing inadequate training, inadequate specification of authority, or encouragement of by-passing.

However, not all foremen are worried about exercising authority, as illustrated by two quotations from supervisors in the same firm: 'I have to shrug off a lot of complaints by habitual complainers,' and 'I don't treat many things as real grievances.' In general, it was our impression that younger foremen used their authority in a more discretionary way than older ones.

To sum up the role of foremen, there is little in our results to suggest that they played an unimportant role in the grievance process, a conception which has sometimes been implied in the literature. On the other hand, their role was limited, and one or two spontaneous comments suggested that it had become more limited in the recent past.

(2) *Middle managers* The role of the line middle manager has been one of the least studied in industrial relations literature, yet *Workplace Industrial Relations,* 1972 noted, and we would agree, that: 'The maximum amount of industrial relations activity occurs at lower manager level, i.e., that directly above first level supervision.'[12] We asked middle managers the amount of time they spent on grievance handling, and their answers are shown here in Table 4.5. Two main conclusions may be drawn from this table. First, the pattern established for supervisors is repeated, in that managers in the carpet industry and in large plants spent more time on grievances than those in other categories. Secondly, managers spent more time handling grievances than supervisors. This does not necessarily mean that they handled a greater number of grievances, but rather that the grievances which did come to them were probably more difficult, and hence

Table 4.5

Time spent handling grievances by middle managers

	Under 2 hours		2–4 hours		Over 4 hours	
	No.	%	No.	%	No.	%
Industry						
Carpets	9	36	5	20	11	44
Chemicals	20	59	10	29	4	12
Food	17	61	7	25	4	14
Size of plant						
Large	14	33	13	30	16	37
Medium	15	68	6	27	1	5
Small	17	77	3	14	2	9
Total	46	53	22	25	19	22

required more time. The main types of grievance dealt with by middle managers appeared to be discipline, most piece-rates, transfers, machine speeds, manning, special allowances, and working conditions.

The middle manager role is more difficult to define than that of foremen, but there did appear to be a spectrum of authority: at one end some respondents said that if an issue was sufficiently important to reach middle management, it was considered useful to consult with the personnel manager or the deputy factory director, since other departments could also become involved. This was particularly true with 'troublesome' departments. Also at this end of the authority spectrum, in several of the smallest plants the factory manager or his deputy was sufficiently close to the shop floor for it to be likely that he would get wind of most grievances which arose and there was no useful role for the middle managers to play. This was a restrictive view of the middle management role. In the middle of the spectrum, where most plants probably lay, departmental managers would deal with departmental issues which could not be solved at supervisor level. At the other end of the spectrum, some middle managers, especially in piecework situations, could exert a lot of authority over aspects of work and would refer upwards only when questions of overall personnel policy were involved. The managers of specialist departments, particularly maintenance or engineering, often found themselves in this situation because their workers had relatively little contact with production workers.

(3) *Senior management* Top management in our plants usually meant the factory manager, but could also cover such functions as the production director, the factory administrative manager or the deputy factory manager. Here we are not dealing with the role of the board of directors, which was strongly criticised by the Donovan Report and later by Winkler[13] for its lack of involvement in industrial relations, although in a number of cases the relevant individual was a member of at least a subsidiary board. One strong impression we gained of the role of top plant management was not that they abrogated their industrial relations function, although they could be criticised for inadequate policy setting and dissemination, but rather that some at least went in the opposite direction and spent too much time dealing personally with relatively trivial issues. For the same reason they were not unaware of possible loss of control through fractional bargaining at lower levels; rather they were so aware of the possible problems of an uncoordinated approach that they may well have contributed to the very lack of acceptance of responsibility lower down which they sometimes criticised.

In a small unit, it is probably difficult to keep even minor issues from senior management's ears, but this situation was not in fact restricted to the small plants. In a number of our plants, the senior manager had some form of 'open door' policy with respect to the senior steward, although not just any steward. He looked upon the senior steward as a confidante and had a close relationship with him. There is a lot to be said for such a policy: the senior manager hears what is happening in the union branch and thus 'keeps his finger on the pulse'; he can also use the steward as a means of communication with the workforce. From the steward's point of view the arrangement also has obvious advantages. We were struck by the number of plants (at least seven or eight) where such a relationship had developed between these two persons so as to make it the key influence in industrial relations within the factory. But, however desirable, it can mean distortion of the procedure, as even relatively unimportant grievances go straight to the top, and some resentment by middle and lower levels of management is inevitable on occasions. In only one of our panel did senior managers explicitly make the point that it was policy to push grievance handling down the procedure. The primary function of the senior manager under the procedure is usually to be the last stage of the domestic procedure, before going outside the plant. But very few of our plants saw the top manager's role in this formal sense. Very few grievances went all the way up the procedural ladder, and in any case the top manager was likely to have become informally involved earlier on. There were three basic ways in which top managers became involved in grievances at an early stage as opposed to being a last resort. One was by giving advice to lower managers in an informal way; the second was when the senior shop steward used his 'open door' powers to go straight to the top; and the third was in his (the top manager's) capacity as head of the works council or equivalent body. All of these could be important ways of involvement, although the first was probably the most significant in the majority of cases.

Union representation

(1) *The shop steward* This section deals with the role of union representatives as seen by management and thus cannot claim to offer a balanced view, although our discussions with the eleven convenors or shop stewards we did interview did not point to radically different conclusions. We attempted to elicit an answer to three questions about the role of the shop steward: the proportion of grievances in which the steward became involved; whether he was the first or only a later contact usually made by an individual wishing to pursue a grievance; and his behaviour, namely whether he acted as a mediator, straight representative or militant. The

only answer which was reasonably clearcut was the first. In 12 plants, 11 of them in the food industry, our respondents estimated that the steward was involved in between 0–30 per cent of all grievances, in 19 plants involvement was estimated at between 30–60 per cent and in 3 plants between 60–100 per cent. In one plant they were seen as playing no role at all in the grievance process, their function being confined to union membership duties. It is interesting that in the one plant which was non-unionised, works council representatives were used in the same capacity as stewards and became involved in most grievances.

The second question, regarding the immediacy of contact of stewards by grievants, showed a mixed situation in the majority of firms but a slight preponderance in favour of first contact in the food industry. This question really relates to individual issues only; group issues would almost inevitably involve the steward. The type of grievances in which stewards became involved also varied; where the steward was typically the first contact of the grievant he was involved in the whole range of grievances, but where foremen were the primary contact and could handle issues such as work allocation and pay queries, the steward would not necessarily be involved. Regarding the way in which stewards used the procedure, it was our strong impression that while they often by-passed the foreman, they would normally go to the departmental manager rather than to top management. Access to the latter was reserved for senior stewards, convenors, and branch officials. Finally, in most situations the role of the stewards was mixed between all three modes of behaviour-mediator, straight representative and militant–but where one predominated this tended to be either that of mediator or straight representative. Nowhere were the stewards felt to be merely militant. The generally moderating role of the stewards again bears out other research in this area.

(2) *The chief shop steward or convenor* The post of senior shop steward existed in either a *de facto* or a *de jure* sense at two-thirds of our panel plants. Sometimes there was a convenor, sometimes the secretary or chairman of the local union branch played the same role. Where it existed, the post was very different to that of an ordinary shop steward. It is perhaps surprising that no comprehensive study has yet been made of what is one of the key posts in the British industrial relations system. As already noted in discussing the role of top management, the senior steward often had direct access to the top and formed an axis with his management counterpart around which much of the industrial relations of the unit revolved, grievances included. Not infrequently, stewards themselves could be by-passed by individuals (or even managers) going to the senior steward. At

least two of the senior stewards we talked to said that a grievant should first see his own steward or foreman, but once the worker had come, it was rather difficult for the senior steward to send him back. For one thing, the post is inevitably political, and it would not be good for his image to refuse to listen; secondly, the senior steward is usually in a much superior position to an ordinary steward with regard to information and power. Thus it is easy to see how the procedure can become distorted.

In four plants, all small, it was felt that the convenor got involved in most grievances, although in the majority of plants he was generally brought in, as procedure would suggest, when the grievance had not been settled at departmental level. His role was obviously also the key one for general grievances of the sort that might be raised at union branch meetings. There may well be some role differences between a working convenor and a full-time one, but the number of plants with a full-time convenor (four) was too few for any conclusions to be reached. Even more than the stewards as a whole, the convenor was seen by management as behaving in a pacifying way, although in some places he was felt merely to play a representative role, and in one plant he was felt to be a militant. Even where militancy was mentioned this was never linked to ideological motives. Rather the key to the convenor's behaviour as seen from the management side may depend on his conception of his own role. In this context, it is worth quoting the very different approaches of two senior shop stewards in one plant, although from different unions. The first said: 'If I didn't think it warranted going higher I'd try to explain my views but if he [the original grievant] still wanted it pushed, I'd still go to the plant manager even though I knew I hadn't a leg to stand on. I can only advise him.' The view of the second steward was: 'I act as a sieve. I have told my men that if the grievant is wrong and the whole shop backed him I still wouldn't go up.'

(3) *The full-time union official* Full-time union officials rarely became directly involved in the grievance process at the plant level unless a very unusual issue came up, such as a bitterly contested dismissal. We cannot comment on their role in the external disputes procedure because the plants in our sample used the external procedure very little, most of them not at all. There were some half-dozen plants, however, where the full-time official made a point of calling regularly and discussing any pertinent matters, and in such cases he would be kept informed and possibly asked to give an opinion on any particularly important grievances.

The full-time official appeared to suffer from two major handicaps. One was that he was a busy man and often difficult to get hold of, especially for relatively peaceful plants such as most of our sample. As a result management did not bother. There was one notable exception where management in a high conflict plant continually sought the aid of the official, but was rarely successful in obtaining him when needed. The other reason was that management genuinely preferred to deal with their own stewards about grievances, since the full-time official was not likely to be well informed.

Deviations from procedure

We now turn to examine deviations from the formal or standard procedure. It should be emphasised again, however, that what are termed deviations may not be seen as such by the participants, even the senior management who were primarily responsible for the official procedure.

By-passing stages of the procedure   This is the deviation most frequently mentioned in the literature, and certainly the most frequent one to occur in practice. A preliminary issue is exactly what it says. In one interpretation, it could mean not even bothering to notify the supervisor before raising an issue with his superior. In another, it could mean merely telling the supervisor of a desire to see a manager about a grievance, without any attempt to explain what is wrong to the supervisor, or give him a chance to answer. Our impression was that supervisors generally objected to the first kind of by-passing but not really to the second, since they often recognised their own inability to decide a certain issue. A second definitional aspect is that in some procedures workers were expected to see the foreman before going to the shop steward, but again, we found that foremen generally did not mind if this did not happen. Indeed, it was even welcomed, since as one supervisor said: 'The steward often tells them if they're being stupid,' implying that the steward was of positive assistance as a screening device, while according to another the steward would put the essence of the case without the long-winded explanation which ordinary workers felt impelled to give. In summary, what foremen appeared to mean by by-passing was somebody going above their heads and thereby causing a loss of face,[14] rather than showing any commitment to the procedure as a formal piece of machinery.

The results of our question to supervisors as to the extent of by-passing as perceived by them suggested that in 15 plants by-passing of supervisors was thought to be common, in 13 it was thought to be occasional and in 6 rare (we did not give any frequential guidance to respondents as to what these terms might mean). It should be added that in several instances managers saw more by-passing than foremen did, which may be true or may be a matter of pride for the foremen, inducing them to underestimate. The extent of by-passing clearly depended to a considerable extent on the attitude of managers rather than that of stewards or grievants, since it takes both sides to make by-passing effective. Many middle managers displayed a distinctly ambivalent attitude towards by-passing. On the one hand they preferred grievants to see supervisors first, and would even ask them if they had done so, but on the other they would not usually turn a man away who had come to state a case or even reject someone approaching them on a visit around the department. This, however, was seen as a human relations exercise, not as a desire to exclude the supervisor or even to coordinate decisions. As such, this attitude of middle managers was rather different to that of senior managers who felt the need to coordinate decisions and thus tended to encourage by-passing for this reason. Naturally, the union could also influence the extent of by-passing. One manager said that his sections differed according to whether workers went through the union or through the foreman in the first instance. He thought this was a function of the respective personalities of stewards and foremen and that where the steward was involved by-passing was more frequent.

Turning to the by-passing of other stages in the procedure, there was also some, albeit unquantified, by-passing of departmental managers. This was clearly very much rarer than by-passing the foreman since the departmental manager has much more authority than the latter, and there is thus less reason to miss him out. Such by-passing might be vertical, to the manager's superior, or horizontal, to a functional or staff manager such as the personnel manager or safety officer. The first would be resented for reasons of pride and status similar to those the foremen felt, the second considerably less so – indeed he might well be welcomed by some managers who did not want their time taken up by non-production issues. Middle managers could also feel by-passed if their foremen used too much initiative or were told to take specific issues direct to someone other than themselves. Thus in one plant where the factory manager had given instructions that all problems arising out of a new productivity deal were to go straight to him, middle managers were resentful that foremen telephoned him directly.

Avoiding procedure altogether   Avoiding procedure altogether was a relatively rare occurrence owing to the elasticity of procedural limits in most situations. It was not generally considered an avoidance of procedure, for example, to go straight to production director level, although it might be resented by those below. This would be by-passing within the procedure. We are therefore looking at those actions which were considered 'beyond the pale' in procedural terms. One example of this was when a firm was suddenly presented with a written letter from a full-time official alleging ten causes of complaint, none or very few of which had even been raised within the plant. This was considered 'beyond the pale' and was much resented by management. Industrial action, it goes without saying, falls into the same category. Another example mentioned in more than one firm was where there existed a fairly clear definition of the functions of the works committee and an issue, usually financial, was raised *ultra vires* to these functions. This was also something which management regarded as not permissible and an avoidance of normal procedure. Again, management rights could be raised as a barrier even where there were no specified limitations. Here, however, the concept of procedure was used in the sense of covering the extent of recognition and the scope of bargaining, rather than in its narrow sense of a grievance review mechanism.

Involvement of persons not part of the procedure   For the most part, as we saw in chapter 3, written procedures directed the grievant straight to line management. But given the much more complex nature of modern production and the increasing division of managerial functions, staff management has in actual practice assumed a larger role in decision making. There are now many specialists chipping away at the traditional line function and this happens in the grievance handling area just as in others. As well as the personnel manager, the wages department, the industrial engineering department, the quality control department, the maintenance department, and the safety department, to say nothing of such subdivisions of the personnel function as welfare and training, may all find themselves becoming involved in grievances because they have a degree of expertise which makes it logical that they should. In an informal problem solving atmosphere such as permeated most of our panel with regard to most grievances, referring to the best available expertise on any issue was a natural thing to do. The senior shop steward in particular (in those plants where the post had become institutionalised) had virtually the run of the plant in terms of approaching any manager he felt to be appropriate.

It is, of course, one of the primary criteria of a staff function that it should advise, assist and serve. Yet the boundary between advice and decision making can be a narrow one. The rate fixer has come to have a responsibility greater than that of most line managers in many piecework-based engineering firms. Myers and Turnbull, [15] in a fascinating study of the role of personnel managers, have shown that even though they possess very little formal authority, they nevertheless made effective decisions on certain issues for a number of associated reasons: (a) they were accredited by line management with expertise; (b) many facets of personnel policy were not welcomed by line managers because decisions on them might impair their relationship with the workers; and (c) unionism and greater size of plants have necessitated greater coordination, and the personnel function is a natural choice for this. Yet Myers and Turnbull found that none of their respondents thought they operated in a line capacity. A similar, although more limited, process seems to have occurred in Britain.

There was no doubt that for many reasons, not least those put forward by Myers and Turnbull, the role of the personnel manager was expanding, even though he rarely had an explicit function in the procedure. We tried to evaluate the roles of personnel managers in the grievance process according to three categories. In eleven plants the personnel manager appeared to act as a top management representative, making or contributing to executive decisions on grievance and other related matters. In a further six his role appeared largely advisory and in some respects mediatory, acting as someone who could take a relatively dispassionate view of a situation. In eleven more the role was minor – restricted to handling trivial issues or providing information – or non-existent. In seven there was no personnel manager.

The extent of involvement of the personnel manager was a function of his personality and experience as much as any formal role structuring by management. As a staff manager he was remote from the shop floor and, not being an integral part of the procedure, he had to prove his worth in handling grievances to line management. One new appointee frankly said he expected it would be two or three years before anyone listened to him. But some personnel managers were long serving employees who had had a lot of experience and knew a great deal about the plant, and hence were worth consulting for their experience or their memory. In a few other plants there were personnel managers who were professionally trained in the sense of having pursued the function as a career, although most had had some training. In the larger firms personnel departments were expanding and younger professional men were coming in at the bottom.

There was certainly some resistance to the growth in importance of the personnel function. One line departmental manager who noted that 'The industrial relations department here is moving from an advisory role to one of arbitration, and I am not too happy about it,' was undoubtedly speaking for many others at middle management level.[16] Moreover, there were echoes of Myers and Turnbull in the ambiguous comment of another manager who noted that the role of the personnel department was 'totally advisory, but we must accept their advice.' Even when personnel managers were not involved there was often some express intention to include them in the future in a coordinating function. But although personnel managers were becoming increasingly involved in the grievance function, it was still relatively rare for them to play a decisive role in grievance handling. In only one of our firms was the personnel manager the key individual in grievance handling, and he had been the assistant works manager in his previous job.

Joint bodies not formally part of the grievance process Although a joint body was specifically mentioned as being a stage in the grievance procedure in only four plants, with a further two or three using them as such in the absence of a written procedure, the function of committees in the grievance process nevertheless went far beyond what these figures might suggest. In almost all plants the works committee, joint consultative committee, works council or similar body handled many issues which could equally well have been handled through the grievance procedure. In addition to these general central bodies, many plants also had subsidiary committees – either in a functional sense, such as safety or welfare, or on a divisional or departmental basis – which also handled relevant grievances, and were also usually outside the procedure.

We did not see the constitutions for all such bodies in the plants surveyed – indeed some hardly had one – but as noted in chapter 3, they fell fairly clearly into consultative and negotiating models, with the latter tending to be of more recent origin. However, even where the original function of the consultative type of body might have been purely the passing on of information and the examination of questions relating to production and productivity, they had since been widened in scope to deal with issues raised by employees.[17] Although it might be made clear that the body could not discuss pay or related issues, this could still leave a wide range of issues on which there could be a potential overlap with the grievance procedure.[18] Fairly typical of this was the plant where the topics noted as being raised in the works council were 'Health, hygiene, holiday arrangements, welfare, safety, working conditions and a lot of technical issues.'

It could be argued that the mode of conducting many of these meetings was in no sense part of a conflict pattern. When asked if the works council acted as a negotiating body for certain types of grievance, the manager quoted above said: 'Negotiating would be the wrong word. We discuss the issues on the agenda, whoever raises them, and come to an amicable arrangement.' But even if these topics were generally not emotive ones, in such cases the fact remained that the issues raised could cause difficulties and they did amount to grievances. There can also be cases where the body, although not part of the procedure, nevertheless has a role to play which is explicitly parallel to the procedure. Thus the stated purpose of one body was 'to ensure the proper implementation of this Agreement,' and hence controversial issues, such as grading and the employment of men as opposed to women, had been brought up there.

There was generally a rough demarcation line between the grievance procedure and the committees, the latter handling more general, non-monetary issues on which decisions were not immediately required. Even so, in many cases it was still unclear as to which mechanism should be used. We heard comments such as one from a foreman who complained that when a meeting of the departmental committee was drawing close, the workers would save all their minor complaints in order to have issues to put on the committee's agenda so that the committee's time was then wasted in discussing trivia. In another case, a manager said that when he could not handle a grievance he usually recommended that it be taken to the works council rather than directly to senior management. It is also possible that in some cases there may be tactical considerations involved in going to the committee. One personnel manager noted that: 'Things are saved for the Works Council which it is thought might not be conceded if taken through normal channels.'

Informal intra-organisational communications This type of deviation is of a rather different order to those examined previously, since it is an integral part of any organisational process but can nevertheless significantly alter the way in which grievance handling operates. On receiving a complaint, a foreman might check with his departmental manager, who in turn, if he felt the issue had any wider significance might check with his own superior, the personnel or some other staff function, or fellow departmental managers. The check might be for information, for a recommendation, or for a positive decision, which would then be relayed to the original recipient who would then inform the grievant. As far as procedure is concerned, the grievance has presumably been settled at the original stage, but it might be the works manager's view which is actually given as an answer, and there might have been several other people whose opinions have been asked before that view was arrived at. Many senior line and personnel managers undoubtedly spend much more time asking in a consultative capacity than actually solving grievances in any face to face way. If in doubt, check, seemed to be the motto of many of our respondents, especially where the union was concerned. There was also the further consideration of reinforcing an answer with someone else's authority. As one foreman said: 'It makes them much happier if I tell them I've had a word with Mr . . . [his superior].' This however carries the implication that the grievant would presumably feel that he had already obtained the superior's view, and to that extent might feel less inclined to the grievance. At levels above that of supervisor, it was often difficult to know where the advisory function merged into the decision making function, and where the formal and the informal aspects of procedure met.

Such communication is a vital and necessary part of the normal process of management and occurs in many other areas besides grievance handling. In this area, however, it does have one important consequence, namely that the concept of review by fresh and disinterested individuals at successive stages is considerably diminished. A works manager might overturn a lower manager's decision if the senior steward comes to see him, but it is less likely if he has already contributed to that decision.

A union also has its own internal communication process. Shop stewards often ask advice from the senior steward, who might be able to recall a precedent or quote union policy, either of which might help resolve an argument. The result might therefore be that what seems like a simple grievance has in fact involved a wide range of people beyond those who actually discuss it with each other.

Conclusions

It is clear from our fieldwork that the grievance process did not operate according to the formal procedural requirements described in chapter 3, where these existed. Some deviation was to be expected, indeed the assumptions of the formal procedure incorporated a certain tolerance for informality, but what was surprising was the extent to which people did not relate to or even know about the formal procedure. Essentially, the actual process is much more complex in terms of the issues, the social organisation of the plant and its underlying normative values than the assumptions of the existing formal procedure can reflect, even in plants with a relatively simple structure. As a result, there was almost everywhere a willingness to permit informal methods of solution to embody the complexity of any given situation. Fig. 4.1 gives a general overview of the typical grievance process as it appeared in practice in the majority of plants visited in our study. The continuous lines represent the formal or official procedure, the broken lines some of the informal lines of communication involved in grievance handling. However, although it indicates

Fig. 4.1 Schematic diagram of the grievance process

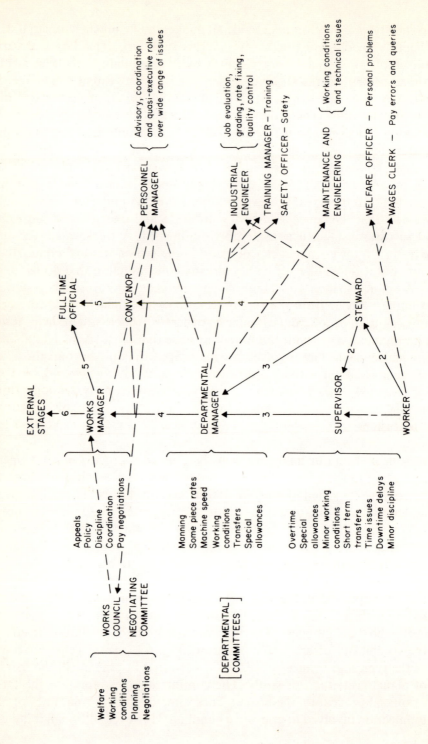

in schematic form the total network, it naturally does not purport to represent the path followed by any single grievance. The level at which any particular issue is likely to be resolved is indicated alongside the various tiers of management. Finally, the stages enumerated do not necessarily describe discrete occurrences involving only the individuals indicated; informal consultation both up and down the management and union hierarchies is likely at any point in the process.

Obviously, a general pattern of the kind given in Fig. 4.1 hides considerable differences between plants. There are as many ways in which these can be examined as there are possible causal variables. We therefore propose to illustrate the way the industry variable appears to influence grievance patterns, and thereafter to consider briefly some of the more notable features of other variables.

The industry variable

The primary factor affecting the nature of the informal process was the type of grievance. Thus technical issues are likely to introduce staff functions, monetary issues are likely to require high level coordination, individual issues are more likely to be settled at the lowest levels. The predominance of particular grievance types is primarily caused by the work situation, which in turn is largely a function of technology (for which the best correlate is in industry). The other major variable affecting the process, management organisation and structure, is also dictated to a considerable extent by technological factors. We saw earlier in this chapter that each industry had its own predominant types of issue, although obviously there were wide variations within as well as between industries; we shall therefore now look at each industry in turn.

The food industry Here the predominant grievances involved work assignments and transfers. These types of grievances were more likely to be individual, less likely to involve heavy cost or other zero-sum creating factors, and require little input of information, action or authority from staff or other departments. Hence the bulk of the grievances were raised and settled between the grievant, his immediate steward and the foreman or supervisor. As we have seen, the food industry had the supervisors who handled the highest proportion of grievances themselves and also, as we shall see in the next chapter, the supervisors who felt the highest satisfaction with the procedure. Relatively few grievances went beyond the department manager to staff officials or plant level management. The staff role was, in fact, fairly limited in many of the plants (with one major exception). However, although most issues were handled departmentally in smaller plants in the industry, a senior shop steward or convenor might be the main union official handling grievances. Fig. 4.2 illustrates this process; here (and in Figs. 4.3 and 4.4) relative thickness of the arrows indicates frequency of involvement in grievances.

Fig. 4.2   A typical grievance process in the food industry

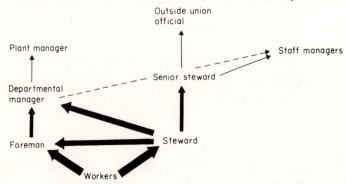

The chemical industry   In this industry grievances over job grading, classification and physical working conditions appeared to be the most common. These types of grievances tended to affect groups rather than individuals, at least some of them were unlikely to be easily handled by immediate supervisors, and some involved direct monetary expenditure, giving them a potential for zero-sum conflict. Decisions sometimes had wider implications than the immediate department and required information on plant-wide policies and practices which was in the possession of 'staff' managers such as personnel, maintenance, etc. Hence supervisors here spent less time on grievance handling than those in other industries, and also formed the highest proportion of those who tended to feel only moderate satisfaction with the procedure.

The typical grievance process appeared to be that many grievances were passed quickly to the department manager level, where guidance was frequently obtained from relevant staff managers. The staff role was probably greater than in the other industries; this would probably have been even more noticeable had the average size of plant not been small. Grievances concerning physical conditions were occasionally raised at works councils and similar joint committees while those concerning job grading might end up at the special joint job evaluation committees. Again, the senior plant level managers played only a limited role. Fig. 4.3 illustrates this process.

Fig. 4.3   A typical grievance process in the chemical industry

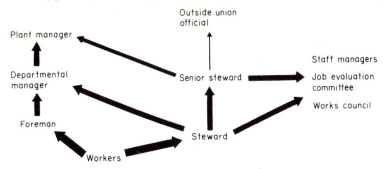

The carpet industry   The most common kinds of grievances in this industry were those affecting incentive earnings, new jobs or piece rates, machine breakdowns and other delays, and faulty raw material, etc. These issues usually affected whole groups of workers, even though only one person might initiate the protest. While some grievances might be corrected by repairing or replacing machines or material, many also had direct cost features which gave them a potential for zero-sum conflict. Such issues, although having implications for higher management as well, involved a good deal of work at first line and departmental level. It will be remembered that both supervisors and especially departmental managers in the carpet industry spent more time on grievances than did their counterparts in other industries. Moreover, higher level line management was much more involved in a coordinating function than in the other industries. Because of the technology and the prevailing piece rate wage system, the work study and maintenance departments were the main staff functions likely to get involved in these types of grievances. Personnel departments played a relatively small role in grievance handling or indeed in industrial relations issues generally.

The typical grievance process, as compared to that in the other two industries studied, more often involved plant level management and the union convenor or senior shop steward. If union officials did not take matters to the top level, it was likely that they would be referred informally by department level management and the 'answers' sent down for them to pass on. This process is illustrated in Fig. 4.4.

We have, therefore, three rather different patterns of grievance handling, although it must be reiterated that these are only general statements to which there are obviously exceptions. Factors such as size of plant, the proportion of women in the workforce, and aspects of personality and union structure, all of which certainly influence the nature of the grievance process, have not been taken into account, nor have factors

Fig. 4.4   A typical grievance process in the carpet industry

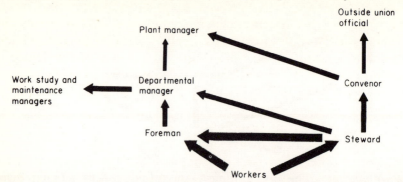

deriving more directly from the type of grievance, such as group as opposed to individual grievances or to the extent to which a particular issue is inherently zero-sum. Nevertheless, we can make some general characterisations of the three industries: the food industry might be said to have a narrow (in terms of the lateral diffusion of decision making) and short (in terms of the vertical diffusion) pattern; the chemical industry's pattern by these criteria is short but more widely diffused; while that for the carpet industry is long in terms of vertical diffusion of decision making and falls between the other two industries in terms of lateral diffusion.

Other variables affecting the grievance process

A second important distinguishing feature was the size of plant which, as already noted, overlaps to some extent with the industry variable. The social structure of a large plant will, other things being equal, be more intricate and contain more organisational levels than a small plant, and this enhances the probability of a longer grievance process. We have seen that large plants tended to have rather more grievances than smaller ones, although not overwhelmingly so. There was more by-passing and more time spent handling grievances in large as opposed to small plants, indicating that the grievances found there are more complex and difficult to deal with. Moreover, middle managers become more involved with grievances in large plants and, while managers generally felt more satisfied with the procedure than supervisors, managers in large plants felt less overall satisfaction with the procedure than did supervisors in small plants. Overall, therefore, the conclusion must be that the process in large plants was considerably more complex, less satisfactory to the supervisory and managerial participants and involved higher levels of authority than the process in small plants.

The other variables we examined earlier in this chapter inevitably involve some degree of collinearity with size of plant and industry; thus in our sample a piecework pay system is closely connected with large plants and the carpet industry, but also seems likely to make an independent contribution to a more complex procedure. In the case of the degree of unionisation variable, it did not appear to be positively correlated with the complexity or usage of the grievance process. Thus while the carpet industry had a complex process, the highest number of grievances, and the most time spent on grievances, it was the least heavily unionised of the three industries, none of its plants being fully organised. The food industry, on the other hand, had in many respects the simplest process, yet half of its plants were completely unionised at the manual level. The implication is therefore that grievances are not primarily a function of union organisation, but rather of the sociotechnical environment.

Notes

[1] In fact we found three managers who kept detailed grievance records on a personal basis, and other instances where some grievances might be recorded, e.g., in a shift logbook, but these hardly constitute a basis for analysis. In any case, while recordkeeping would help at the higher stages of procedure, it would raise an inevitable issue of completeness at the lower levels, a problem highlighted by Peach and Livernash, op. cit.

[2] P. Ash, 'The parties to the grievance', op. cit.

[3] The only remotely comparable estimate is the government social survey report, *Workplace Industrial Relations 1972*, which asked about the number of grievances and claims in four categories–many, some, a few, none (p. 50). Amongst foremen, 5 per cent said many, 10 per cent some, 71 per cent a few, and 13 per cent none. Amongst lower managers 19 per cent said many, 21 per cent some, 58 per cent a few, 2 per cent none.

[4] Unfortunately we were unable to obtain sufficient data to replicate the analysis of departmental differences found in the study of Peach and Livernash, op. cit.

[5] Ash, op. cit. concurred with this feeling in his finding that grievants were primarily workers who had not settled down.

[6] The basic statement of this view is R.W. Revans, 'Industrial Morale and Size of Limit', *Political Quarterly*, vol. 27, 1956. More recently, however, the existence of any simple relationship has been challenged by G.K. Ingham, *Size of Industrial Organization and Worker Behaviour*, Cambridge University Press, 1970.

[7] Trying to define an overall level of conflict presents several conceptual problems. Taking our 'common', 'occasional' and 'rare' categories, there are difficulties in weighting their relative importance and assigning a cut-off point for differentiating levels of conflict. Even if this is done, the result only relates to numbers of grievances, whereas there are likely to be very considerable differences in the relative significance of different types of grievance. This factor could, of course, vary greatly between plants, but we would suggest that in general terms two important considerations are the extent to which a grievance type is likely to be the subject of group or individual complaints, and the extent to which it is zero-sum in nature. We tried to construct two tables showing overall levels of conflict, one merely relating to grievance frequency, the other taking into account the estimated relative significance of grievance types, but we do not think the results are sufficiently reliable to be reproduced here.

[8] The extent of the desire for informality can go as far as setting up a separate informal mechanism, parallel to the procedure. Thus the avoidance of disputes clause of one company procedure stated that:

> It is not the intention of the Disputes Procedure to prevent or discourage employees from continuing to have direct contact with Management. It is accepted by both parties that the most satisfactory solution to a problem is reached between the individual and manager affecting that individual. The procedure for avoiding disputes is available in the event of these two parties being unable to agree.

It should be added that the formal procedure in question suggested precisely this approach of individual to manager, so that other than stressing informality the relevance of this addendum is difficult to understand.

[9] The problem of adequate definition of authority does not only spring from possible faults in the wording of our questionnaire. The CIR noted in its review of procedural references: '. . . we found that unnecessary escalation of problems was often due to uncertainty on the part of managers, particularly middle managers and supervisors, as to their industrial relations role. This in turn reflected general uncertainty as to the areas in which they could take their own decisions.' (CIR report no. 90, *Final Report*, pp. 7–8).

[10] The *Workplace Industrial Relations, 1972* report, op. cit., suggested a much lower capacity by foremen to handle grievances or claims without reference to higher management. Thirty per cent of foremen were found to do this 'very often', 34 per cent 'fairly often', 26 per cent 'seldom',

and 10 per cent 'never' (p. A23). The difference between these figures and ours may be accounted for at least partly by the nature and the context of the questions asked. As already explained, we encouraged respondents to take a liberal view of grievances as complaints, whether they came within the normal range of union activities or were merely individual issues. For the purposes of the report the question was not asked if the foreman did not have any stewards, and the context of the questionnaire was very much one of a union–management bargaining relationship. The likelihood is therefore that the term grievance was taken by many respondents to involve a degree of formality, union orientation, and fractional bargaining which was absent from our study. We would certainly agree that most union-oriented issues tended not to be solved by foremen.

[11] Government Social Survey, *Workplace Industrial Relations*, SS. 402, HMSO 1966, p. 103. The reasons for the difference are probably similar to those given in note 10 on proportions of grievances resolved. Another check on time spent is provided by Thurley and Hamblin, who also noted that little time was spent on disputes by supervisors, with the exception of a single instance in the engineering industry, and went on to say: 'Most supervisors regarded the operatives' personal problems and general welfare as one of their main concerns; but in fact this was a "low priority" matter, and the amount of time spent on it decreased as the pressure of other jobs increased.' (K.E. Thurley and A.C. Hamblin, *The Supervisor and His Job*, HMSO 1963, p. 15.)

[12] *Workplace Industrial Relations, 1972,* op. cit., p. 50.

[13] Donovan Report, op. cit., p. 41; J. Winkler, 'The ghost at the bargaining table', *British Journal of Industrial Relations*, July 1974.

[14] We asked supervisors their views about by-passing on a four-point scale: 'very annoyed', 'mildly annoyed', 'not bothered', and 'prefer it that way'. Predictably, the great majority were 'very annoyed'. Only one 'preferred it that way'. Another who said he was 'not bothered' added 'any more', clearly a case of resignation rather than disinterest.

[15] C.A. Myers and J. Turnbull, 'Line and staff in industrial relations', *Harvard Business Review*, July–August 1956.

[16] Most of the literature supports the view that the personnel function should remain advisory. See for example CIR report no. 34, *The Role of Management in Industrial Relations*, p. 17.

[17] If they had remained purely consultative bodies they might well have died out altogether, as McCarthy has argued. (W.E.J. McCarthy, *The Role of Shop Stewards in British Industrial Relations*, RCTUEA Research Paper No. 1, p. 22.)

[18] The difficulty of any specific statement of function is well illustrated in the following statement of intent from the consultative body in one of our plants: 'Joint Consultative Machinery should not be regarded merely as a means of ventilating grievances. If the business resolves into an exchange of recriminations the main objects will fail. By this it is not meant that well-founded complaints against management policy nor questions of workshop discipline should be excluded. Morale is undoubtedly an important factor governing productivity and one that must receive consideration along with other factors. Coming within this category, too, are questions of promotion and dismissal.'

5 Towards a contingency theory of procedural effectiveness

It is clear from our fieldwork that the grievance process did not operate according to the formal procedural requirements described in chapter 3, insofar as these existed in the various plants studied. The assumptions of the formal procedure may incorporate a certain tolerance for informality, but if this goes too far the formal procedure becomes irrelevant to a considerable degree. We have seen in chapter 4 that the actual process is much more complex than the assumptions of the existing formal procedure can reflect, even in plants with a relatively simple structure. Essentially, we would agree with Marsh's observations on the informality of domestic grievance handling:

> But it is also because managers in general are disinclined to treat procedures for handling grievances with the same degree of precision with which they might regard, for example, a procedure for accounting or stock control. So far as managements are concerned, it seems that procedures for handling grievances are commonly regarded more as a convenience than as an instrument of regulation. In extreme cases, it seems that procedures are virtually disregarded until workplace pressures, and in some cases unconstitutional stoppages, force attention to be paid to them.[1]

Yet neither this quotation nor our prior analysis entirely explains why this was so. This chapter therefore attempts in its opening sections to delve further into this question by examining three cognitive dimensions relating to grievance handling, namely knowledge of the procedure, satisfaction with the process, and a re-examination of the underlying assumptions. In the succeeding section we examine the wider implications of our findings prior to trying to create a practical framework for procedural analysis in chapter 6. The objective of the later sections of this chapter is to set up a contingency theory of procedural effectiveness and, after a general discussion, to take up the specific issue of the desirable degree of formality.

Knowledge of procedure

An obvious prerequisite for the efficient operation of a procedure is that all concerned should know what it entails. However, in view of the absence of written and widely communicated procedures in many cases, the lack of training in the use of procedure even where it was written down, [2] and the ambiguities associated with the concept of procedure in terms of what ought to happen or what did happen, this was certainly not something which could be taken for granted.

We therefore questioned respondents about their own clarity of awareness of what procedures to follow when faced with a grievance, and also asked how they perceived the procedural knowledge of their subordinates in the workforce. The overall results are given here in Table 5.1. This shows

Table 5.1

Knowledge of procedure

	Middle managers		Supervisors		Total	
	No.	%	No.	%	No.	%
Respondents viewing their *own* knowledge of procedure to be followed as:						
Very clear	63	71	78	59	141	64
Fairly clear	22	25	40	30	62	28
Rather unclear	4	4	12	9	16	7
Very unclear	0	0	2	2	2	1
Total	89	100	132	100	221	100

that over 70 per cent of managers but less than 60 per cent of supervisors were 'very clear' about procedure. However, only a few professed themselves to be either 'rather unclear' or 'very unclear'. It may seem surprising that the procedure was thought to be very clear by such a large proportion of respondents when many firms did not have a written procedure. However, this begs the question of what the term 'procedure' meant to respondents, since the existence of a written procedure did not appear to make a great deal of difference to their practical knowledge of what to do. When respondents were re-categorised according to whether their plant had a written procedure of any kind or not, 70 per cent of those in written procedure plants were 'very clear' as opposed to 60 per cent in plants without written procedures. Although this difference was accentuated by a larger number who were 'unclear' in plants without a procedure, it is still not large enough to argue that the existence of a written document is the critical factor in making people aware of procedure, and the only conclusion that can be drawn is that many people were not referring to the written procedure as such, but rather to the 'standard practices' or, since neither the written procedure nor the 'standard practices' were necessarily the framework within which grievances were in fact resolved, the 'actual' process. The inherent ambiguity between the formal and the actual was well underlined by one respondent who said: 'The procedure is understandable, yes, but not clear because the letter and the spirit are two different things here. The procedure is only followed when it suits us, i.e., management; if it doesn't we don't follow it.' Moreover, when we asked the question, it was very rare for respondents to quote the written procedure as such. In several of the firms with written procedures, the respondents (in particular the supervisors) were not given a copy, and were probably only dimly aware of its existence. In one plant, where all the supervisors said the procedure was very clear, three of them admitted that they had not read the agreement in which the procedure was written and which had been distributed the previous week. In another plant, the works manager said that the procedure was not generally distributed because it was not intended for individual workers, but rather for the 'union and management negotiators'. This situation may, of course, have changed as a result of the 1971 Industrial Relations Act.[3]

Satisfaction with procedure

A second aspect which might help to further explain the grievance process as we found it is the level of satisfaction expressed about it. We must, of course, recognise that satisfaction is likely to be a function of other aspects of the work situation beyond the narrow technical operation of procedure, and we therefore asked four more detailed questions of prospective importance and also gave respondents an opportunity for open-ended comments.

The specific question on overall satisfaction, which centres on the actual rather than the formal process, was: 'All in all, how satisfied are you with the present procedures for the handling of employee grievances and complaints as they actually operate from day to day?' Respondents

Table 5.2

Satisfaction with procedure

	High	%	Moderate	%	Low	%
By totals						
Managers	59	69	23	27	4	4
Supervisors	66	50	48	37	17	13
Respondents	125	58	71	33	21	9
By industry						
Managers:						
Carpets	16	64	8	32	1	4
Chemicals	24	75	6	19	2	6
Food	19	66	9	31	1	3
Supervisors:						
Carpets	20	49	12	29	9	22
Chemicals	18	50	16	44	2	6
Food	28	52	20	37	6	11
By size of plant						
Managers:						
Large plants	25	58	15	35	3	7
Medium plants	16	76	4	19	1	5
Small plants	20	83	3	13	1	4
Supervisors:						
Large plants	31	44	27	40	9	16
Medium plants	15	47	11	34	6	19
Small plants	20	61	10	30	3	9
By formality of procedure						
Managers:						
High formality	16	59	9	33	2	8
Moderate formality	18	60	9	30	3	10
Low formality	27	85	5	15	0	0
Supervisors:						
High formality	14	40	18	52	3	8
Moderate formality	28	56	13	26	9	18
Low formality	25	53	17	36	5	11

were asked to indicate their level of satisfaction on a 1–10 scale; we then created three admittedly arbitrary categories: 1–5 represented low satisfaction, 6–7 moderate satisfaction, and 8–10 high satisfaction. Although this is somewhat asymmetrical in its distribution, it related better to the pattern of responses than a more even distribution, since those giving a grade as low as five usually expressed strong reservations about the procedure, whereas those who said eight had few comments and intended it as a high mark.

The results are shown in Table 5.2 and disclose a reasonably consistent pattern. Supervisors are clearly less happy with procedure than middle managers but this is to be expected, given the responses in the previous sections of this chapter and the consensus in the literature. Those in large plants were less satisfied than those in smaller ones; this again might be expected. Somewhat more of a surprise is the tendency for those in plants with more formal procedures to be dissatisfied. This may be explicable in either or both of two ways. First, those plants with formal procedures may have created them for the purpose of meeting the needs of the plant. Hence there could be more perceived latent conflict. Alternatively, these respondents may be better able to appreciate deviations from the procedure. However, whatever view is taken of our classification system, overall satisfaction was clearly far from general. This is not surprising in itself, but it does differ considerably from both the 1966 and 1972 government Social Survey reports which asked roughly similar questions.[4]

Table 5.3

'How do you feel about the amount of authority you are given to handle grievances which come to you?'

	Not enough		Just right		Too much	
	No.	%	No.	%	No.	%
Managers	15	21	56	79	0	0
Supervisors	41	39	64	61	0	0
Total	56	32	120	68	0	0

As well as the issue of overall satisfaction, we wished to examine some more detailed aspects of respondents' perceptions of their roles in the grievance process with especial reference to their attitudes towards the way they were organised to deal with grievances. The four questions, the

Table 5.4

'Do you feel you are given sufficient guidance, help, advice and training by upper management in the handling of employee grievances?'

	Not enough		Just right		Too much	
	No.	%	No.	%	No.	%
Managers	11	19	50	80	1	1
Supervisors	24	28	59	71	1	1
Total	35	24	109	73	2	3

Table 5.5

'When a grievance is passed to your boss or higher do you feel that you are adequately consulted and involved by them as they try to handle it?'

	Always		Usually		Occasionally		Rarely	
	No.	%	No.	%	No.	%	No.	%
Managers	33	54	20	33	7	12	1	1
Supervisors	42	45	26	28	18	20	6	7
Total	75	48	46	31	25	16	7	5

Table 5.6

'When a grievance is settled or an agreement reached between higher management and the union do you feel that you are adequately informed about the settlement and what went on?'

	Always		Usually		Occasionally		Rarely	
	No.	%	No.	%	No.	%	No.	%
Managers	37	55	25	37	4	7	1	1
Supervisors	40	39	29	28	29	28	5	5
Total	77	45	54	32	33	20	6	3

categories of choice, and the answers given are set out in Tables 5.3 to 5.6. As with the question of overall satisfaction, most managers and supervisors were happy with the various elements of their role, but again supervisors were consistently and significantly less satisfied than managers. The extent of dissatisfaction, while not particularly high, certainly gives no grounds for complacency, especially in view of the relatively peaceful nature of the plants surveyed. There is no direct basis for comparing these results with others, although the very limited comparison with *Workshop Industrial Relations, 1972* which is possible again suggests that our respondents were less satisfied.[5]

When the results are broken down by industry and size of plant, large plants and plants in the carpet industry generally registered higher levels of dissatisfaction, although, as already pointed out, these two factors may interact because of the large average size of carpet plants. Thus some three-fifths of supervisors in the carpet industry felt they had inadequate authority. However, going against this general pattern, criticism of the extent of guidance and training was highest in the chemical industry, while five of the six supervisors who were only rarely consulted were employed in the food industry.

At least as interesting as the figures themselves were the open-ended comments which were made in connection with the extent of satisfaction. The comments can be broken down into four categories: those to do with the procedure itself; those dealing with the behaviour of the workforce and management respectively; and those concerned with roles. Most of the comments were spontaneous; procedural issues were not given a great deal of thought, and some comments had little to do with procedures as such. Nor did all respondents make comments. What follows must be understood as representing a minority, albeit a substantial one. On the other hand, the level of expectation as to what constituted a desirable state of affairs was sometimes quite low, and this may have inhibited comments. An example of this attitude was a supervisor who replied: 'No strikes, no sitdowns here, so no changes needed.'

The most frequent comment about the procedure itself was a variant on the theme of increased formality, whether this was expressed positively–as simply a desire for a more formal procedure, a detailed works rule book, or written grievances–or negatively–the comment that 'people don't know whether to go to the steward or the foreman first', that there were 'too many things which are not covered,' or that 'some groups aren't covered'. In only one case was there a complaint about too much formality, namely that the discipline appeals procedure was far too elaborate. On the other hand, whilst there was a fairly widespread desire for more formality, it was clear that people did not envisage long elaborate written documents and it was also apparent that they did not wish to be tightly constrained by procedures.

The second category, that of perceptions of the behaviour of the workforce in procedure, was perhaps less strongly represented than might have been expected. There were a number of remarks about people not sticking to procedure; a typical one was: 'It would be a good procedure if only it was adhered to.' By-passing was the main issue. There were also a number of comments to the effect that the stewards were too strong, or that there were too many of them. There was only one comment regarding the inadequacy of the local union. A more general feeling, reflecting the level of decision making in some firms, was that the procedure could be abused by too much trivia: 'Senior people's time is being spent too much because these small things escalate all the way up, and they appeal to senior management, then executive management and the representative must come with the supervisor, so that you get at least five people around the table wasting time.' On the other hand, there were some comments pointing in the other direction to the general trend expressed so far. One manager noted that his shop stewards were so inadequate that it was difficult to get any impression of workers' feelings, while a supervisor in another plant said: 'The union is so weak here that workers don't have a chance in procedure.' These last points are illuminating in that they strongly suggest that procedure by itself may be an inadequate means of protection, and that it requires institutionalised union power to make it effective.

In contrast to the relatively restrained comments on worker behaviour, criticism of one level of management by another was definitely stronger. Most of the criticism related to weakness, an inability or unwillingness to enforce agreements or take decisions or impose discipline. This last was a particular comment of supervisors, who felt that their decisions were not being backed up adequately. Sometimes there was self-criticism: 'One gives in too much'. While all this may not be directly related to procedure, there was no doubt that the lower ranks of management saw behaviour and procedure as parts of the total managerial process. Other than the weakness argument, there were three other sources of comment. One, almost as common as weakness, was criticism of communications, mainly vertically downwards but also laterally to some extent. The second was to blame management for delays in solving issues: 'Things get distorted by building up through too much time lag', and one respondent saw delay as a deliberate management tactic. Finally, there were comments on the need for training in grievance handling.

The final, and much smaller, category related to roles within the procedure, and especially to supervisor authority and status. Several comments focused on the uncertain boundaries of authority. One foreman, rather poignantly, said that management told foremen to assume responsibility in theory but in practice did not permit it, and other comments suggest that this ambivalence could be more widely shared. The other issue was one of status. In one or two cases foremen felt that their authority was undermined because they earned less than those they supervised.

The overall results of these attitudinal questions show that although there was no major feeling of inadequacy of procedures, there is also not too much cause for complacency on the part of British management. Knowledge of procedure, the various aspects of involvement, and overall satisfaction levels all indicate that the management side of the relationship in the plants under study was by no means as well organised as it might have been. Nevertheless, our questions do help to indicate why the process was acceptable; it was, at least in many cases, the only standard of comparison, since otherwise there was variously no procedure, or what there was was seen as extremely vague and general or was not thought of as the basis of behaviour. However, there was on the whole sufficient satisfaction with the process for it not to be seriously challenged by middle and lower level management.

Management's assumptions of the function of grievance procedures

The views of middle and lower level management on the existing process suggest acquiescence in it, but they are not responsible for initiatives in this area. We did not ask attitudinal questions of senior plant managers, largely because there were too few of them to form a satisfactory group for reporting purposes, but in order to understand the reasons for the process we also need to take into account their perspectives. At the time of our visits several companies were considering or had just instituted procedural changes. There was certainly an interest in the structural aspects of the subject which was not present lower down. Nevertheless, for the most part senior managers accepted the process as it existed, in spite of the deviations mentioned. It is thus desirable to re-examine here the assumptions we made in chapter 2.

We would suggest that there are three possible ways in which senior managers conceive of the grievance process. The first involves looking at grievance handling essentially as an extension of the administrative process.

This is frequently the case where an issue arises which is something less than a claim to change the status quo. This 'administrative' model of grievance handling springs primarily from the nature of management organisation in many plants. As we have noted in earlier chapters, junior management's inability to resolve grievances is in considerable part due to lack of authority or competence with respect to particular issues. British companies have relatively few detailed written documents which would enable supervisors to give unequivocal answers to grievances. Since there often tends to be uncertainty about the limits or interpretation of a decision, some upwards reference of grievances by supervisors is likely. As we have seen, senior management frequently has to offer advice or interpretation concerning previous decisions, or in lieu of an existing policy.

The very great majority of management decisions on grievances were undoubtedly accepted without challenge. However, if a decision was challenged or clarification requested management was quite willing to accept the right of the workers to do this and would approach the subsequent resolution process in a problem solving and placatory manner. The result was a request to share in the process of decision making by adding the worker point of view when amplification was required. As such, this was of considerable value to management. Very rarely in our plants did it appear to be a case of 'we will not accept that decision' on the part of the workforce, while management, from its point of view, did not see workers and managers as two separate sides, but rather as a single administrative process. Grievance handling was thus only to a very limited extent an adversary proceeding.

In this administrative process, it mattered less that the grievance procedure was followed (since there was no conscious intention of manipulation) than that the best answer was achieved in the shortest possible time. Moreover, the logical person to amplify or re-evaluate a decision need not necessarily be someone in the direct line of the procedure, and, given the problem solving approach, it might appear sensible to go straight to that manager. It is a model of this sort which we envisage as accounting for much of the informality and deviations from procedure which existed, and which in numerical terms represented the predominant model for grievance handling. Thus according to this viewpoint the grievance procedures in the large number of plants in Britain where conflict is not endemic are not so much 'instruments in the process of obtaining concessions from each other'[6] as extensions of the administrative and decision making processes, which tidy up and clarify the situation and ensure that human relations considerations are take into account.

A second model of the grievance process as viewed by top management could be termed the equity model. This is more akin to the way American grievance procedures operate, or at least to the conventional picture of the way they work. Where more or less formal rules exist, embodied in the collective agreement, in stated management policies, or even in well defined custom and practice rules, some grievances will call for interpretation of these rules. It may be that a worker has a grievance concerned with the makeup of his pay packet, a transfer, or his allocation of overtime. The process here contains a judicial element with a decision based on existing standards, rather than requiring what is essentially an *ad hoc* judgement. Even so, while there may be some case for formalisation in this process, it may also be that the division of effective authority does not coincide with the procedure. Thus the pay office is the logical place to sort out a grievance about the makeup of the pay packet, although the foreman may have some part to play, such as confirming a given amount of overtime. As a result some degree of informality is desirable in this model also.

The third model might be called the claims or power model. Claims in the sense of worker initiated challenges to the status quo can and often do arise through the grievance procedure, and it is these which managers regard as a threat to their power, and are frequently unwilling to legitimise by setting up a special procedure to deal with them. Moreover, these are precisely the types of issue which are most difficult to resolve through the stages of the procedure. It is unlikely that lower level managers would be able to provide answers in many cases, and also unlikely that senior managers would want them to do so. In order to take a plant-wide view and coordinate policy, senior managers are likely to want claims to go rapidly to the top, irrespective of the formal procedure. Here again, therefore, there is a strong case for informality and deviating from the procedure. However, such claims were not common amongst our panel and hence we are unable to speculate at length on the way they affect procedures.

We would not wish to assert that these three models of the way in which managers view the grievance process are easily delineated in any given situation. They are not, and each situation is likely to be a mixture of views. In the majority of our plants the predominant view can be characterised as the administrative model, but the power model may be more apposite for conflict prone plants, just as the equity model is more appropriate for the United States. It is, of course, quite possible that the models may operate at different levels within the same plant. However, in looking at the distinction between process and procedure, we must examine more than the views of management alone.

The union point of view in adhering to the procedure (insofar as we were able to ascertain it) usually seemed to be one of strongly favouring an informal approach. In particular, the senior stewards whom we interviewed greatly valued access to senior management. The possibility of a certain amount of 'forum shopping' on issues where there is no single clear authority is also an attractive aspect of the informal process. The works council, significantly in the light of criticism of such bodies as powerless, was on several occasions mentioned as a place to which grievances could be taken. (This is significant in the light of criticism of such bodies as being powerless.) Only in the situation where management took a formal or autocratic line did stewards tend to want the grievance procedure laid down in detail, although there were cases where they would have preferred specific elements such as time limits, and of course they often welcomed a specification of their rights to certain facilities. In general, however, the stewards we spoke to strongly favoured an informal approach. [7]

Given that both sides favoured informality, it paid both sides to maintain this approach as long as the conflict generated did not become too severe. When we say this, we have in mind both social and economic costs. Socially, a problem solving approach helps to maintain the cohesion of the plant, preventing the development of an adversary relationship, and perhaps even persuading management that a unitary conception of the firm is not only possible but actually works. From an economic point of view, informality seems to save time and effort of all concerned, and therefore to involve lower transactions costs than formality. This, however, may be a false conception; informality does incur costs, which may be shared disproportionately between the parties, especially when viewed in the longer term.

A further factor adding to the informality of the process in our sample was the nature of interaction over a grievance. In most cases a procedural stage merely consisted of going to see a particular manager. Frequently this would not even involve making an appointment (although some managers insisted on this). Meetings themselves were in the nature of informal discussions. Since minutes were not taken, no written forms were necessary, there was no agenda, and no specification of who ought to be present, it was difficult to say in most cases that a stage of the formal procedure was in progress. It is sometimes argued that there are advantages in having informal meetings to oil the wheels before formal sessions, but with the possible exception of the last in-plant stage, we found few formal sessions as such. Also contributing to informality was the fact that the handling of grievances often took place in the wider context of a discussion covering a range of issues of a consultative and informative nature. This was particularly true where senior managers and senior lay officials had a close working relationship, and the opportunity to feel each other out on wider issues added to the informal nature of grievance resolution.

As a result of the above points, we would argue that the view of procedure as a review mechanism for re-evaluating a disagreement at successive stages and levels on both sides was only a small part of the total conception of the grievance process in our sample and the least important from the point of view of the participants. Looking at the grievance procedure in terms of any of the three models we have put forward (with some reservations about the equity model), it is logical to take a problem either directly or as quickly as possible through the procedure to the person who can best solve it. It was certainly our impression that few grievances in practice went through more than two stages of procedure. If they were localised and individual matters, it was highly unlikely that they would get beyond departmental level. If, on the other hand, the grievance was seen as being a significant one, either involving an issue of principle or covering a fairly large number of people, it was not likely to start at the supervisor level. The picture which emerges is that there are a number of loci of decision making, some of which are part of the procedure, others of which are not, which are likely to be approached in given circumstances to settle a grievance.

To take the discussion one stage further, in general it can be said that the major part of the grievance process as it actually operates is essentially an information processing system which gets information on grievances to the person(s) with authority to make decisions on them. Different types of grievances and different structures of power and authority create differing informal paths from the grievant to the effective source of authority on his complaint. Steps in the process *prior* to the involvement of the key decision maker function as gatekeeper or channel switching actions designed to stream the complaint to the right person; they may also act as data collating steps which save the decision maker from having to undertake his own primary investigation. Most of the obvious flaws in actual grievance processes involve such factors as issues going to the 'wrong' people (meaning either those who do not have effective authority or people who have authority but not the requisite skill, experience or knowledge to make reasonable decisions); breakdowns in the channelling and switching steps which delay the grievance from reaching the proper source of authority;

or inadequate data gathering on behalf of the decision maker so that he makes ill-informed judgements.

We now return to the possible mixing of the three models put forward earlier. Prior to the point of effective authority, the interests of the two sides are likely to run parallel in pushing the problem to the point of collective resolution, although some members on either side (such as a foreman or steward) may resent their inability to affect the decision. Up to this point the grievance is part of the administrative process. After a grievance has reached the effective authority on the issue and provided his decision is rejected by the grievants or their representatives, the process immediately changes from problem solving within the administrative process to one of review and negotiation in which the divisions between the two sides become clearly drawn. This is the point at which the issue is no longer presented as a problem or question but rather as specific 'demands' along with possible threats or promises of a *quid pro quo* nature.

Subsequent actions therefore cease to have the primary function of information processing and instead are aimed at the manipulation of power in a negotiating process. Higher level management seeks to back the decision of the individual with effective authority. The union implicitly realises that it is no longer appealing an issue up the hierarchy in order to get to the effective authority; it is now trying to weaken the credibility and legitimacy of that authority and gain influence over it by dealing with higher levels of authority. When the problem solving phase of the grievance process is flawed as described above, the bargaining phase appears much sooner and is likely to be much more difficult. In our particular sample of plants this second phase occurred relatively infrequently and in most cases the bargaining which did occur was not of a punitive variety. Nevertheless, a number of establishments were considering reviewing their procedures, largely on account of such occurrences.

Finally, if the foregoing represented the views of management towards the procedure, what then was its purpose in practice? There are four aspects to this. First, the procedure provided a lowest common denominator of grievance handling patterns: it was the most obvious path for most grievances, even if it could not express the complex total pattern. The obligations of the Industrial Relations Act were in all probability viewed as providing such a denominator. Secondly, it provided a means of checking deviations, albeit not a very strong one. Managers could and did ask grievants if they had seen their supervisors and use the procedure in support. Thirdly, there was the opportunity of using the procedure as a fall-back position if there were constant abuses of the informal system. We did not hear of this happening, however, and we would largely discount it as a serious possibility in the absence of re-structuring. Fourthly, a procedure was thought to be a means of improving industrial relations (a view based on the Donovan Report and the Industrial Relations Bill) but there was not the same enthusiasm as, for instance, for productivity bargaining, and nowhere was the same effort put into selling procedure to the workforce.

Our conclusion is therefore that generally speaking the effect of the procedure was neutral. One exception to this was one plant where an over-elaborate procedure had probably generated conflict by pushing upwards issues that could easily have been settled lower down. There were also several instances where it could be argued that too much informality had resulted in senior managers taking on too much of the burden of decision making, although such over-centralisation probably also had other causes. However, this is merely one view of the results of procedure. Procedure itself had not been an issue as far as we heard, either in bargaining or in grievance handling. The closest instance to conflict over procedural issues appeared to have been attempts to raise matters at works councils which management argued were beyond the jurisdiction of such bodies. The lack of procedural formality did, however, result in the dissatisfaction of some lower level managers over their loss of status due to by-passing, not being consulted by superiors or not being kept informed about settlements.

An alternative is to consider whether following the procedure would have produced different results, either substantively or attitudinally. There is a considerable amount of evidence that breaking procedure can be of considerable value to a workgroup, especially if industrial action is taken or threatened. It produces not only a quicker answer but possibly a more favourable one. The CIR report on Birmid-Qualcast companies illustrated this, and it was also noted by McCarthy.[8] However, in our own panel it was not at all the practice to push a grievance to the point of threatening industrial action. Grievances were essentially treated in a problem solving rather than an adversary fashion, although many managers did feel that stewards would go to whoever would give them the most favourable answer if there was any choice in the matter. In general, informality probably did not make much difference to the substantive outcome of grievances. The same answer was obtained which would have been arrived at if the procedure had been followed. Such problems of coordination, over-centralisation, and inadequate definition of policy and authority as existed were the fault of management organisation and structure rather than the procedure as such. As a result, respondents generally did not feel that the procedure was being abused by the stewards in the sense of being manipulated for tactical advantage; if anything, such comments as there were on this point suggested managerial manipulation.

Towards a contingency theory of procedural effectiveness

We now move from consideration of our fieldwork to an attempt to develop a contingency theory of the effectiveness of procedure. Our argument is as follows. The context in which workers, union representatives, and management relationships exist generates both the conflict within the relationship and the power to affect its outcome. This conflict will be resolved by mechanisms which will resemble to a greater or lesser degree the formal or expected processes for resolution. If the latter are too far removed from the former, they will either be ignored or, if attempts are made to enforce them, they will exacerbate the conflict by precipitating secondary conflict over the procedural forms themselves. It follows that the procedure ought to be closely related to the actual behavioural process, but just how formal it is, along what dimensions, and how closely it should be followed are key issues in contingency analysis. In essence, we would argue that informality has increasing disadvantages with increasing conflict and a deteriorating attitudinal climate. It is also important to note that a conflict relationship can change in degree and kind so that the procedures for resolution become out of date. As Marsh, Garcia, and Evans noted in their study:

> What has happened in engineering is that the *volume* of domestic negotiations has grown while other elements of the system have remained constant. This has overloaded the York Procedure and led to strain in workshops in which the institutions have been unable to cope with the increased load of negotiations and grievances. [9]

Finally, procedural change is a part, not the whole, of structural reform; it will have different effects in different situations and will not of itself be sufficient in some. This section, then, sets out to examine the preconditions for procedures to be effective before an attempt is made in the following chapter to make this more practical by examining the advantages and disadvantages of formalising the major elements of procedure.

In encapsulated and polarised form, our view of the factors which surround the grievance process can be seen in Fig. 5.1, which in many respects brings together and recapitulates earlier arguments. Fig. 5.1 is composed of four sections: (i) the contextual conditions; (ii) the implications of the context of grievances; (iii) the implications for procedure; and (iv) the effects of the attitudinal climate on the impact of procedure. In this construct, the contextual conditions are seen as being the major influence, with the additional climate affecting the mode of operation of the procedure. It is possible that the attitudinal climate can be a more independent factor, influencing the frequency and type of grievances, but in common with most of the literature we would argue the attitudinal climate is a secondary factor and is largely a function of the past environmental context. However, while a change in the procedure or its mode of operation cannot change the environmental situation directly, it can affect the attitudinal climate. To the extent that this is deliberate, it may be viewed as a form of attitudinal structuring as described by Walton and McKersie.[10]

Fig. 5.1 only states the polar contextual positions and not the many intermediate situations. There is a wide spectrum of conflict situations which require different procedural solutions in both breadth and depth of procedures. However, it by no means follows that procedural change is either desirable or will be sufficient in itself. There are some situations, usually involving very small companies, where procedures are likely to be irrelevant to the highly personalised relationships; there are others, usually where a good informal relationship has been developed, in which over-formalisation will lead to a premature adversary relationship; in yet another category where high conflict prevails we would suggest that procedural change alone will not solve the problem–rather a wider ranging reform is necessary to remove some of the sources of conflict and prevent the procedures from being overloaded. Indeed, with respect to this last point, it would be sensible to re-examine all other elements of the industrial relations system before introducing procedural changes.

The degree of formality

One of the key issues in this discussion of the reconstruction of procedure concerns the merits of formality and informality. There is considerable confusion over this subject, since not unnaturally everyone wants to have the benefits of both approaches without the disadvantages. It has become almost obligatory to say that there must be flexibility and informality even in the working of formal procedures. Management, for its part, wants to preserve informality in the problem solving stage of grievance resolution, but to reserve the right to fall back on formal procedure when 'attitudes are struck'. Workers and their representatives

Fig. 5.1 Contingent conditions affecting the nature of disputes procedures
and their effects on conflict

---

(1) Contextual conditions

1 Large size, multiplant, geographically dispersed organisation.

1 Small size, single plant.

2 Unstable, diverse, complex external environments (scarce resources, great economic fluctuations, frequent innovation in products and production technology, changing values in workforce and community).

2 Stable, relatively predictable external environments (requires adequate economic stability, low rates of product and technical change, stable values in workforce and community).

3 Highly differentiated, complex organisational structure.

3 Simple, hierarchical organisational structure.

4 Technology creates considerable worker control over workplace and quality, requires special training, creates potential for group cohesion and gives strategic position in work flow.

4 Technology inhibits growth of cohesive, powerful workgroups.

(2) Characteristics of grievance issues
Contextual conditions will:

1 Increase likelihood of work grievances developing.

1 Relatively low rate of grievances likely to develop.

2 Increase likelihood that issues will be shared by high power groups.

2 Low probability that grievances will be shared by high power groups.

3 Increase likelihood that issues will be seen as potentially 'we–them', 'zero-sum' type.

3 Low probability that issues will be seen potentially as 'zero-sum' type.

(3) Procedural characteristics
Contextual conditions and grievance characteristics create need for procedures which:

1 Are jointly determined.
2 Require considerable delegation of authority and responsibility down management and union hierarchies.
3 Create differentiated roles among managerial levels, staff positions, union positions, and joint bodies.
4 Create differentiated procedures for particular types of disputes.
5 Create detailed specification of terminal stages favouring arbitration or mediation, no strike/status quo clauses, penalties for non-adherence, etc.

1 Formal procedures may be simple, less formal or in some cases non-existent; no detailed specification of roles; no differentiation by issues; coordination and control based on existing authority hierarchy; no detailed specification of terminal stage. However, any formal procedure should parallel existing authority structure as it actually operates, thus allowing issues to quickly pass to nearest person with authority and knowledge to make decisions on the matter.

(4) The impact of procedure in different attitudinal climates (based on Derber et al.)

Attitudinal climate	Degree to which procedure is enforced by management	
	Consistent	Inconsistent
Aggressive	Can promote conflict if no normative agreement on procedures. Containment of conflict if there is.	Procedural manipulation.
Repressed hostility	Individualist withdrawal.	Procedure largely ignored.
Moderate	Relatively stable equilibrium with mixed distributive and integrative approaches.	Unstable informal equilibrium with possibility of erratic actions.
Cooperative	Procedure followed in problem solving approach.	Informal problem solving.
Passive	Acquiescence.	Acceptance of differing standard patterns.

want certain aspects of the relationship enshrined as rules, especially those established as matters of custom and practice, but also find it useful to have access to persons not part of the procedure or to by-pass procedure in the interests of more rapid resolution. It is doubtless also convenient to be able to argue that procedure is uncertain and inconsistent and has not been followed by management when sanctions are applied.

The advantages of some degree of formality obviously underlie the whole concept of a procedure as discussed in chapter 2. But there are also other more practical reasons for a more formal approach in certain circumstances. Perhaps the most important of these is concerned with moving along the spectrum of conflict. As a plant becomes more complex in its social organisation by virtue of growing size, changing technology, or widening scope of union–management interaction, it becomes more difficult to make decisions on an *ad hoc* basis and the possibility of conflict through uncertainty increases. Points of detail need to be verified, comparative information obtained, old precedents re-examined. To enable this to be done efficiently, some structure for the presentation of and response to grievances is necessary, at least at the higher levels. Yet even at the higher level, the framework for coordinated behaviour is often not present. Instead, there has been a strong tendency to treat each individual case on its merits in spite of the obvious desire and need to coordinate decisions which is a contributory reason for issues being pushed upwards. As a result, precedents tend to be set which produce anomalies between the various parts of the workforce.

Arising out of this type of situation, as Fox has pointed out, 'Managerial and work-group control systems may co-exist without ever coming to terms with each other.'[11] Procedures are the best, possibly the only, way of bringing the two separate control systems to terms with each other, but if operated too loosely or if they give inadequate definition of roles they merely perpetuate the dualistic system. However, as a joint control system designed to reconcile conflicting needs they can, if properly designed in mutual recognition of the respective roles, provide a balanced point of linkage between the parties. As Flanders put it in a succinct paradox, it may be necessary for management to share control in order to regain it.[12]

A further reason for formality is that if the two sides have different conceptions of procedure (for instance, if they differ as to how far procedural deviation can be taken), the procedure itself becomes a major issue of disagreement. Moreover, if the procedure solves only the easy issues on which there is a considerable amount of common ground, but fails on difficult ones because both sides manipulate it to their advantage, then the procedure is of little value when it is most needed in institutionalising conflict. The strength of the American system lies not in the fact that it is rigidly applied at all levels, although there has been a trend towards more formality as agreements have grown more complex, but in the fact that it provides a safety net if problem solving fails. The British safety net has been the industry-wide procedure, but its deficiencies were clearly exposed by Donovan. If the safety net fails frequently, there is no joint control system.

On an even more pragmatic level are three other, perhaps less significant arguments in favour of rather more formality. One, which would appear to have lain behind the requirement in the Industrial Relations Act for firms to instruct workers in the method of formulating grievances, is that workers might be inhibited from putting forward grievances if they do not know the procedure. The second is that lower level management is likely to feel increasingly aggrieved if they are continually by-passed as a result of informal methods, and a grievance system which ignores these levels is likely to run into trouble in the longer term. [13]

The other side of the coin, the argument for low formality, has until recently been even more persuasive. Essentially it amounts to saying that labour relations are primarily human relations, that the situations arising are so complex, so varied, so uncertain in their frequency and intensity, that they cannot be forced into a pre-determined set of procedural channels. To try to impose a formal structure could be to destroy a relationship wherein mutual trust is necessary for change, adaptation, and evolution; it could, for instance, create a premature adversary climate by putting people on opposite sides of the table, making them conform to rules which emphasise their separate status. An informal problem solving approach, on the other hand, which does not structure interaction, can be more effective in bringing the two sides together. At the lowest levels in particular, it is not feasible in most instances to operate in a legalistic way; a foreman needs flexibility to avoid cumbersome rules, or to permit minor transgressions of them on occasion, if he is to obtain willing co-operation. [14] The problem, of course, is to identify the point at which the benefits of such informality become outweighed by the costs in terms of loss of control. A second point in favour of informality is that it frequently minimises the time and efforts of all concerned. It can enable the grievance to go straight to that person most likely to solve it; it is therefore speedy and effective in Donovan's terms. (It should be noted, however, that a differentiated formal procedure can also do this.) A third point is that a structured procedure is still perfectly capable of being manipulated; McKersie and Shropshire have shown how a company can be forced to return to a more informal mode of operation, especially at the lower stages of procedure.[15] If formal or informal sanctions must be consistently applied to enforce conformity to procedure then the latter is likely to defeat its own purpose.

Finally, it is sometimes argued that moves towards formality and rationalisation are against the best interests of the workforce because formality creates a re-establishment of managerial control which must in turn mean a diminution of that of the workforce. With respect to this last factor two points need to be made. First, although it must be accepted that in many circumstances stewards may have a vested interest in the maintenance of informality, as suggested by the above, it by no means follows that they have a vested interest in uncoordinated decisions. Brown's study of Coventry showed that where the joint shop steward group was strong, there was in fact less uncontrolled drift.[16] Scott et al. also showed in their study of coal mines that higher morale was associated with a higher degree of organised and a lower degree of unorganised conflict.[17] Stewards do not like anomalies, which make their job *vis-à-vis* their members much harder.[18] What most stewards *do* want is the opportunity for joint regulation, of contributing to a move towards an equitable equilibrium. To argue that stewards desire anomalies in order to pursue their quest for power is to misconceive all the research that has been done about the self-perceived role of the vast majority of shop stewards in British industry. Most stewards value their informal powers not as an end in themselves, but as a means of achieving the ends desired by their members, which for many of the most common grievance issues need not be incompatible with the more effective operation of the enterprise.

Pulling together this discussion on informality, it can be said that some informality is both inevitable and desirable as an expression of human relations, not merely technical ones, as recognition that no procedure can fit the needs of all situations, and as a prerequisite for a problem solving approach to grievance resolution. But except in situations of very low conflict, in small plants where a highly personalised relationship and good communications upwards and downwards can enable formality to be dispensed with, informality is not something which should merely be allowed to happen without thought on a random basis. To do this, which is all too common in Britain, is to invite uncertainty and ultimately trouble. Without a careful watch on developments uncertainty is likely to be created along with a power vacuum which will be filled by continuous bargaining in an attempt to find the limits of existing rules and permissible behaviour.

130

In conclusion it can be said that the relative value of the formal versus informal attitudes towards grievance handling is obviously a complex issue. However, two facts which do seem to stand out are first, that informality is preferable lower down the procedure because it is at this level that human relations considerations are most important, formality is more valuable higher up the procedure since it is there that the costs of deviation are likely to be greater, and secondly, that the degree of formality should be tied to the level of conflict on a contingency basis. Finally, a change in procedural structure will not do away with informality, but may instead create a new kind of informality.[19] Instead of the parties operating on an informal basis because there is no clear structure to follow, informality can be used to supplement, not supplant, the procedure; to have informal discussions between the stages in the knowledge that there is a definite machinery to back these up and set limits to procrastination which might occur without such stages; and to prevent a formal system from being unduly legalistic.

Notes

[1] A.I. Marsh, *Disputes Procedures in British Industry,* RCTUEA Research Paper No. 2 (Part 1), HMSO 1966, p. 19.

[2] We did ask a general question of senior managers about the extent of training in the plants, and in only three was it felt that there was a good deal of training in industrial relations. In thirteen of the plants it was felt that there was little or no training, in seven a moderate amount and in ten little or none for supervisors but a moderate amount for managers. Moreover, from questions on how procedures were communicated we would be fairly certain that there was no instruction of individual workers in the use of procedure except perhaps for the supervisor saying that he was the person to see if there were any complaints, or somebody from the personnel department mentioning that a procedure existed. Only in six or so plants were employees given an information handbook or a copy of the collective agreement incorporating the grievance procedure.

[3] But see B. James and R. Clifton, 'Labour relations in the firm; the impact of the Industrial Relations Act', *Industrial Relations Journal,* Spring 1974 and CIR Report No. 69, *Small Firms and the Code of Industrial Relations Practice* for limits on the effect of the Act.

[4] To the question of the 1972 Report: 'On the whole, do you think that the procedure for dealing with the workers' grievances and claims works well or not?', 87 per cent of foremen thought that the procedure

worked well; 93 per cent of foremen answered in the affirmative to a similar question in 1966. We cannot account for this high level of satisfaction, especially given the high level of by-passing and other challenges to the authority of foremen which emerged from the surveys, and the fact that three-quarters of the foremen who were by-passed according to the 1972 Survey disapproved of it.

[5] Comparisons can be made on two scores. Foremen were asked in the 1972 investigation whether they were satisfied with the amount of authority they had to deal with issues raised by stewards: 49 per cent said they were satisfied, 49 per cent said they were fairly satisfied, and 1 per cent were dissatisfied. (Yet 43 per cent of foremen in establishments with more than 500 employees said there were issues raised by stewards which they had to refer to higher management but which they thought they ought to be able to settle themselves.) In the other comparison, 69 per cent of foremen said they were kept 'well informed', while 28 per cent said they were not.

[6] Marsh, op. cit., p. 19.

[7] When asked by the *Workshop Industrial Relations, 1972* investigation to give *one* way of improving industrial relations, only 9 per cent of stewards mentioned a category including a more efficient formal procedure and the rapid settlement of grievances. This must, however, be taken only as a very indirect indication, since it might still be a desired objective but not the main priority.

[8] See the CIR Report No. 4, *Birmingham Aluminium Casting (1903) Company Ltd, Dartmouth Auto Castings Ltd, Midland Motor Cylinder Company Ltd,* Cmnd. 4264, January 1970, especially para. 45; and W.E.J. McCarthy, *The Role of Shop Stewards in British Industrial Relations,* op. cit., p. 25.

[9] A.I. Marsh, E.O. Evans and P. Garcia, *Workplace Industrial Relations in Engineering,* Kogan Page, London 1971, p. 63.

[10] Walton and McKersie, op. cit.

[11] A. Fox, *Industrial Sociology and Industrial Relations,* RCTUEA Research Paper No. 3, p. 14.

[12] A. Flanders in evidence to RCTUEA, *Selected Written Evidence,* HMSO 1968, p. 555.

[13] It is often argued that grievances should be settled at as low a level as possible (S. Slichter, J. Healy and E. Livernash, *The Impact of Collective Bargaining on Management,* p. 732). An empirical study which purported to validate this proposition is J. Turner and J. Robinson, 'A pilot study of the validity of grievance settlement rates as a predictor of union–management relationships', *Journal of Industrial Relations,* September 1972.

[14] The classic statement of this (from the United States) is J. Kuhn, *Bargaining in Grievance Settlement,* Columbia University Press, New York 1961.

[15] R.B. McKersie and W.W. Shropshire, 'Avoiding written grievances: a successful program', *Journal of Business,* no. 2, 1962.

[16] W.A. Brown, 'Piecework wage determination in Coventry', *Scottish Journal of Political Economy*, February 1971, p. 28.

[17] W.H. Scott et al., *Coal and Conflict*, Liverpool University Press, Liverpool 1956, p. 39.

[18] Thus the 1966 government Social Survey investigation found that of those stewards with all or most of their members on payment by results over half were in favour of replacing that system by some other method. (W.E.J. McCarthy and S.R. Parker, *Shop Stewards and Workplace Relations,* RCTUEA Research Paper No. 10, p. 43.)

[19] To draw an analogy with productivity bargaining, McKersie and Hunter argue:

> The evidence we have been able to collect suggests that productivity bargaining does not change the *locus* of the control system as between management and labour, but that it exerts a dramatic impact on the *kind* of control that is exercised. Prior to productivity bargaining, decisions were made in terms of precedent, customary practice, or the dictates of stewards and foremen. Such a control system could be characterised as haphazard and personal. By contrast, under productivity bargaining, the control system becomes much more deliberate, rational, and professional. It remains just as much a product of joint influence, but the process of joint regulation has been placed on a much more systematic and impersonal basis.

(R.B. McKersie and L.C. Hunter, *Pay, Productivity and Collective Bargaining,* Macmillan, London 1973, p. 287.)

6 Practical issues in procedure development

This chapter takes up the practical issues of developing a procedural structure. As noted in chapters 1 and 2, this is an area in which only very limited guidance is available from the existing literature. There are of course model procedures, but few of these make allowance for different situations; the most that is done, as in the case of the USDAW model, is to suggest more and less sophisticated approaches. No determinative model is possible or intended here; for such a complex issue all that can be done is to indicate in broad terms procedural structures which might be appropriate for particular contingencies. Even so, it is as well to echo Fox's warnings: 'We have to begin by recalling once more that no single direct relationship exists between structural characteristics and human responses. Ideologies, frames of reference, and aspirations mediate to determine how the structural context is perceived.'[1] This chapter is based initially on the inputs to formulating a procedural structure, taking into account general organisational factors and the various different possible constituents of a procedure. It then considers scenarios in which organisational and procedural elements might be brought together. (An appendix at the end of the book provides a further checklist of actions which may be useful in a procedural review.) Inevitably, we go beyond the immediate findings of our own study, since, as we have emphasised, our panel did not represent a total range of potential situations. We have therefore made use of examples from procedures published in such journals as *Incomes Data Service Briefs* and the *Industrial Relations Review and Report,* and also relevant CIR reports.

General organisational considerations

It is clear that considerations must begin well beyond the immediate sphere of industrial relations. We have discussed the central role of management structure and particularly the distribution of authority in the process of grievance handling, and have also noted that informal management behaviour often differed from formal management organisation. Yet the starting point of any discussion must be the formal structure and distribution of authority. A great deal has been written in recent years about influence on management organisation, much of it refuting the views of earlier management theorists that universal rules could exist. Nevertheless, it is perhaps possible to mention at least four influential determinants of structure, with an indication of their potential implications for procedure.

The first determinant is size of unit. In structural terms Blau[2] has defined its influence in two generalisations: (a) increasing organisational size generates differentiation along various lines at decelerating rates; and (b) differentiation enlarges the administrative component in organisations to effect coordination—the latter because increasing size is subject to the 'law of diminishing control', which must be offset by compensating mechanisms. It is commonly accepted that small units can have more personal contacts, shorter lines of control, and consequently higher morale, and while it does not always follow that industrial relations are necessarily better in smaller than in larger plants,[3] the predisposition must be towards greater informality in small plants and greater formality in larger plants of the type which would permit differentiation and coordination in handling different types of grievances.

The second dimension is technological: Woodward's major contribution was to show that firms which conformed to the model organisational structure of their technological classification were likely to be more successful than those on the extremes of the organisational spectrum.[4] Thus production control in process production is largely built into the technology, leaving a minimal supervisory function; in unit production control should be decentralised to supervisors and workers themselves because many different functions require on the spot judgement and because central coordination is not critical; in mass production, on the other hand, both close supervision and a high degree of coordination are necessary. There are similar implications for the relative significance of different functional groups within management. Woodward not only found that structure is tied to technological needs, but also that the social problems of the enterprise were likely to vary according to technology. The probable implications for procedure are: a high staff and planning input but with some degree of flexibility in process production; concentration on coordination by line management and hence a fair amount of formality in the mass production category; and informality with line control at a low level in unit production.

The third factor is the market environment. If a company is operating in a market in which products are homogeneous and competition is largely on the basis of price, its structure is likely to be dominated by line production managers and accountants with an objective of maximum output for the minimum feasible price. Cost control systems are likely to be effective and every additional cost will be scrutinised. The position will be very different where the main consideration is quality. Here experience will be likely to play a more important role than cost, and individual or small group bargaining will be more easily tolerated. Clearly, procedural formality and coordination would be seen as more important in the first situation than in the second.

The last dimension might be called routinisation, and is in some respects a composite of the other three. In the literature it has perhaps been best expressed in Burns and Stalker's concepts of organic and mechanistic environment.[5] The greater the stability of the organisation, whether in size, technology or market position, the more suitable a mechanistic organisational structure, close to Weber's bureaucratic ideal, will be. On the other hand, the need of the organisation to react rapidly may make a formal structure, a rigidly defined hierarchy, and clearcut specifications and procedures for all tasks and interactions completely inappropriate. At this organic end of the spectrum roles may be self-defined, communication largely personal, and status highly uncertain. Again, the implications for procedural structure are fairly obvious.

These exogenous factors can in turn help to create a considerable range of possible management structures along either or both vertical and lateral divisions of authority, from simple line organisation to functional to 'matrix' management, and each has implications for authority and thus for procedure. It must nevertheless be remembered that in many respects formal organisation is of less value in discerning the division of power down the hierarchy than is the informal organisation, with its emphasis on personal and transitory political relationships within management. Most plants are unlikely to be able to define specifically the range of authority open to a foreman or manager, although this has been done in great detail by companies such as Ford. Woodward found that some two-thirds of her sample lay on the organic part of the scale; this corresponds to a rough impression of our own panel. Nevertheless, we are generally of the opinion that there is too much informality in the structure of British management and that a better defined organisation is necessary to deal with the issues posed in industrial relations. In particular, internal management communication and control systems need improvement. Even if it is thought desirable to have an informally operated procedural system, effective management control systems are likely in most instances to be a prerequisite for success.

A further question is how far the industrial relations function is tied to other aspects of management structure. Baker and France have shown that it is perfectly possible to have a centralised management structure for most purposes but a decentralised industrial relations system.[6] Woodward for her part found that the firms in her sample often had difficulty in fitting the personnel department into their preconceptions of organisation structure. Nevertheless, industrial relations is a part of the overall management structure and hence must relate to it, and will also be governed by influences such as those discussed earlier. In any case, authority in industrial relations is much wider than the personnel function alone, and it is this wider authority which the procedure must also try to reflect.[7]

Beyond management a second organisational structure which must be taken into account is that of the union. In many respects this is a secondary influence since, as McCarthy has noted,[8] unions tend to base their organisation at the level at which management makes economic decisions. However, this is less true now than in the past. Much of the pressure for reconstructing plant level institutions has come from the increased power of workgroups, and recent trends to decentralise power within British unions have tended to support this development. The nature of the union also tends to influence its structure. A white collar union, for instance, is more likely to give more importance to the full-time official than a production union, because there is often less opportunity for white collar workgroups to be as cohesive in the work situation as operatives. The same is probably true, if to a rather lesser extent and for rather different reasons, of craft unions.

Another important facet of union policy and structure may be the existence of more than one union in the plant, with either rivalry or cooperation or little contact between them. The less the rivalry and comparison between unions, the lower down the management hierarchy decisions can be taken; the more coercive comparisons there are, the greater the need for centralisation and coordination. Moreover, where there is more than one union in an establishment, it is sometimes argued that each union should have the right to process its own grievance without the involvement of any other union. Thus the TGWU pamphlet *Plant and Productivity Bargaining* states: 'In multi-union establishments we should ensure facilities which allow our union to progress matters through all stages of procedure without having to negotiate through the representative of another organisation.'[9]

This raises particular problems where there is a multi-union grievance committee, or where a small union does not have enough members to justify senior steward representation. In practice, however, unions are frequently less rigid than their statements of principle lead one to believe.

Coercive comparisons do not, of course, exist only between members of different unions, for instance, workgroups can be competitive between themselves, but membership of different unions may well exacerbate this rivalry. Procedures will need to reflect the willingness of unions and workgroups to act together. There would appear to be three possibilities: a single procedure in which each union nevertheless separately processes its own grievances; a single procedure in which at some stage a joint inter-union body participates, and separate procedures for each union. If separate procedures are necessary, equivalence between them is desirable, otherwise advantages accruing to one union may become a bone of contention to the others.

Of most immediate relevance for the procedure is the bargaining structure, and indeed for some purposes the bargaining structure and the grievance procedure are likely to overlap. Bargaining in Britain is often (and for some issues usually) based on the procedural structure. However, the two are not the same, especially as regular periodic negotiations and formal written collective agreements become more common.

Bargaining structure is not entirely a matter of choice for a company, but is subject to similar types of pressures as management structure. It is a well-recognised fact, strongly propagated by the Donovan Commission, that the traditional basis of industry-wide bargaining has in large part broken down, thus creating important strategic policy decisions for companies and unions as to the appropriate level of bargaining or combination of levels of bargaining, since different issues may well be best determined at different levels. Yet the old structure has by no means entirely collapsed. In many industries conditions will continue to be determined primarily at industry-wide level for reasons of product market homo-geneity, thus maintaining the need for some procedural mechanism at this level.

One level of bargaining to have received considerable attention recently is the company level, [10] which, with some important exceptions, tended to be ignored in the traditional system. This looks likely to become more significant in the future, especially in relation to comparability claims between plants and the widening scope of bargaining over issues such as pensions. A Department of Employment study of bargaining reform noted that all the firms in its sample 'sought as far as possible, in the interests of bargaining consistency, to centralise negotiations at company level on all matters which might have company wide implications.'[11] Moreover, as companies follow the Donovan injunction to determine labour policy at board of directors level, it is likely that strong central staff departments will grow up to develop and advise on such policy, and this will also operate in favour of stronger company level control. Such a development has, of course, implications for the structure of procedures, in that it is a trend towards greater formality and also towards a company level stage. Against this, there is the inertia created by past practice which has tended to deny the advisability of procedures at the company level and to suppose that policy can be separated from procedural decisions. Thus as the CBI has noted:

> . . . in the case of federated multi-plant firms we see little advantage in their setting up company procedures beyond establishment level. The role for the company lies much more in the field of laying down a sound industrial relations policy for the company as a whole and in providing advice on that policy at establishment level, not in direct intervention in the procedures.[12]

It was not the intention of this study to analyse to any significant extent the issues underlying management, union or bargaining structures. All are inherently difficult issues, and social science is far from providing any definitive answers to any of them. Writings such as those of Woodward, and Burns and Stalker in managerial organisation, Roberts and Leiserson in union administration, and Chamberlain and Weber in bargaining structure have pointed to various important factors, but in such highly pragmatic areas as those surrounding the grievance process it is perhaps not surprising that more conclusive analyses have not yet emerged.

The elements of procedure

We now turn to examine the various potential component elements of procedural structure, commenting on them primarily in respect of the level of conflict in the particular relationship (which we have suggested is the main consideration for the requisite degree of formality) and to a lesser extent referring to the issues of management, union, and bargaining structure in the preceding section. For purposes of discussion the components are broken down into five main areas: basic structure; the roles of participants in procedure; the scope of procedure; procedural differentiation; and the impact of the procedure.

Basic structure

The number of steps in the domestic procedure   The purpose of a series of steps is to ensure that those with effective authority within the two parties can be reached in an orderly way and also to provide for a review of decisions by a new level of authority at each succeeding stage. In addition, it may be desirable to provide that the matter in question may be referred back at any stage to one of the previous stages if the parties consider this will be helpful (such a provision was incorporated in the 1972 Hoover–CSCU agreement). Further provisions for more immediate access to persons with effective authority may also be desirable for some types of issue–thus it has become increasingly common to have different numbers of stages for individual and group grievances, as in the 1971 Lever Brothers–ASTMS agreement, which had three stages for collective grievances and five for individual grievances.

The lowest feasible number of steps within a plant is probably three: supervisor; departmental or other middle management; and senior management. The decision reached is almost entirely a function of the size of plant and the number of levels of management and not, in this instance, of the level of conflict. Essentially, wherever there is a significant level of *effective* authority, there should be a step. However, too many steps within the internal plant procedure could lead to delay and repetition and encourage by-passing. In general the guiding rule should probably be: if in doubt, choose fewer rather than more steps and add to them later if necessary.

The final stage in the procedure Here the choices already become multiple and are far from easy to choose between. There can be a last step internal to the plant; another last step internal to the company; an external last step specific to the plant incorporating third party conciliation or arbitration; or the traditional method of the industry-wide dispute procedure. There may also, even if it sounds paradoxical, be combinations of these. Thus certain issues could be designated for plant-level decision, while others could go to industry level. This was suggested by the EEF in negotiations over engineering procedure some years ago. Alternatively, there could be an option, but no obligation, to go beyond the plant. Thus the TGWU states as part of its policy: 'The procedure should end at the place of work, after which the union is free to take such action as the circumstances warrant. The union should have the voluntary option to seek outside conciliation or, possibly, arbitration by a mutually agreed arbitrator.'[13] Apart from the procedure itself, there is often a mutual reluctance on the part of both management and union to go beyond the plant. Even conciliation is not readily welcomed, as a survey by Goodman and Krislov discovered,[14] and unions tend to be more reserved than management in their views. Even though the amount of conciliation

140

carried out by the DE and more recently the ACAS has greatly increased, Goodman and Krislov note that in over 90 per cent of stoppages conciliation facilities have not been used. Nevertheless, attitudes towards the actual work of conciliation officers is positive and there are signs that it is increasingly being accepted, although not necessarily as a normal stage of procedure.

The question of arbitration in particular requires further discussion.[15] It has typically not been the practice in Britain to use arbitration for plant level issues, partly because of the existence of industry-wide procedures and partly because the parties have preferred to keep matters within their own hands. The lack of differentiation between rights and interests issues and the unwillingness of unions to give up the right to strike have been further factors. To the extent that arbitration has been used it has taken a number of different forms: under the Industrial Courts Act, under JIC procedures, and now increasingly on an *ad hoc* basis at the company level under the auspices of the ACAS, following an attempt at conciliation. Relatively few cases have been over interpretation of the agreement, although it is possible that the proportion is increasing. Seven of our plants did make provision for arbitration (five voluntarily, two compulsorily), but it was not used in practice at the time of the fieldwork. There has nevertheless been a rapid increase in the number of procedures culminating in arbitration and also in the number of arbitrations arranged by the ACAS. The two are not necessarily the same thing, however, since many of the ACAS cases have arisen in ways other than as the last stage of procedures, and there are certainly very many procedures with arbitration as a last step which have never made use of it.

But even with the increase in interest in the subject, there is as yet little evidence of a widespread move towards arbitration in the way in which it is used in North America, in spite of an undoubted increase in more formal collective agreements at plant level. Arbitration appears to be seen as an option to be held in reserve for exceptional circumstances rather than as a normal last step, or, as American unions see it, a *quid pro quo* for a no-strike clause. There is also a tendency to regard it as a voluntary rather than a compulsory step, in that both sides should agree before an issue can go to arbitration and one side cannot insist on it unilaterally. Indeed, arbitration is frequently mentioned as a rather remote possibility, as in the Dunlop manual engineering agreement of 1972: 'Although arbitration will not normally form part of this procedure, if both parties agree a matter may be taken to a mutually acceptable form of arbitration.' There is, however, some slight move towards arbitration as a compulsory step, as in the NUBE agreements concluded with some building societies.

141

A variant on this is the Henry Wiggins 1974 agreement with its manual unions, where the union (but not, apparently, the management) can impose arbitration. Once arbitration is accepted, the parties normally agree in practice to be bound by it; the Pilkington–GMWU agreement of 1972 is unusual in that it provides for advisory arbitration in which 'both parties will use these findings as a basis for further negotiations.'

The TUC, in *Good Industrial Relations,* warned that: . . . 'it must be recognised that an excessive reliance on arbitration can weaken the effectiveness of the negotiating procedures in resolving disputes,'[16] something for which there is a certain amount of evidence to be found in the United States. There is, however, no evidence of such a development in Britain to date. Moreover, the cost, delays and increasing formalisation of the arbitration process in the American system,[17] are not likely to present the same problem in Britain, at least not with the system currently operated by the ACAS. The costs of the arbitrator are paid by the ACAS (although many procedures stipulate that arbitration costs will be shared by the parties), and he is normally expected to produce a written report within a week to ten days. Presentation of evidence is usually informal and little use is made of lawyers. One British problem which does parallel the situation in the United States is a shortage of arbitrators, but the expansion of the ACAS panel should help to ameliorate this.

Our view is that arbitration could usefully be written into the procedure in most instances. Even small peaceful plants occasionally have to deal with many issues for which there is no easy solution and it might be valuable, at least as a reassurance to those who might be tempted to take direct action in the absence of any procedural escape valve, to state that in the event of failure to agree at plant or company level some form of outside arbitration will be sought.

Time limits at each stage of procedure   The prompt settlement of grievances is essential to good relations and the problem of frequent delays, amounting to apparent procrastination, was one of the features of industry-wide procedures most heavily criticised by the Donovan Commission. We would, however, note that in our experience delays did not seem to be a major problem, even from the point of view of the stewards we talked to. Nevertheless, one steward did say of foremen that it was essential that they give some immediate answer to a grievance, even a conditional one, rather than merely saying they would see about it, since it was important for the steward to have something to report back. Time limits provide an obvious guarantee for the grievant, and the TGWU has made specification of time limits a part of its policy on procedures, noting parenthetically: 'This is in the employer's interests as well as the members', since delays invariably cause more grievances.'[18] Time limits can also be valuable to management in that if grievants are reassured that they will have a reply within the prescribed period, management is given a known breathing space within which to prepare a reasoned answer. On the other hand, some delay may be inevitable on occasions, and it may therefore be desirable to add that limits can be waived by mutual agreement. Time limits also add to the formality of a procedure, and thus may inhibit flexibility in instances such as disciplinary cases, which may need very rapid resolution. A further possible use for time limits is in initiating or appealing the grievance. Thus the contract might specify that a grievance must be submitted within ten days of the incident at issue, or that a grievance will be considered settled if there is no appeal within ten days of the decision at the previous stage.

Time limits are probably not necessary for small plants with an informally operated procedure and a cooperative relationship but they would seem to be one of the first sensible additions in the range of possibilities for formalisation, and thus suitable for plants which have a moderate grievance load as well as those with a high one. The length of time limits should ideally vary according to the stage, with somewhat longer limits for the later stages.

Recording of grievances As noted earlier, very few records of grievance handling were kept in our panel, and those few individuals who did keep a record did so on their own initiative rather than as a result of company policy.[19] In general, record-keeping would appear to be a very rare practice in British industry. Yet grievance records can be extremely valuable both as a check on past practice and, something which seems to be done very rarely in Britain, as a diagnostic device to analyse underlying problems within a department or plant.[20] But the most important use of records is as a means of achieving coordination and consistency in grievance handling. The CBI in its pamphlet on disputes procedures noted that: 'It is advisable to keep a record of the proceedings at all stages above supervisor level, together with a note of those attending, for future reference.'[21] The Birdseye–ASTMS agreement of 1971, going further, stated that at *every* stage records would be kept. On the other hand, there are some definite disadvantages in this, especially at the shop floor level, since it is very much harder for a foreman to engage in cooperative interaction with his workers, which involves a good deal of give and take and bending of rules or practices on both sides, if he has to record these for his superiors. Even higher up, there are bound to be occasions when both sides would be loath to have a 'shabby, shoddy' compromise recorded. And if the difficult issues are not recorded there seems little point in recording the simple issues.

Again, increased formalisation through the recording of grievances does not seem to be called for where there is low conflict, and even in plants where there is a moderately high grievance load it does not seem advisable at the foreman level. Most foremen advise their managers of important grievances and their disposal, and this would appear to be a sufficient safeguard for ensuring that issues of any significance are included in the manager's record-keeping. For plants with a moderate grievance load, individual record-keeping could well suffice, but where there is a high level of grievance conflict some consolidated recording system might be preferable, with records available to the unions as well as to management. The most logical place for this to be done would be in the personnel department.

Written or oral grievance presentation and answers This question is obviously closely tied to the previous one, but differs from it in that the latter can merely be an *ex-post facto* method of recording what has happened, whereas the present one involves written documentation within the resolution process itself. The Industrial Society has recommended that a 'procedure report form' should be used in the event of failure to agree at supervisor level.[22] Written grievances help to clarify the issue, prevent it from expanding beyond its original scope, and make the process of recording easier, but they have the disadvantage that a successful informally operated process tends to negate the value of documentation.[23] It also more obviously sets the parties on opposite sides of the fence and adds a degree of legalism by apparently reducing what is intended to be a problem solving exercise to an exchange of documents.[24] We would suggest that written grievance presentation is only needed in high conflict plants, and that even here it should be above only the first level. There would also seem to be a stronger case for requiring management to write replies than for the grievant to be required to fill in a form as a precondition to taking the grievance above the first level. Such requirements are relatively rare at the present; the Henry Wiggins–ASTMS 1972 agreement was unusual in that it required all grievances to be written, dated and signed, and for management to make replies in writing.

Cooperation clause A partial alternative to having time limits or written grievances, and one which is suitable for small companies, is to have a statement of intent avowing cooperation in grievance handling to the effect that the two sides will cooperate in the prompt resolution of all grievances in an amicable manner, or, as in the 1973 Beecham–ASTMS agreement, that every attempt will be made to settle the matter at the earliest possible stage. These may be seen merely as 'motherhood' clauses of little practical significance, since such an intent is certainly implicit in the whole concept of procedure. Nevertheless, an explicit statement of intent may have some virtue where no procedure has previously existed.

The roles of participants in the procedure

Line management In many of the procedures studied, the member of management to whom a grievance should be taken was not specified explicitly, except that the worker's 'immediate supervisor' was almost inevitably designated the first stage. It seems to us that a more specific designation is desirable, such as 'departmental manager' at the second stage, followed by 'divisional manager' or 'plant manager' at the third stage. For example, the 1972 BLMC framework agreement specified that 'the management shall make clear provision as to the managers to be approached and involved at each stage.' This does, however, raise the problem of authority. The procedure itself cannot define the authority of any member of management; this is an issue for managerial organisation. In a sophisticated procedure with the requisite degree of procedural differentiation it is possible to specify in the procedure that the designated representative of the company shall have authority to settle any grievance properly taken to him under the procedure. Such a clause exists in some American agreements, such as the 1971 US Steel–USW contract.

A further issue in connection with line management participation is whether those who have given answers at a lower level should be present when higher level decisions are made. There are obvious disadvantages in that this may make it more difficult to reverse a decision, and in that it tends to negate the review aspect of procedure in the minds of grievants, but the point was made by at least two foremen we talked to that they deserved the chance to defend their position and to know about the decision as soon as it was made, and Slichter, Healy and Livernash report finding this practice in their study.[25] Perhaps a preferable alternative is an efficient management organisation which ensures that lower managers are consulted and kept informed even if they are not present at meetings.

Staff management For the most part, the role of staff management in the procedure may be to advise and sit on committees dealing with their special area of competence. There are bound to be some exceptions to this, the wages department being an obvious direct point of answer to pay queries,

145

but the most important issue is the role of the personnel manager with regard to participation in the basic procedure. Probably a minority of procedures specify a definite role for the personnel function, although some, such as the 1971 Birdseye–ASTMS agreement, state that appropriate members of the personnel department may be present at any stage. As we noted in an earlier chapter, the actual role of the personnel manager is often considerably greater than the formal function he is assigned, especially where the individual concerned has a good deal of experience and a high level of personal acceptance, and in several of our plants senior management expressed an intention to further increase his status and that of his department. On the other hand, middle management in many plants would prefer not to see this role increased and formalised, and some commentators have argued the undesirability of allowing line management to evade its responsibilities in the personnel field.[26] Our view is that the personnel manager's importance in the procedure should increase with the level of conflict, since he is in the best position to carry out the necessary function of coordination and may possess certain special knowledge in some areas where grievances arise, e.g., job analysis and evaluation. Thus his role should remain *ad hoc* in low grievance plants, while there is a case for including him in a formal role as part of a management committee at the higher levels in plants with a moderate grievance load, and while he should certainly be given an explicit function where there is a high level of conflict. Moreover, the more coordination is necessary and the more grievance records are kept, the more desirable it is that the personnel role be strong, both in an advisory and in a direct participatory sense.

Employers' association representatives   In general this role seems likely to diminish in grievance handling, but for small companies there is still much to be said for giving such representatives an optional position at the last stage of the internal procedure, especially in a mediatory role.

Shop stewards   The formal role of the steward does not raise major problems. Perhaps the most common issue about the role of the shop steward is whether the grievant should go to him before or after seeing the foreman. However, this is largely a pseudo-issue. There are grievances for which the steward is the only realistic representative, as, for instance, in the case of group issues; there are also others where the individual may feel more comfortable dealing with the foreman himself. The sensible solution would therefore be to state as part of the first stage that the employee and/or his representative should approach the foreman. The steward would also in most cases be the most appropriate person to approach the departmental manager. Procedures frequently require that a steward shall have been employed for a given period, usually a year, before standing for office, and in some cases where immigrants constitute a large proportion of the labour force a further requirement is the ability to speak and be understood in English, as in the 1971 Birmid-Qualcast agreement.

Senior shop steward/convenor/branch secretary   By contrast this is one of the most difficult roles to fit into formal procedure, since an informal role can be, as in several of our plants, highly beneficial for rapid resolution of grievances. Most managements would prefer the senior shop steward not to become officially active until a grievance has left the departmental level, even though in many instances he is likely to become informally involved earlier, especially in the smaller plants. Frequently he has a *de facto* roving commission, especially in larger plants. Indeed, it is often because the senior steward, having become involved at a low level, sees a senior manager as his natural counterpart that by-passing occurs rather than because a department steward himself goes over the heads of his foremen and manager. There may be a theoretical argument for trying to restrict the access of the senior steward to the shop floor, but this is unlikely to work in practice. A better solution would be to increase the efficiency of the departmental stewards by training and by giving adequate authority to the lower levels of management. The official role of the senior steward/convenor is probably best expressed within the grievance or negotiating committee as leader of the union side.

Full-time union official   In general, where there is an established shop steward system there seems to be little need for a full-time official to have a specific role in the procedure, except to have optional representation on the grievance committee (if one exists) or at the last internal stage, like his counterpart from the employers' association. This will not, however, be sufficient for cases where the steward system is weak. Access to and representation by the official is probably necessary no later than the immediate post-departmental stage.

Grievance committee   One of the most important considerations in the procedure relates to the possible role of a joint union–management committee within it, as the last internal stage of procedure. It is, of course, possible to have a consultative or works committee which has no official role in the grievance procedure but nevertheless handles grievances; this happened a good deal in our panel. It is also possible to have a negotiating committee for arriving at collective agreements which has no official role in the grievance procedure. Again, there can be joint committees, sometimes with quite elaborate constitutions, which carry out all three functions. In such cases, of course, the distinction between rights, interests, and consultative issues inevitably becomes blurred.

The advantages of such committees is that they permit those separate individuals who might have some interest in a solution, or something to contribute to one, to be present. Moreover, on the union side in a large plant, or where there is more than one union, it is not feasible to leave decision making to a single individual and hardly convenient to be constantly reporting back. Moreover, the existence of a representative body of senior stewards on the grievance committee enables a degree of coordination of decisions to take place which would be very difficult were all issues solved on an individual basis.

At the same time, there are considerable disadvantages to a grievance committee. It is not as flexible as a small *ad hoc* group; it may be difficult to convene rapidly; and depending on its size it may be a difficult forum at which to have informal discussions. Indeed, if its size is not kept reasonably small, it may become very difficult to make any decisions at all. There is thus some danger that it will be by-passed, either to save time or to avoid sensitive issues. There may also be the difficulty of a multi-union situation in which a union insists that grievances be handled only under the *aegis* of its own union. Small unions may also easily feel dominated by large ones.

Whether grievance and negotiating committees should be separate or the same body is an important issue with a range of possibilities. At one end, where the relationship is relatively sophisticated and formal and some distinction between rights and interests disputes is emerging, there is a case for separate negotiating and grievance committees. Where no such distinction exists and where there is a high level of conflict, a joint committee for negotiation and grievances is logical. Where most important negotiating decisions are above the level of the plant at industry or company level, the committee is likely to be a grievance/consultation committee. At a low level of conflict, an informal procedure with a consultative committee to handle general issues may be all that is required. It is our view that grievance committees are generally to be welcomed, for although they are relatively rare in formal procedures, informally a committee of one sort or another frequently plays a key role in grievance handling.

The individual grievant   Should the individual be allowed to conduct his own case without reference to the union and what are the union's rights in this case? There is the legal issue of who owns the grievance, but this is also a structural question. If the individual union member does insist on processing his own grievance, the union should be entitled to be present, and, at certain appropriate levels such as the grievance committee, it should participate in decision making. The bigger problem in both practical and legal terms is that of the aggressive non-unionist or member of a minority breakaway union. Should he be permitted (or forced) to use the procedure, or should there be a separate one to cover such cases? This is probably an issue which can be decided only on an *ad hoc* basis and not in the formulation of procedure, although the 1974 Alenco–APEX agreement does specify that: 'In the event of a non-union staff employee having a grievance, the company reserves the right to resolve the problem with the employee concerned and to take whatever action is considered to be justified.' A further aspect of the role of the individual grievant is whether he has any right to be present at hearings, especially at the later stages. This is not normally incorporated in procedures, although it may happen informally, but the 1974 Scottish and Newcastle Breweries–GMWU agreement states that the aggrieved and his immediate superior may be present at any stage if they so wish.

The scope of procedure

British procedures are typically open-ended in that they do not prescribe any formal limitations for issues that might be raised under them. This, however, merely serves to conceal difficult problems of scope, involving management rights, overlapping jurisdictions, the status quo issue, and the difference between claims and grievances. It is one thing to admit an issue into the procedure; it is quite another to admit that the issue is merited. Because British procedure is oriented to negotiation rather than adjudication of grievances, the decision which emerges will reflect the relative power of the two sides whenever an adversary relationship exists. Limits on discussion are therefore set on an arbitrary and pragmatic basis only, although power will vary according to the issue and how close it is to the interests of each side. Not infrequently, both sides try to reserve an area of unilateral control; a good example of this was illustrated in the CIR's report on shipbuilding. Only a very few companies in Britain have tried even to define management rights in the contract of employment, and indeed the general academic and union view is probably that this is in any case an outdated concept;[27] nevertheless, most firms try to impose a sphere of managerial rights.

The conventional North American model has laid down a scope of coverage for procedure by frequently trying to define what is admissible as a grievance, by setting aside areas of management rights, and, above all, by differentiating between rights and interests issues. The Donovan model certainly looked to an increasing formalisation of the agreement, which would in turn lend itself to a closer definition of procedural scope. However, it is by no means obvious that this will happen. Given British traditions, it is probably sensible to have an open-ended definition of a grievance, no exclusive management rights, and the possibility of negotiations on non-contract issues as they arise. Nevertheless, an emerging differentiation between rights and interests issues is desirable if the grievance procedure is to produce predictable and consistent results and escape from the *ad hoc* evaluation of issues in isolation or based upon half-forgotten precedents which has plagued the British system in the past. A status quo clause would in many respects be a natural counterpart to a differentiation of this sort, since it crystallises the differences between action under an existing agreement or understanding and a *de novo* move by management. The difficulty about the rights–interests split is of course the argument of mutuality and continuous bargaining.[28] Yet the move towards recognition of a time interval between substantive negotiations, embodied in the Labour government's social contract, has already undermined this presumption.

The issue of status quo is currently one of the most difficult in industrial relations, since in practice it subsumes many of the above questions. It was primarily this issue which resulted in the abandonment of attempts to reform the industry-wide engineering agreement. The TUC has argued that a clear status quo clause is a necessary pre-requisite for tackling the problem of unofficial strikes, but the CBI has argued that there are 'grey' areas where there is an impact on employment, but where flexibility and quick implementation of decisions are required in the interests of both employer and employees, and that a status quo clause in such cases would seriously prejudice efficiency.[29]

The CBI argued in favour of consultation in all areas of management decision as one alternative, but it is also suggested that a specific definition of what was covered by status quo was necessary. Here the matter stands, and seems unlikely to achieve national level resolution: a plant-by-plant definition will be required instead. Our own view is that a general status quo clause should be conceded, but that if there are issues which are central to the efficiency of a plant, such as the right to transfer workers, management must be prepared to argue the case for specific management rights at the time, rather than try to introduce it later.

A facet of procedural scope which will probably become more important in the future relates to the possible overlap of the procedure with coverage by legislation, such as the Redundancy Payments Act, the

Employment Protection Act, or others covering employment. In order to reassure employees of their rights, it may be advantageous to include a clause to the effect that the provisions of the procedure will in no way prejudice the statutory rights of the employee. Another facet relates to the ability of management to raise grievances under the procedure. This is sometimes done in the United States, and the CBI has recommended it as being desirable in British agreements, especially where management 'apprehends a possible stoppage of work but the matter has not yet been raised by the employees.'[30]

Procedural differentiation

We have noted that different types of issue require different modes of resolution and that these can be made the subject of separate procedures. The advantages of such differentiation are clear where there is an issue of significance and frequency; the sub-procedure is likely to be able to conform more effectively to the 'actual' process and the needs of the parties. Moreover, not to have some degree of differentiation may well be to ask too much of the lower levels of the grievance procedure. There are, of course, disadvantages to this. Blurred boundaries between procedures are almost inevitable for complex grievances. Different procedures may make for inconsistent overall management and union policies; indeed if different people are responsible for them they may invite some degree of rivalry over authority. Finally, of course, the more specialised a procedural structure becomes, the more bureaucratic it becomes and the more its administration may become an end in itself.

The extent to which differentiation will be appropriate in any given case will vary according to a number of factors involved. In some instances grievances might require accelerated treatment through basic procedure; in others specialists without a role in the normal procedure might need to be brought in. Alternatively, issues which might have a major but sudden impact on the workforce, such as redundancy, may be thought to require a special procedure to minimise confusion when they do occur. Obviously a separate procedure should be introduced only where it is really needed, and it is unlikely that British companies would wish to take procedural differentiation to the extent which sometimes occurs in the United States.[31] A second aspect of procedural differentiation which is probably sensible for all plants is that issues covering a group of employees wider than the jurisdiction of the management representative at any given stage would commence at that stage where a manager has executive authority over the whole group. This is almost inevitable in any case, and will help

to forestall feelings of annoyance at by-passing. The 1971 Pilkington–
ASTMS agreement, for instance, identified three types of issue: individual
grievances, those affecting a number of employees, and matters of
common collective interest. Beyond this, there is much to be said for
recognising the role which existing specialist committees play in handling
grievances in their area, and these can be built in as a separate stage.
Thus if an issue regarding safety cannot be resolved by the foreman, it
might be passed to the safety committee and if it is not settled there, it
might be re-examined at, say, the fourth step of procedure. It is arguable
that the nature of such committees will be transformed from a problem
solving to an adversary one but this is not necessarily the case.
Another possibility in this category is that a temporary committee may
be formed to oversee some aspect of change, and it can then act as a
forum for grievances which arise during the time the change is being
implemented.

Discipline is almost certainly the leading candidate for a separate
procedure. Since the 1971 Industrial Relations Act it is becoming almost
as obligatory to have a disciplinary procedure as a grievance procedure.[32] Discipline is the most personal and perhaps the most
emotive of issues to arise in the plant, and a considerable number of
serious disputes are still caused by it (although we found none in our
panel). There is a particular need to ensure that justice is seen to be done,
and the open forum provided by a formal procedure helps to provide this.
A further reason for this found in some instances where joint regulation
of the grievance procedure is the practice is that the union may not want
to be associated with decisions on discipline. But the most compelling
reason normally adduced is the need for rapid review, especially in the
case of dismissals. The Department of Employment has recently produced
a valuable document on the subject of discipline entitled *In Working Order*,
which looks in some detail at the considerations in creating this
particular aspect of procedure.[33]

The impact of the procedure

Formalisation of procedural usage   As we have noted, flexibility is normally
assumed in a procedure, and rarely explicitly permitted or disallowed. We
have quoted earlier the case of one of our plants where informal
approaches to management were encouraged. The Goodyear and Royal
Insurance agreements concluded with ASTMS in 1971 also encouraged
such informal settlement prior to initiating the procedure. On the other
hand, procedures sometimes demand rigorous adherence, for example, the

Sainsbury's–USDAW agreement of 1971, which stated that the parties 'will not be prepared to deal with matters covered by this Agreement other than through the machinery laid down in this Agreement.'

The status of the grievance decision   Senior managers frequently worry that precedents may be created at lower levels which will effectively set new standards, and this is one of the reasons for centralisation of decision making. Yet, as we have seen, centralisation can also destroy the effectiveness of a procedure by encouraging by-passing. One possible procedural solution, especially for companies wanting to lower the level of decision making, is to state that precedents will not be recognised unless made at a given level of the procedure.[34] This might not always be sustainable in practice, and there is some danger that issues could be pushed up to reach the level of creating a precedent, and that it would be difficult to reverse a decision once made. Nevertheless, if adhered to, this could ease the use of initiative by foremen.

No-strike clause   In Britain there is an implied, if not always explicitly stated, no-strike agreement until the procedure is exhausted. This is the essence of voluntarism. Indeed, the procedure becomes something of a contradiction unless it is intended to follow it through. The TUC, in *Good Industrial Relations,* accepted this premise with one qualification:

> Where an adequate 'status quo' provision is incorporated [disputes procedures] should preclude a strike or any other form of industrial action by workers, or a lockout or any other pressures brought by management until all stages of procedure have been exhausted. Workers, however, can be reasonably expected to observe such a procedure only if it contains adequate 'status quo' provisions which are adhered to by management.[35]

In return for this, the union might be expected to agree to announce orally and in writing that it will disavow unofficial industrial action, order the workers to return to work, and refuse any financial relief in the event of a strike being threatened.

Sanctions   The critical question about procedures is of course what happens when they are broken. Can sanctions be written into the procedural structure? Perhaps the most usual sanction against industrial action is to refuse to negotiate until the action is over, and some procedures do explicitly state this. Another approach, adopted in the 1971 Pirelli–AUEW agreement, is to specify that the personal record of the individuals concerned will be endorsed, and yet another, found in the 1971

Shell–ASTMS agreement, is to incorporate the procedure into the individual contract of employment, thus requiring that the procedure be exhausted as well as due notice given before industrial action can be undertaken. But other than these mild forms of sanction, which are unlikely to constitute a severe deterrent in practice, there is little consensus about breaches of procedure. Ford tried to make certain payments contingent upon there being no unconstitutional action. This provoked a violent reaction from the union side and has not been operated by other companies.[36] Kuhn, in his analysis of fractional bargaining, concluded that only a concerted effort by management with tacit union support to cut the attractiveness of unconstitutional action by disciplinary measures against all participants could be successful.[37] However, discipline creates the problem of whether it can be sustained in the face of group sympathetic action. Unions may induce workers to return to work pending negotiations, but they are not willing to countenance discipline or forego the right to strike. If there is widespread breaking of procedure, this is a sign that the relationship as a whole needs re-evaluating. Few managers can now be under any illusion that the law can help here, whatever their views prior to the Industrial Relations Act.

External impact   Procedures are designed to regulate the parties involved, but there may be aspects which affect other relationships. One such aspect relates to working in the event of a strike by other unions. Thus the 1974 Alenco–APEX agreement states that the company agrees not to request APEX members to undertake any work normally outside the terms of their employment in the event of an industrial dispute in which these members are not directly involved. Another aspect refers to sympathy strikes; in reference to this the 1974 Lesney agreement with the hourly-paid unions states that 'no industrial action shall be taken in support of disputes external to the company, other than those national level issues outside the control of the parties to this agreement.'

Procedural review   Most procedures do not make explicit reference to possible revision. However, some capacity for this is desirable, since, as we have argued, conditions in a plant are likely to change over time. In the case of the Lesney agreement mentioned above, the parties to the procedure agreed to review its operation after a year, while one of the functions of the company and plant committees set up in the 1970 Birmid-Qualcast procedural agreement was to provide a continuous review of the grievance procedure.

The above list of elements is not intended to be exhaustive; in particular, it omits ancillary features normally associated with the operation of procedures, for instance, workplace facilities such as union rights of access, time off for stewards, bulletin boards, telephones, office space, and so on, although most of these have been adequately covered by the CIR.[38] The communications and information networks within and between the parties but outside procedure might also have been mentioned, along with industrial relations training, or the obligation to distribute procedural agreements to all employees (which the Industrial Relations Act did not by any means manage to achieve), or the various possible sub-committees that might be set up within the procedure. On a different plane, the elements of this section, like the scenarios in the following question, are primarily oriented towards plant level procedures, industry-wide procedure, or company–plant relationships.

Finally, we have tended here to advance a general case for the various elements, but they are, of course, likely to be seen in different lights by the two sides, and indeed by different groups within the parties, since, as was pointed out in chapter 2, the parties are unlikely to be homogeneous. It may therefore be helpful to present in tabular form some of the main issues on which conflict is likely to arise, and to state the potential disadvantages from the point of view of the parties. This is done here in Fig. 6.1.

The formulation of alternative procedural structures for various contexts

Before trying to draw together the various threads of procedural formulation, some words of caution are necessary. It must be reiterated that there is no such thing as an ideal procedure, only a balance of advantage between often conflicting considerations. Moreover, no procedure is likely to be right at all times in the context of a constantly changing economic, technological, and political environment. Finally, and most importantly, procedures help to distribute power in a relationship, so that what is a 'good' procedure for one party may not be so for the other. While employers can be expected to initiate procedural change, they will very rarely be able to impose it. Thus while we would say that in general terms the elements of procedure must be seen in relation to environmental and attitudinal conditions, including and in particular the level of conflict, and while we shall shortly present some scenarios to illustrate this, we would nevertheless accept that there is a potential dichotomy between the optimum and the ability to achieve it. This is also implicit in other comments on procedural structure.

Fig. 6.1 Potential disadvantages of elements of procedure

	Disadvantages to management	Disadvantages to union
1 Number of stages	—	Too many stages cause delay.
2 Final disposal mechanisms:		
(a) Internal control	Provides no ultimate means of solving disagreements. Limits managerial control over own policy.	—
(b) Industry procedure	Takes decision out of managerial control. Possible inconsistencies.	Delay. Also industry decisions may not reflect local circumstances.
(c) Arbitration		Takes decisions out of union control. Possible inconsistencies.
3 Specification of actors involved at different stages	Real authority or expertise may be too complex to be expressed in procedure.	—
4 Recording of process or written grievances	Can be cumbersome and encourage avoidance.	Cumbersome. May inhibit individuals from pursuing grievances.
5 Time limits	May be unrealistic for certain issues.	May still not provide a sufficiently speedy answer for issues of immediate concern.
6 Specification of scope of issues covered	—	May reflect conceptions of management rights and inhibit wider interests of union.
7 Differentiation by issue or grievant	Possible confusion over correct procedure for particular issue. 'Forum-shopping'.	Possible confusion.
8 Differentiation by rights and interests issues	—	Distinction may be seen as unrealistic.
9 Status quo clause	May create difficulties in applying existing agreements.	—
10 No-strike or lockout clause	Difficult to enforce.	Limits union options.
11 Grievance committee	Means joint regulation of grievances.	May cause inter-union difficulties.
12 Role of external union/management representatives	Reduces internal control.	Reduces internal control.

Marsh and McCarthy suggested 'acceptability' and 'appropriateness' as the primary criteria for procedures,[39] while Flanders commented:

> One of the important points that can be made about what is a good procedure for collective bargaining is that it should correspond as closely as possible with the de facto structure of collective bargaining. When a procedural agreement assumes that decisions can be taken and regulations made effective at levels where there is not the requisite power or authority, it will soon be circumvented or discredited. This is not to deny that in favourable circumstances the negotiation of a new procedural agreement may be the means of changing an existing bargaining structure.[40]

Yet the question remains, what happens if 'acceptable' is not 'appropriate', or vice versa, or, in Flanders' terms, what should happen if the *de facto* structure of bargaining is inefficient or undesirable to one party or the other and yet the circumstances are not 'favourable' for negotiation. There is no denying that the problems of achieving change are formidable, and we shall examine these in the final section of the next chapter.

We now present a number of scenarios in which the various elements discussed in this chapter are brought together. These scenarios are at best illustrative, and even then by no means include all possible types. Rather they represent in very general terms the points on a possible spectrum of conflict and organisational complexity, and our best estimate as to what type of procedure might be appropriate in a given case. As such, they are an attempt to go beyond the rather bland disclaimer of the CIR that: 'There is no single formula for the reform of procedures since . . . each situation varies according to circumstances.'[41] A more complex matrix, although theoretically possible and indeed highly desirable for purposes of guidance, is nevertheless precluded by lack of knowledge of the interaction of the variables. It is very much to be hoped that future work will enable further steps to be made in diagnosing these complex interrelationships.

Scenario 1

Environmental conditions Small plant, simple management structure, most terms and conditions dependent on industry-wide bargaining.
Attitudinal conditions Close relationship, easy communications and access to appropriate authority, low level of conflict expressed through grievances. Weak union or even non-unionisation.
Procedural structure A simple grievance procedure written into the works rulebook, essentially operated by the individual employer. A works

committee to handle more general issues as part of the wider function of consultation, with some capacity for the committee representatives to act as shop stewards in the absence of formal shop steward structure. Foremen may also perform this role.

Scenario 2

Environmental conditions Small plant, though larger than in Scenario 1. Still a simple management structure and a short chain of management command, but some need for coordination. Weak staff function. Still little plant level negotiation; major decisions made at industry level. No local agreement.

Attitudinal conditions Informal problem solving approach on both sides. Union(s) has majority but not 100 per cent membership. One dominant shop steward carrying out most union functions, with ready access to senior management.

Procedural structure Simple procedural agreement detailing steps and providing for union representation. Joint consultation style works committee takes up many grievances although not formally part of procedure. Procedure uses industry-wide disputes mechanism as terminal point. No strike or lockout clause.

Scenario 3

Environmental conditions Medium sized plant, i.e., 300-plus employees. Line management still dominant, but personnel manager exists with an administrative and welfare role. Diffusion of authority requires coordination policy. Some supplementary plant bargaining but not brought together in plant agreement. Plant possibly member of multi-plant company, with simple industrial relations coordination of information from headquarters.

Attitudinal conditions 100 per cent unionisation creates need for some formality, especially where grievances intermittently become claims. However, issues still generally left to proceed to point of decision making in an informal way.

Procedural structure More detailed procedure with time limits, differentiated procedure for discipline. Procedure still gives industry-wide disputes procedure as terminal step, and occasional use still made of this in practice.

Scenario 4

Environmental conditions More complex management structure in medium to large plant (around 1,000–2,000 employees). Staff play a planning coordination role in industrial relations. Most effective bargaining done at plant level, although minimum conditions determined at industry level. Plant level agreement(s).

Attitudinal conditions Moderate level of conflict, generally cooperative. Joint regulation a reality, especially at shop floor level where effective shop stewards exist. Records kept of grievances.

Procedural structure More sophisticated procedure, with time limits, rights of shop stewards defined in terms of time off, payment, visits to other departments. Explicit recognition of joint shop stewards committee. More procedural differentiation, e.g., job evaluation committee where job evaluation used. Specification of disciplinary standards in works rulebook. Third party intervention a possible last step in procedure.

Scenario 5

Environmental conditions Large plant, part of multi-plant company. Complex management structure, with personnel department playing a key role not only in advice and coordination but also in deciding non-standard grievances. Detailed plant agreement, but with some decisions made at company level. Membership of employers' association only for research and legal services.

Attitudinal conditions High level of conflict manifested in numbers of grievances, but industrial action only intermittent and associated with large group claims rather than fractional bargaining by small groups. Generally cooperative atmosphere in day-to-day relations. Formality in operation of procedure, but informal meetings in addition to clarify issues.

Procedural structure Complex procedure, with different issues going to different points of authority and starting at different levels. Grievance committee as last stage of internal procedure, with arbitration/conciliation as external stage. Clear status quo clause, with specification of issues covered by it. Formal planning and information consultative meetings for union on company progress and forward planning.

Scenario 6

Environmental conditions Multi-plant company, with close technological ties between plants. Much policy and decision making at company level. Close specification of authority within management. Not members of employers' association. Labour relations member of main board of directors. Staff as trouble shooters.

Attitudinal conditions Numerous unions sometimes coordinating, sometimes competing, especially at lower level. Shop stewards combine throughout company. A good deal of fractional bargaining in spite of a fairly complex agreement, with frequent stoppages by small groups. Armslength relationship, a good deal of mutual suspicion. Challenges to managerial prerogatives.

Procedural structure Complex procedure with codification of scope of issues covered in order to try to differentiate rights and interests issues, status quo clause, considerable differentiation according to issue. Precedents not binding unless accepted at a given level. Possibility of named arbitrator as last step in procedure, which also includes possibility of step at company level.

Notes

[1] A. Fox, *Beyond Contract: Work, Power and Trust Relations,* Faber, London 1974, p. 356.

[2] P.M. Blau, 'A formal theory of differentiation in organisations', *American Sociological Review*, April 1970, pp. 201–16.

[3] We noted this with regard to our own panel in chapter 4. An *increase* in stoppage rates proportionate to the numbers of manual workers employed has also been pointed out by Marsh, Garcia and Evans in their study of engineering (*Workplace Industrial Relations in Engineering*, op. cit., p. 25). See also G. Ingham, *Size of Industrial Organization and Worker Behaviour,* op. cit.

[4] J. Woodward, *Management and Technology*, HMSO 1958.

[5] T. Burns and G.M. Stalker, *The Management of Innovation,* Tavistock, London 1961.

[6] H. Baker and R. France, *Centralisation and Decentralisation in Industrial Relations,* Princeton University Press, Princeton NJ 1954.

[7] It might also be asked to what extent the overall management structure should be affected by its industrial relations system. On the whole the literature on management organisation does not take account of this factor, although in two of our plants industrial relations considerations had apparently been of importance in designing the organisational structure.

[8] W.E.J. McCarthy, *The Role of Shop Stewards in British Industrial Relations,* op. cit.

[9] H. Urwin, *Plant and Productivity Bargaining,* TGWU Policy Statement, 1970, p. 17.

[10] See, for instance, CIR Report No. 85, *Industrial Relations in Multi-Plant Undertakings,* HMSO 1974; and A.W.J. Thomson and L.C. Hunter, 'The level of bargaining in a multi-plant company', *Industrial Relations Journal,* Summer 1975.

[11] Department of Employment, Manpower Papers No. 5, *The Reform of Collective Bargaining at Plant and Company Level,* HMSO 1971, p. 23.

[12] CBI, *Disputes Procedures,* 1970, p. 13.

[13] TGWU, *Plant Level Bargaining,* 1970, p. 28.

[14] J. Goodman and J.K. Krislov, 'Conciliation in industrial disputes in Great Britain: a survey of the attitudes of the parties', *British Journal of Industrial Relations,* November 1974.

[15] The American literature on this subject is extensive. Most useful, perhaps, is R.W. Fleming, *The Labor Arbitration Process,* University of Illinois Press, Urbana 1965; and P. Prasow and E. Peters, *Arbitration and Collective Bargaining,* McGraw-Hill, New York 1970. For Britain the best recent work is W.R. Hawes, 'Some recent developments in local arbitration in Great Britain', unpublished MA thesis, University of Warwick, 1971.

[16] TUC, *Good Industrial Relations: A Guide for Negotiators,* 1971, p. 15.

[17] See Fleming, op. cit.

[18] TGWU, *Plant Level Bargaining,* op. cit., p. 28.

[19] The only exceptions to this were for meetings of works committees, where a 'shift-log' was kept to record all occurrences for the new shift, and one company which required a weekly labour relations report.

[20] Cf. J.W. Kuhn, 'The Grievance Process' in J.T. Dunlop and N.W. Chamberlain, *Frontiers in Collective Bargaining,* Harper and Row, New York 1967, pp. 259–60.

[21] CBI, *Disputes Procedures,* op. cit., p. 12.

[22] Industrial Society, *Model Procedural Agreements,* 1969, p. 28.

[23] One of our panel plants had printed 1,000 grievance report forms but at the time of our visit none had been used.

[24] McKersie and Shropshire in their study of the International Harvester plant in the United States found that written grievances had resulted in the piling up of grievances at higher levels, and that a return to oral grievance handling forced the parties to deal with complaints expeditiously and at the scene of their occurrence. (R.B. McKersie and W.W. Shropshire, 'Avoiding written grievances: a successful program', *Journal of Business,* April 1962.

[25] S. Slichter, J. Healy and E.R. Livernash, *The Impact of Collective Bargaining on Management,* Brookings Institute, Washington DC 1960, p. 726.

[26] Thus the CIR has argued that grievance decisions 'should be seen to come from the line manager concerned. The line manager's job is to manage and his managerial influence will be lessened if certain decisions are referred to others.' (CIR Report No. 34, *The Role of Management in Industrial Relations,* 1973, p. 17.)

[27] One example of an extensive management rights clause in Britain was the 1969 Massey Ferguson–AUEW agreement at the Perkins diesel plant. It stated: 'The function of management vests in the Company and includes, amongst other things, maintaining order and discipline and controlling efficiency. The following sub-clauses are included as illustrations of the functions and responsibilities of management . . .' The agreement then proceeded to define these areas, including as major headings such topics as transfer of employees, short term transfers, improvements in working practice, work study, efficiency in skilled and other areas, and training. For the argument that management rights in the sense of reserved areas of control is an outdated concept see W.E.J. McCarthy and N.D. Ellis, *Management by Agreement,* Hutchinson, London 1973.

[28] The principle of mutuality, to quote the TGWU: 'means that all aspects of working conditions and pay should be permanently negotiable . . . The policy is not one of a once-and-for-all bargain, but a continuous process of bargaining in which the union keeps open all its options to deal with new circumstances and opportunities for gains for its members as and when they arise.' (TGWU, *Plant Level Bargaining,* op. cit., p. 7.)

[29] CBI, *Disputes Procedures,* op. cit., p. 24.

[30] Ibid., p. 8.

[31] For instance, the US Steel–USW agreement of 1971 contained eight variations on the basic procedure, and listed nine joint committees which dealt with specialised topics.

[32] This has resulted from unfair dismissal cases in which the procedure followed in the dismissal is a criterion as to whether the decision was reasonable *(Earl v. Slater and Wheeler (Airlyne) Ltd* (NIRC) [1972] ICR 508). Paragraphs 131–4 of the Code of Practice laid down the basic framework for a disciplinary procedure which was used as a point of reference by many industrial tribunals.

[33] Department of Employment, *In Working Order,* Manpower Papers no. 6, HMSO 1973.

[34] This was the case in a plant visited during a pilot test for our fieldwork questionnaire.

[35] TUC, *Good Industrial Relations*, op. cit., p. 15.

[36] Ford also tried to enforce the agreement legally, but was rebuffed by the courts *(Ford Motor Co. Ltd v. AUEW* [1969] 2 QB 303).

[37] J.W. Kuhn, *Bargaining in Grievance Settlement,* Columbia University Press, New York 1961.

[38] CIR Report No. 17, *Facilities Afforded to Shop Stewards,* Cmnd

4668, HMSO 1971. The Code of Practice referred to such facilities in paragraphs 116–117, while the TUC listed desirable facilities in its 'Good Industrial Relations', and also in a 1971 booklet 'Facilities for Shop Stewards'.

[39] A.I. Marsh and W.E.J. McCarthy, *Disputes Procedures,* op. cit., p. 3.

[40] A. Flanders, 'Measured daywork and collective bargaining', *British Journal of Industrial Relations,* November 1973, p. 372.

[41] CIR Report No. 90, *Final Report,* HMSO 1974, p. 8.

7 Future models for British procedures: a comparative perspective

This final chapter extends the discussion of grievance procedures to possible future patterns and broadens it to include international comparisons which may be of relevance to the British situation. So far we have provided a contingency based approach to the structure of grievance procedures, using the plant and its immediate environment as the main focus. However, wider considerations are also relevant, since changes in public policy and other political and cultural developments will clearly affect the context within which procedures evolve. We therefore propose to examine four possible models of development which are not entirely mutually exclusive. First, there is a continuation of the traditional British system, with some incremental changes. Secondly, there is the North American pattern of much more comprehensive and formal plant based relationships. Thirdly, there is the European, and for our purposes predominantly German, model of providing institutions of participation at company and plant level. Finally, there is the radical model, which presumes the end of capitalism and an economy based on workers' control of the enterprise. In addition to these possible models of future development, we conclude by examining the practical steps which might be taken in the process of procedural reform.

The traditional British model

In chapter 1 we examined the origins and development of the traditional British system of industrial relations based on voluntarism and the role of procedures in that system, and also briefly analysed the differences between the British system and its counterparts in other developed countries, using Kahn-Freund's differentiation between static and dynamic approaches. We then left the review at the point where we carried out the fieldwork for the present study, namely at the time of the passage through Parliament of the Industrial Relations Act in 1971. Our model now picks up the threads of the trends in the voluntarist system noted

164

in chapter 1, that is, it assumes no fundamental structural changes in plant level relationships.

The picture painted by Kahn-Freund of the British system must be considerably modified in the light of more recent events. In a number of spheres and as a result of several different pieces of legislation in previously laissez-faire areas of industrial relations the law has encroached, largely in defence of the individual through the system of industrial tribunals, although also with considerable implications for collective relationships in the Employment Protection Act and the Trade Union and Labour Relations Act. However, the major attempt to introduce restrictions on collective action, including the possible imposition of legally enforceable procedures, was of course defeated by the repeal of the Industrial Relations Act.[1] Equally importantly for the autonomy of the parties, a series of incomes policies since the early 1960s has limited the exercise of free collective bargaining. But in spite of these changes, and in spite of some moves towards the more formal framework recommended by the Donovan Commission, this is certainly not sufficient to be characterised as a substantial move away from the traditional dynamic framework.

There has been a good deal of change in the British industrial relations system in the last few years, probably more than during any other equivalent period. It has encompassed the interrelated aspects of bargaining structure, greater substantive formalisation in comprehensive agreements, codification of custom and practice, the extension of scope of bargaining, payment systems, fixed term agreements, and greater managerial sophistication and resources, as well as change in the immediate areas of procedures. Some of the recent procedure agreements were quoted in the previous chapter; as the frequency of quotation may suggest, a considerable proportion has been in the white collar sector where most recent gains in recognition have been made. The CIR, and more particularly the Manpower and Productivity Service of the DE, both of whose work has now been transferred to the ACAS, have advised on the reconstruction of many procedures.

Nevertheless, change has been incremental and piecemeal in nature, with relatively few companies initiating major reviews of their industrial relations structure. Wilders and Parker, reviewing changes between the Workplace Industrial Relations surveys of 1966 and 1972, noted a continuation of general trends towards more structured plant level institutions, but nevertheless concluded that: ' . . . of the Donovan Commission's enthusiasm for the formalisation of factory-wide agreements there was remarkable little evidence.'[2] A survey by the Department of Employment of the impact on institutions of the Industrial Relations Act and the Code of Practice found that neither had produced many procedural or substantive changes in plant level industrial relations, although they had produced a greater consciousness of industrial relations issues, especially among senior management.[3] Disciplinary procedures had received the greatest attention, doubtless as a result of the trend in legal decisions to require an adequate appeal procedure as an important factor in unfair dismissal cases. Otherwise the most common procedural change was the formalisation of individual as opposed to general or collective grievance procedures. This of course also had a legal impetus in s20(2) of the Act. The survey also noted that:

> The design of these individual procedures has in general followed the relevant but rather general recommendations of the Code [paras 124–5]. But at times this was not so, and the procedure might indeed be fairly crude; for example, a major oil refiner had introduced at all its sites a simple two-stage procedure with no mention of conciliation, no time limits and no formal provision for representation.[4]

More generally, the report noted that: 'Approximately one quarter of the firms in the survey noted some moves towards formalisation of grievance/disputes procedures during recent years', but what was meant by 'formalisation' was not too clear, although 'it seems from such statements as "tidying up" and "putting things in order" that in most cases it did not involve a radical break with the past'.[5]

It can thus be seen that attempts to reconstruct procedures have not in general been very wide in scope nor deep in analysis and that if one accepts, as we do, the Donovan contention about the importance of plant level institutions and grievance resolution in particular, it is clear that much still remains to be done. However, the priority given to plant level reform has, if anything, diminished in the recent past. Procedures played no role in the provisions of the Employment Protection Act, although the TUC had suggested that a registration requirement might be included, while the demise of the CIR removed the main investigatory body in this area. Its replacement, the ACAS, does not have the same facilities for either general or detailed research. There is therefore a strong likelihood that change in this area will continue to be incremental, will be dependent on the initiatives of the parties at establishment level, and will be within the general mould of the traditional system.

It is not the function of this section to analyse in depth why change has been so limited. However, a number of possible reasons may be mentioned: the Industrial Relations Act, which produced an atmosphere of industrial confrontation; successive income policies, which in part took away from management the responsibility for the outcome of bargaining; some reduction in wage drift, which has also diminished the plant as a focus of public attention; political and legislative uncertainty, which induced a mood of waiting upon events; inadequate leadership by governmental and other bodies to give guidance in the structuring of reform; the role of regulatory legislation, which has transferred many erstwhile grievances to industrial tribunals; challenge to the Donovan assumption of underlying consensus and pluralism; and, last but not least, managerial and union unwillingness or inability to face up to change. There can be no doubt that plant level reform has been difficult to achieve in the last few years. Nevertheless, the evidence all points to the increasing importance of the workplace. The need for improved procedures will therefore not diminish.

The American model

In Britain's search for new industrial relations policies the experience of the United States provided a natural starting point, since it appeared to have resolved those problems of operating a decentralised system of industrial relations which Donovan had identified as being the most pressing in Britain. In particular, the capacity of the American grievance resolution system to operate in a largely voluntarist way, with only occasional references to the law, made it a very attractive model for Britain to examine, and it is therefore hardly surprising that the 1971 Industrial Relations Act borrowed a number of concepts from the American system with the clear intention of trying to create a similar institutional structure here in Britain.

The American system is based on a number of distinctive factors, which have been comprehensively analysed by Bok.[6] One such group of factors is cultural, e.g., the lack of solidarity and class consciousness amongst the American working class, the general acceptance of the capitalist ethos, the consequent lack of a socialist or labour party, and the decentralised nature of the political and, to a lesser extent, the economic system. The result has been a somewhat narrow, economically based union movement with its strength at the local rather than national level. Employers for their part have depended far less on associations as the basis for their activities, although these do exist in many industries, but are little concerned with industrial relations. The United States is also, more than most countries, organised according to legal norms–with only four times the population of Britain, it has twelve times the number of lawyers. Moreover, law has long been acceptable as an integral part of the industrial relations system because of the benefits it provided to unions through the seminal Wagner Act of 1935 in defining and enforcing rights of representation and bargaining for what had been a weak and hesitant labour movement up to that time. From that Act date most of the concepts later to be copied in the British Industrial Relations Act–bargaining units, exclusive bargaining agents, unfair labour practices and the obligation of bargaining in good faith, backed by the National Labor Relations Board. Most relationships in American manufacturing industries grew up under this system, which as interpreted by the NLRB favoured a plant oriented structure based on the right of the individuals within the bargaining unit to be represented by unions of their own choosing. Indeed, the role of the State in establishing the basic structures of industrial relations, and the procedures for arriving at those structures, has been greater in the US than in almost any other modern western country (with the possible exception of Canada, which mirrors the US structure in most respects and, in addition, imposes compulsory conciliation in all interest disputes before industrial action is allowed).

Yet in spite of the legal background to the industrial relationship, the American system has maintained a very considerable degree of voluntarism, since the role of the law has been to bring the parties together in the bargaining chamber by means of certain obligations designed to ensure the *process* of bargaining and not to impose substantive or procedural conditions on the parties. Nevertheless, given the legal nature of mutual obligations, it was not unnatural for a contractual relationship to emerge, based on a comprehensive collective agreement for a fixed period,[7] and a relatively clear, although by no means absolute, differentiation between contract negotiation and contract administration. At the heart of contract administration lay the grievance procedure as the mechanism for day-to-day operation of the collective agreement and what has come to be its concomitant, the use of third party arbitration as a final means of disposal if the parties could not agree on the interpretation of the contract. By the end of the Second World War the spread of grievance machinery and arbitration had become such as to make this an integral feature of the system. The latest survey carried out by the Bureau of Labour Statistics in 1964 showed that 99 per cent of the 1,717 agreements surveyed included a grievance procedure and that 94 per cent included arbitration.[8]

The grievance procedure itself is almost invariably multi-stage, reflecting the levels of authority in the organisation. Like the rest of the collective agreement, it is much more formal and detailed than that normally found in Britain. Time limits between stages generally exist, procedural differentiation to cover different types of issue is common, and such aspects as the scope of procedural coverage, management rights, and the status of the grievance decision are also frequently included. An effort is made to solve grievances as close as possible to their point of origin, and it is generally the case that foremen and stewards are well acquainted with the terms of the collective agreement, using it as the starting point for grievance discussions. Underpinning the process is the peace obligation represented by the acceptance of a no-strike clause by the union and arbitration as a final means of settlement by the employer.

In this system the arbitrator is dependent on the terms of the contract; although in earlier periods clinical or mediatory arbitration was common, in recent years, as agreements have become more complex, it has become increasingly judicial in nature. However, it is by no means the case that all issues are arbitrable; in a large number of cases certain subjects are specifically excluded, giving the union the right to strike after the earlier steps of the procedure have been carried out. But, generally, the crux of the system is that arbitration is seen as a *quid pro quo* for a no-strike clause. The instance of an arbitrator as a last recourse during the life of the agreement means that management cannot depend on imposing its views by power and is thus forced to consider its actions before the event as well as to justify them afterwards. This is a vital factor; as Kuhn has noted: 'Workers are, perhaps, as interested in an assurance of justice *before* the act as in justice through the grievance procedure *after* the act'.[9] It is precisely this facet which has all too often been missing in Britain. It is also this belief in the efficacy of the system which has reversed the concept of status quo which is of such importance in Britain:

> The understanding of the parties, and the almost universal ruling of arbitrators, is that an employee must obey an order so long as it poses no threat to his personal safety and that discipline may be imposed for failure to obey without regard to the propriety of that order under the agreement . . . His right to recover depends on a later . . . determination as to whether the order was improper.[10]

However, the system is by no means as mechanistic as the foregoing may imply. In particular, there is the function, present in all systems, of interstitial rulemaking through the grievance process. As Kuhn put it:

169

'Thus, the grievance process has evolved from a policy procedure for worker protection into a means for on-the-job joint determination of work conditions.'[11] Indeed, this concept was accepted by the Supreme Court in its description of the grievance procedure as 'a part of the continuous collective bargaining process' and as 'the means of solving the unforeseeable by molding a system of private law'.[12] Kuhn's earlier work on *Bargaining in Grievance Settlement* has been frequently quoted throughout this book, and it represents a fascinating example of the extent to which fractional bargaining can be taken even in a country where, to quote Kuhn: ' . . . the judicial and administrative functions in almost all unionized firms have greatly improved over the past fifteen to twenty-five years and are not susceptible to basic improvements'.[13] Fractional bargaining is the norm rather than the exception in the American system, but it would be wrong to assume that it is usually or even frequently carried to the lengths described by Kuhn. Wildcat strikes do exist, and may constitute up to a third of the total, but many occur over issues which would not in any case be arbitrable. Yet there is still a good deal of less hostile informality in the grievance process, and it would be a mistake to see it as a purely judicial hearing under the agreement. It must be added, however, that the judicial component increases when the higher stages are reached.

There is little doubt that the American system does work well and it is hardly surprising that it has been seen as a suitable mentor for Britain by various American commentators,[14] to say nothing of providing an implicit model for the Donovan Report and an explicit model for the Industrial Relations Act.[15] Yet the attempt to transfer the system has manifestly failed. This was partly because of the wider political and social reasons described earlier and partly because there was no adequate *quid pro quo* for the unions, so that the British labour movement was unwilling to accept the constraints on its actions which the Act imposed. But it was also partly because the British legislation did not in fact reproduce the intricate balancing system which exists in America. Various instances illustrate this,[16] but one in particular, covering the relationship between the individual employee and the union under the grievance system, is worth recounting in some detail.

In the 1967 case of *Vaca v. Sipes*[17] the Supreme Court tried to set the boundaries of the union duty to the individual of 'fair representation'. In this case, Benjamin Owens was discharged for health reasons. He filed a grievance, presenting medical evidence that he was fit to work. The union backed his claim, but after it had sent him at its own expense to a specialist of his own choosing and that specialist reported that Owens' blood pressure was too high for him to do any work the union decided to drop the case. Owens then sued the union for refusing to take his claim to arbitration. On appeal, the Supreme Court decided against Owens, reversing the judgement of the lower court and arguing that 'a breach of the statutory duty of fair representation occurs only when a union's conduct towards a member is arbitrary, discriminatory, or in bad faith.' The fact that a grievance may at some stage be found to be meritorious is not of itself evidence of a breach of that duty.

The position is therefore that in the United States the union essentially owns the grievance,[18] and while there is a definite duty towards the individual, the essential relationship is the collective one. By contrast, the role of the individual under British law has been very much greater; this reached a highwater mark in the Industrial Relations Act where the primacy given to the individual as opposed to the collectivity was one of the main objections of the unions against the Act.

Under s20 of the Industrial Relations Act employers were required to provide information to employees about the redress of their grievances, and the interpretation of this in conjunction with individual rights under s5 in the relatively small number of cases which arose threatened to severely curtail the bargaining function of the recognised union and to greatly increase that of small unrecognised but registered unions. Under the Act there was no conception of exclusive representation and no obligation on the part of the union to represent non-members (as there is in America) so that individuals who were not members of the recognised union could pursue their right to be a member of and take part in the activities of the other (registered) trade unions. In the Crouch case not only were minimal activities and facilities to be granted in respect of such individuals, but the courts decided that it would be discriminating to provide additional facilities to the recognised union, although some allowance should be made for its greater size and sole bargaining rights.[19] It followed that if there was no obligation on the part of the union to let such a non-member pursue his grievance through the normal procedure, a separate procedure would have to be created. Taking this a stage further the NIRC argued in *Howle v. GEC Engineering* that: 'To have two sets of grievance procedures, one which allows an employee to be represented by his union and the other which does not, is, on the face of it, to discriminate unfairly against those denied union representation.'[20]

Even so, the dangers of this approach were well illustrated by the Howle case. Howle had tried to obtain negotiating rights for UKAPE, an unrecognised union, and on being rebuffed had tried to use the grievance procedure to negotiate his own salary, bringing along an official of UKAPE as his representative. The Industrial Tribunal argued that this was an attempt to negotiate, but this verdict was reversed by the NIRC which concluded that: 'The Tribunal has fallen into the error of equating "negotiating rights" with the right to represent and negotiate on behalf of a member in an individual grievance. They are quite separate functions.'[21] In practice, of course, these functions are far from easily separable, especially in Britain where the distinction between disputes of right and interest is infrequently used. What was being done in these cases was to virtually eliminate the control of the recognised union over the grievance process, to prevent it from ensuring that the process is used in the interests of its membership, and to permit a non-recognised union to gain *de facto* negotiating rights, all under the guise of individual rights. It is arguable that this interpretation of s5 was not intended by Parliament but the fact remains that, far from creating consistency and stability through the grievance procedure, this approach, if the Act had not been repealed, would have threatened the role and in some cases the very existence of the recognised union. Thus although ostensibly drawing on American experience, the Industrial Relations Act in fact totally ignored the lessons to be learned from the other side of the Atlantic in a key area which lies at the heart of the successful operation of the American system.

The European model

In what might be called the 'Donovan' period of 1968–72 it was generally the case that Europe was less frequently seen as an example of how a reformed British system of industrial relations might function than the United States, with its relatively efficient decentralised system. However, in the last two or three years interest in Europe has increased greatly, in part owing to British membership of the EEC, but also partly because of a changing focus of interest away from plant level reform on the Donovan basis towards institutions of industrial democracy, for which Europe, and particularly Germany, provides a more obvious point of departure than the United States. Although less directly concerned with the grievance process as such than the American analogy, this new emphasis does also have important implications for it.

The leading European countries inevitably differ a good deal between each other, but some general points of similarity can be traced. Perhaps the key factor of European industrial relations from our point of view is that in contrast to both Britain and the United States, unions there have tended to be weak at plant level–indeed, there is often a gap between the union and plant level institutions, with unions in recent years struggling for admission into the plant. Plant institutions for their part have rarely had a bargaining role–this has belonged to the union at national or district level. There is rarely an explicit plant procedure for grievances, rather there is often a multiplicity of procedural paths. Thus McPherson has said of the French situation: 'The grieving employee . . . has free choice among at least six alternatives for the direct presentation of his grievance. He may take it to his foreman, the plant manager, or to a steward; or he may omit discussion at plant level and turn at once to the factory inspector, a union district official, or even the Labor Court.'[22] In several other countries the works council would also be a frequent recourse for employee grievances. As might be expected from this nebulous structure, grievances are generally less frequent and the process of less importance than in either Britain or the United States. Writing in 1964, Sturmthal noted of France and Germany jointly that: 'It is perhaps not more than a mild overstatement that the effectiveness of grievance handling is in reverse proportion to the number of available grievance procedures.'[23] In practice, informal methods are probably more important than all the procedures. Stewards also play a less central role, although they have had a statutory role in France since 1946 and although their significance in all European countries has increased considerably in recent years, especially in Germany and Holland, as the union has sought a more positive role at plant level. This in turn has led to a conflict between the stewards or the union shop committees on the one hand and the works councils on the other in the area of grievance handling.

Thus in Europe, as in Britain, although occurring somewhat later in time, there has still been a challenge to the existing predominantly centralised arrangements (noted by one commentator as 'a widespread shift in the location of initiative and power from the central organization to the periphery, from trade unions to formal or informal work-place committees.').[24] Indeed most European countries have used legislation to validate what they see as a changing balance between centralisation and decentralisation, since one of the key focal aspects of the legislation has in each case dealt with the plant level. Germany, France, Italy, the Netherlands, Norway and Sweden have all passed such legislation since 1968. One of the purposes of this has generally been to give unions an increased role at plant level; another has been to develop the institutions of industrial democracy. To this latter topic and its implications for Britain we now turn.

The development of industrial democracy promises to create a new authority structure within the plant which will inevitably have implications for the grievance process. Here most attention has been focused on the German situation, since its system of co-determination is the main basis of the proposed European company legislation and also the most frequent model for discussions of this topic in Britain. Of the two aspects of co-determination, the best known relates to membership of the board of directors, on which German law states that one-half of the members of the supervisory board shall be worker representatives in the coal and steel industries, and one-third in other industries. The present German government has promised to extend the greater representation to all industries. The other aspect is the system of works councils which has potential lessons for plant level institutions. The Works Constitution Act of 1952 set up a system of works and company councils, and the rights given to the councils were greatly extended by a further Act in 1972. Various levels of participation are granted. The highest level is that of co-determination, meaning that any measure proposed by the employer has no binding effect until approved by the works council. If no agreement is reached, the law prescribes determination by an arbitration committee. To a British eye, the areas covered by co-determination are extremely wide ranging; there are also additional rights to be consulted in certain areas, and further rights of access to information, besides certain miscellaneous rights such as the right to inspect personnel records and the right to be involved in the creation of the grievance procedure.

There has as yet been little published information on how this system is working. It should be borne in mind, however, that, on the whole, the works councils were not notably aggressive in their pursuit of the more limited rights granted under the 1952 Act, and that many tended to take a cooperative approach with the employer, based on *Betriebsegoismus* or loyalty to the goals of the enterprise. Moreover, there is a legal obligation on both council and management to work together for the benefit of both the company and the workers in a way which could be considered a unitary rather than an adversary conception of the enterprise. Nonetheless, it is clear that the legislation does set out the rights, obligations and functions of the parties at plant level in a way which has been almost totally absent in Britain. Moreover, it does so in a very wide variety of procedural areas, giving rights which, when taken together with the rights to board membership, provide one possible formula for industrial democracy.

What are the implications of this approach for Britain? As Roberts has pointed out: 'While there are recognisable differences between the Works Council and a British Joint Shop Steward Committee, the similarities of function tempt comparison.'[25] One major difference relates to the role of the union. In Germany the works council is separate from the union and is elected by all employees, although in the great majority of cases works council representatives are members of, and are backed by, the union. The 1972 Act has also extended the rights of the full-time union official within the plant. It is also the case that the shop stewards committee in Britain, although its members are nominally elected from within the union hierarchy from national to grass roots level, often shows a disposition to operate on a semi-autonomous basis. To continue Roberts' argument:

> It is contended that formal recognition of such joint bodies, while clearly necessitating the abandonment of long established management and trade union prerogatives, could effect beneficial changes in the use of labour and capital, in the gains from improved industrial efficiency and in the general industrial relations climate at plant level.[26]

The implications for management prerogatives can be considered in the British context in the same way as they would for conflict resolution. Whereas most grievances are appeals *after* the event, the obligation to jointly determine or at least consult *before* the event would greatly alter both the nature of the decision, the responsibility for it, and the mode of its interpretation. Moreover, the implementation of the rights given to the employee body would in all probability necessitate increased formalisation of the role of shop stewards, improved information networks, procedural agreements, the codification of the collective agreement, and the formulation and dissemination of management policy. Not only can it reasonably be expected that such changes themselves would have desirable effects on the conduct of industrial relations, but it might also be expected that the greater involvement of the workforce in decision making would be conducive to acceptance of the outcome of decisions and would contribute substantially to the achievement of industrial democracy.

Of all the political parties in Britain the Liberal Party has been most enthusiastic about such a structure; the TUC, however, has been much less welcoming:

> An attempt to introduce a general system of works councils in British industry would lead to one of two things. Either they would duplicate

existing structures at plant level, in which case Works Councils would clearly be superfluous; or they would displace and supersede existing trade union arrangements; this latter approach would be even more unacceptable to the trade union movement. [27]

This is indeed dismissive, yet the TUC, and the Labour movement in general, appears to have thought little about possible future developments in plant level relationships, arguing only that the collective bargaining model now in existence should be developed in the workers' interests. It has somewhat grudgingly accepted the concept of two-tier boards and worker representation on the supervisory board, but both here and at plant level it is clearly worried about the implications of some degree of joint responsibility for decisions, with many preferring the adversary model, and also about the relationship between the unions and such bodies and the role of non-union members and managers. Yet the TUC can surely be under no illusions that the state of British plant level institutions leaves much to be desired, and the works council model, with the advantages it could bring in worker involvement, would seem to warrant further investigations. Management in Britain, for its part, has tended to take the opposite view to the TUC, being prepared to accept works councils, but generally opposing worker membership of the board of directors.

Part of the interest in the co-determination question arises from the stated intentions of the EEC to introduce legislation in this area. An original proposal for a European Company Statute was issued in 1970, and in April 1975 the Commission produced an amended proposal. The purpose of the Statute is to make possible cross-frontier mergers, holdings, and common subsidiaries; it does not seek to replace national laws, but will exist alongside them, and will be voluntary for those multinational companies which wish to take advantage of it. On the industrial relations side a pattern of a European Works Council and board representation is suggested, with one-third of the supervisory board members as representatives of the shareholders, one-third as representatives of the employees and the last third coopted by both groups. An electoral system is proposed for the employee representatives.

It is this co-determination model which at the present looks most likely to be introduced into Britain, although its precise form and particularly the role of works councils, if any, is far from clear. The Labour government intends to introduce legislation on company law and a committee of inquiry on industrial democracy was announced in August 1975. Its terms of reference are unusually explicit: 'Accepting the need for a radical extension of industrial democracy in the control of companies by means of representation on boards of directors, and accepting the essential role of trade union organisations in this process . . .' This emphasises the board representation aspect of industrial democracy, and the implications for procedures may not emerge until the final shape of the legislation is determined.

The radical model

The final model we wish to examine starts with a different assumption from the previous three by rejecting the pluralism which is the essence of the other models. As portrayed in recent British academic writings, the pluralism of these models, although in many respects oriented towards reform, is based on the values of what is inherently an unfair society, and because it involves 'only marginal adjustments to a structure the basic elements of which are unquestioned [it] has a predominantly conservative orientation.'[28] This view therefore rejects the concept implicit in the Donovan Report 'of a widespread basic consensus which needed only the "right" institutional forms in which to emerge.'[29] Many writers of this school would reject the concept of industrial democracy embodied in the co-determination approach as vehemently as those concepts embodied in the traditional or American models, and would agree with Mandel that '"Workers' control" and "Participation" are exact opposites.'[30]

Most of this writing is more explicit in its criticisms of pluralism and the present system than it is in its own formulation of what should replace it. Certainly there is no discussion of the grievance procedures which should be incorporated in any new economic organisation. The two basic alternatives presented are a centralised and a decentralised socialist system, with most writers recognising that there is a genuine difficulty in providing for both central planning and grass roots democracy. Of the two, the bulk of recent attention has been given to the decentralised approach of workers' control. The theoretical basis for this approach has come from writings such as those of Gramsci and the most widely quoted practical analogies have been drawn with the Yugoslavian system, which we shall use as a basis for discussion, even though there is some disillusion amongst commentators with various aspects of the system.

Leaving aside the wider aspects of relationships with the State, the Communist Party, and the local community, the Yugoslav system is based on workers' self-management of publicly owned enterprises within an economy based on social planning and the market mechanism. The supreme authority within each enterprise is the workers' collective which consists of all the members of the enterprise. The three major organs, however, are: the elected workers' council, which sets policies on fundamental issues such as production and financial plans, allocation of income, government of the enterprise, and so on; the management board, elected by the workers' council, and responsible for translating these policies into day-to-day operations; and the director, whose function is to carry these out. A more recent development has been the emergence of a working unit, which may represent a production department or a professional service unit, or, in large enterprises, an entire plant. This addition overcomes to some extent the problems of representation in large scale enterprise by introducing further elements of direct democracy into the system of self-management. Relations between these units are on the basis of contracts and payment for services rendered. With a complicated pattern of different bodies taking decisions at an increasing number of different levels there is a clear need for conflict resolution procedures. Thus disputes between work units can be dealt with by an arbitration commission appointed by the workers' council, or in certain cases by a referendum. Externally, disputes between enterprises can be referred to permanent courts of arbitration, or to a hierarchy of economic courts.

On a less formal level the relations between the director and the self-management bodies are in many respects the key to the operation of the enterprise. In many cases the director, although in theory he has no right to make decisions, effectively controls and manages the plant. In any case his role, which involves ensuring efficiency and maintaining national planning objectives as well as responsibility to the self-management bodies, is full of conflicting pressures.

From the point of view of the individual and the small group, there must sometimes be difficulty in identifying the body to which a grievance should be directed. There is little quantitative information available on grievance handling, but Gorupic and Paj report that a 1967 survey revealed that appeals were lodged against decisions of workers' councils in 1·6 per cent of cases relating to work issues, and that 44 per cent of the appeals were upheld.[31] Writing more generally of grievance handling, Sturmthal has noted:

> There is an almost embarrassing wealth of grievance procedures available to him [the worker]: the workers' council, the managing board, the director, the union, the Communist Party. Which of these,

if any, Stepan selects depends on a great many circumstances. If he is a member in good standing in the party, he will most probably turn to it with his complaint. Where the director is a strong personality, he may be the court of appeal against decisions of the foremen and department heads. In the early stages of the council system, the workers' council was often enlisted in support of personal grievances. Sometimes . . . the employee may even follow the course suggested by the law and appeal to the managing board against decisions of the director. One of the frequently used methods of presenting grievances, particularly those of a whole group, is not listed among the publicly acknowledged ways of grievance handling: the workers present themselves en masse at the director's office and demand redress . . . Equally noteworthy is the fact that the union is hardly ever mentioned by anyone in connection with grievance handling.[32]

On the last point, Poole, writing more recently, has suggested that the union has become a more important means for workers to express grievances and pursue their interests.[33] Hunnius also notes the use of the courts for certain specified grievances.[34]

What emerges from the Yugoslav experience is the prevalence of conflict and the complexity of procedures for reconciling it and providing for the necessary coordination of activities. Indeed, Gorupic and Paj argue of the ambiguous relations within the enterprise between the management cadre, the work units and the central self-management bodies that: 'This situation entails the possibility of conflict as a normal phenomenon, and thereby the need for some kind of procedure for the current solution of conflicts as a component part of the activity itself.'[35] Not least of the focal points of conflict is the individual; whatever the satisfactions inherent in the system, it is clear that they do not obviate the same types of day-to-day grievance issues as in western economic systems.

The four models reviewed above are not entirely incompatible with each other, nor do they exhaust the possibilities for structural and procedural change. Mention might be made, for instance, of the reconstitution of work organisation and flows within existing technology, and the possibility of self-managing work groups on the shopfloor without fundamental change in the whole company structure. Experiments in Scandinavia are possibly the most developed in this direction, although again little is known of their implications for procedural forms. Another model might take into account the growing importance of the multinational corporation and the need for new procedures of conflict resolution where ultimate control is very remote and lines of communication very long. But whatever the overall pattern which emerges in a world of rapid change, we would strongly argue that the position of the individual in the work environment will continue to be a central issue in both political and economic development and that for him to achieve the self-fulfilment which is the goal of all societies it is critical that larger organisational questions should not obscure his personal and day-to-day needs, demands, and grievances.

In other words, whatever the economic or political model, grievance procedures will be necessary to take account of the individual and the small group. Even for larger groups, grievance procedures are a necessary mechanism for *ad hoc* bargaining, which will continue irrespective of the comprehensiveness of the collective agreement, factory plan, or statutory regulation. At the very least, change in this area should not have to wait until the resolution of larger political issues. In the final section of the book, therefore, we take up the practical aspects and mechanisms of change in the establishment.

The challenge of change

On a general plane the problems of change are acquiring a literature of their own. In the 1970 Reith Lectures, Donald Schon noted: 'In all domains of experience, transforming a familiar system means passing through zones of uncertainty . . . the situation of being at sea, of confronting more information than you can handle.'[36] Cyert and March, in their pathbreaking *A Behavioural Theory of the Firm*, base their theory of decision making within organisations on the response to uncertainty:

> Organizations avoid uncertainty . . . They avoid the requirement that they correctly anticipate events in the distant future by using decision rules emphasising short-run reaction to short-run feedback rather than anticipation of long-run uncertain events. They solve pressing problems rather than develop long-run strategies . . . each problem is solved as it arises; the organisation then waits for another problem to appear.[37]

On the next stage, searching for a solution, Cyert and March state that:

> We assume that rules for search are simple-minded in the sense that they reflect simple concepts of causality . . . search is based initially on two simple rules: (1) search in the neighbourhood of the problem symptom and (2) search in the neighbourhood of the current alternative.

These two rules reflect different dimensions of the basic causal notions that a cause will be found 'near' its effect and that a new solution will be found 'near' an old one.[38]

It follows from these points that although organisations do 'learn', adaptive behaviour tends to be of an incremental rather than a far-reaching nature. Moreover, British management has often been conservative in comparison to its international counterparts. Thus the American sociologist Dubin has written: 'Among British executives there is likely to be greater emphasis upon the value of the present and the utility of existing conditions. The view of history is essentially to accept the present as a culmination of past developments, and, therefore, as representing the highest achievements attainable.'[39] Whatever the truth of such comments, we would certainly argue that a positive strategy of reform is a necessary prerequisite for successful change.

The mechanics of procedural reform are not unlike those of productivity bargaining. Management must normally initiate the process, although doubtless there will be occasions when shop stewards will point out to management the problems of an existing procedure or demand their own desired changes. It would in any case be desirable to tell the union informally that a review is planned. An immediate question arises as to whether to make an inside review or to go outside the plant for advice. If the plant is one where day-to-day pressures effectively prevent a studied evaluation there is clearly an argument for going outside, to the employers' association, to a firm of consultants, or to the ACAS. In general we would argue that the last of these is the best alternative. If an inside review is possible, we would suggest that a working party be formed, preferably under a director to ensure that the results are adequately explained at board level. Even so, the crucial people are the personnel department representatives from either or both company or plant level. Line management should also be represented, and we would press for the inclusion of a foreman in view of the importance of first-line supervision in industrial relations.

Stage two is the evaluation of the plant situation. We would suggest an explicit written evaluation of the many facets of the plant's environment, with lessons drawn separately from various technological, organisational, market, and union factors, some of which may be contradictory. Any evidence on the operation of the current procedure should be examined. What are the key grievances, at what level are they solved, how does this conform with the 'official' procedure and organisational structure? A questionnaire could be given to all members of management with industrial relations responsibilities to elicit such information.

Stage three is one of initial policy formulation and discussion within management. What are the options and to what goals should they be directed? Does the plant have an overall industrial relations policy, either to act as a base or as something whose premises are to be challenged? Does the 'actual' grievance process reflect a desirable distribution of managerial authority and responsibility?

At this stage also, a further issue will almost certainly arise. Does the evidence suggest that other aspects of the plant industrial relations system also require reform? This last is a particularly important point, since there is little advantage in procedural reform by itself if the source of the substantive conflict, such as an inefficient wage system, remains unreformed. Moreover, when the union makes its views known, it will undoubtedly and rightly point to other defects which it wishes to see remedied, and these might form part of a *quid pro quo*. On the other hand, to allow reform to concentrate on substantive issues from the outset will run the risk, as appeared to happen with many productivity bargains, that procedures will be forgotten. In general we would agree with McCarthy's argument:

> It seems to me that successful bargaining change is made most likely when both sides are prepared to bring virtually everything into account that could possibly help to break the log jam of perceived vested interests and unthinking conservatism that too often stands in the way of a good agreement . . . But there is also another and more positive reason for doubting the general value of separating the processes of procedural change from substantive reform. To my mind the main aim in adapting procedures is to keep them in line with substantive change. Procedures are, for the most part, adequate, or inadequate, to the extent that they fit existing collections of substantive agreements . . . In other words, most of the needs for procedural reform is rooted in prior substantive change. It follows that we should encourage both sides to think of the two processes as inter-related.[40]

Stage four is to introduce the union. It is arguable that this could be done earlier, but on the whole we think management should take the initiative and prepare its own evaluation and a range of possible options before asking the union for its views. The union should be told what is happening, since it will certainly hear in any case, and it would of course be fatal for management to decide on a single course of action as a result of its own evaluation. The union should be invited to join a reconstituted working party and should have the right to challenge or supplement the evidence management has gathered; if necessary, further research could be undertaken at the union's instigation within the discussions of the working party, since what McCarthy said of bargaining structures is also true of procedures:

> But stewards and their members know only too well that one reason why managements desire comprehensiveness and order is because they hope that it will result in less wage drift and few competing claims. Not unnaturally those on the shop floor who have done rather well out of the existing system will tend to look coldly on such proposals for change. Once again they will have to be offered compensating advantages before they agree.[41]

The working party clearly cannot work in isolation at this stage. There is indeed a case for making it known that anyone in the plant with views on restructuring should be able to put them to the working party. Shop stewards should report back on developments to their members and management representatives likewise to the board of directors or at least the senior plant manager, while the full-time union official should have the opportunity of an *ex officio* seat on the working party, even if he cannot attend regularly. Within the working party the key roles, if the evidence of the DE pamphlet on plant level reform is accurate, will probably be those of the personnel manager and the senior lay union official; indeed, the DE pamphlet stated: 'It cannot be overstressed that recognition and acceptance of the important new roles they must play is a pre-requisite of successful bargaining reform at this level.'[42]

Once the new structure is developed, the final stage of introduction and implementation becomes crucial. The dangers here are also well illustrated in the DE monograph:

> In many cases, however, agreements were confusingly constructed, inadequately indexed and cross-referenced, and often ill-written. In such circumstances it is not surprising that considerable misunderstanding soon became evident following their introduction. Moreover, although conventional communications channels proved inadequate to the task, few firms undertook any special training or communications exercises to ease the change, and some who did, failed to plan them as thoroughly as was later found to have been desirable. This particularly applied to the training of shop stewards, who were to play a crucial part in the successful operation of agreements. The quaint reluctance of most of the firms to distribute copies of the

agreement to their workforce can only have contributed to the difficulties which most encountered in the introductory stages.[43]

In conclusion, it remains to stress what a plant level grievance system can and cannot do. It cannot solve the underlying causes of conflict, whether these result from dissatisfactions at the plant, industry, or economy level, or whether they are due to economic, technological or ideological factors. It is very limited in the extent to which it can institutionalise conflict if there is not a basic consensus about the legitimacy of the roles of the parties. It cannot of itself make up for deficiencies in the structure of the relationship. Nor can it necessarily persuade people that short term goals cannot sometimes best be achieved by procedural abrogation. On the other hand, an effective procedure is a *sine qua non* for any organisation facing conflict, or for any organisation wishing to minimise the results of conflict when it becomes obvious that management is treating their complaints seriously, workers learn what problems can be effectively solved, how long it will take, and what the solutions are. To put it in Kuhn's words, 'they build up reasonable expectations concerning the grievance system and come to rely on it to protect their rights, through tradition, past practice, and the collective agreement.'[44] To achieve this will be a long task, but there are few which are more worthwhile.

Notes

[1] See A.W.J. Thomson and S.R. Engleman, *The Industrial Relations Act: Review and Analysis*, Martin Robertson, London 1975.

[2] M.G. Wilders and S.R. Parker, 'Changes in workplace industrial relations, 1966–1972', *British Journal of Industrial Relations,* March 1975, p. 22.

[3] Department of Employment, 'A report into the workings of the Industrial Relations Act and the Code of Practice', *Industrial Relations Review and Report*, Nos 83 and 84, July 1974. See also B. James and R. Clifton, 'Labour relations in the firm: the impact of the Industrial Relations Act', *Industrial Relations Journal*, Spring 1974, which suggests that the Act had an even more limited effect on small firms.

[4] DE Report, op. cit., p. 10.

[5] Ibid.

[6] D.C. Bok, 'Reflections on the distinctive character of American labor laws', *Harvard Law Review,* vol. 84, April 1971.

[7] The obligation to bargain in good faith includes the requirement that the parties must reduce their agreement to writing (*H.J. Heinz v. NLRB,* 311 US 514, 1941).

[8] US Department of Labor, Bureau of Labor Statistics, Bulletins Nos 1425–1, *Grievance Procedures*, and 1425–6, *Arbitration Procedures*.

[9] J.W. Kuhn, 'The grievance process' in J.T. Dunlop and N.W. Chamberlain (eds), *Frontiers of Collective Bargaining*, Harper and Row, New York 1967, p. 257.

[10] D.E. Feller, 'A general theory of the collective bargaining agreement', *California Law Review,* May 1973, p. 778.

[11] Kuhn, 'The grievance process', op. cit., p. 261.

[12] *United Steelworkers v. Warrior and Gulf Navigation Co.,* 363 US 574 (1960).

[13] Kuhn, *Bargaining in Grievance Settlement*, op. cit., p. 50.

[14] A.M. Ross, 'Prosperity and British industrial relations', *Industrial Relations*, February 1963; J. Garbarino, 'Managing conflict in industrial relations: US experience and current issues in Britain', *British Journal of Industrial Relations*, November 1969; L. Ulman, 'Collective bargaining and industrial efficiency' in R.E. Caves and Associates, *Britain's Economic Prospects*, Brookings Institution, Washington DC 1968; J. Stieber, *Grievance Arbitration in the United States,* RCTUEA Research Paper No. 8, HMSO 1967.

[15] For analogies between the Industrial Relations Act and American legislation see W.B. Gould, 'Taft–Hartley comes to Great Britain: observations on the Industrial Relations Act of 1971', *Yale Law Journal*, vol. 81, July 1972.

[16] See Thomson and Engleman, op. cit., especially chapter 6.

[17] *Vaca v. Sipes*, 386 US 171 (1967).

[18] In *Republic Steel v. Maddox*, 379 US 650 (1965) the Supreme Court decided that an individual cannot bring a suit unless he has tried to use the contract grievance procedure and can show that the union has refused to take action.

[19] *Post Office v. Crouch*, CA (1973) ICR 366 and HL (1974) ICR 378.

[20] *Howle v. GEC Engineering Limited* (1974) ICR 13, 20.

[21] Ibid.

[22] W.H. McPherson, 'Grievance settlement procedures in Western Europe', *Proceedings of Industrial Relations Research Association*, vol. 15, 1962, p. 28.

[23] A. Sturmthal, *Workers Councils*, Harvard University Press, Cambridge, Mass. 1964, p. 161.

[24] Quoted in M. Kidron, *Western Capitalism since the War* in

J. Barbash, *Trade Unions and National Economic Policy,* John Hopkins Press, Baltimore 1972, p. 175.

[25] I.L. Roberts, 'The Works Constitution Acts and industrial relations in West Germany: implications for the United Kingdom', *British Journal of Industrial Relations,* November 1973, p. 365.

[26] Ibid.

[27] TUC, *Industrial Democracy,* 1974, p. 40.

[28] R. Hyman and I. Brough, *Social Values and Industrial Relations,* Blackwell, Oxford 1975, p. 177.

[29] A. Fox, 'Industrial relations: a social critique of pluralist ideology' in J. Child (ed.), *Man and Organization,* Allen and Unwin, London 1973, p. 196.

[30] E. Mandel, 'The debate on workers' control' in G. Hunnius, D. Garson and J. Case, *Workers' Control,* Vintage Books, New York 1973, p. 355.

[31] Quoted in 'Workers' participation in management in Yugoslavia', *International Institute for Labour Studies Bulletin,* no. 9, 1972, p. 151.

[32] Sturmthal, op. cit., p. 118.

[33] M. Poole, *Workers' Participation in Industry,* Routledge and Kegan Paul, London 1975, p. 158.

[34] G. Hunnius, 'Workers' self-management in Yugoslavia', in Hunnius, Garson and Case, op. cit., p. 292.

[35] Quoted in *IILS Bulletin,* no. 9, op. cit., p. 162.

[36] Donald Schon, *Beyond the Stable State,* BBC Reith Lectures, 1970.

[37] R.M. Cyert and J.G. March, *A Behavioural Theory of the Firm,* Prentice Hall, Englewood Cliffs NJ 1963, pp. 119–21.

[38] Ibid.

[39] R. Dubin, 'Management in Britain: impressions of a visiting professor', *Journal of Management Studies,* May 1970, p. 184.

[40] W.E.J. McCarthy, 'Changing bargaining structures' in S. Kessler and B. Weekes (eds), *Conflict at Work,* BBC, London 1971, pp. 91–2.

[41] Ibid., p. 90.

[42] Department of Employment Manpower Paper No. 5, *The Reform of Collective Bargaining at Plant and Company Level,* HMSO 1971, p. 85–6.

[43] Ibid., p. 80.

[44] Kuhn, *Bargaining in Grievance Settlement,* op. cit., p. 46.

The intention of this checklist is to provide a series of questions which may be of use in the review and reform of procedures. It is not a synopsis of the book, since the major conclusion drawn has been that a procedural structure should be tailored to the level of conflict, the environmental context and the organisation of the plant, and no checklist could possibly cover the many disparate situations which could arise.

I   Diagnosis: is procedural reform necessary?

It should be noted in regard to the following list that negative answers do not necessarily mean that procedural restructuring is not desirable for other reasons than procedural issues alone, e.g., a change in management organisation, a new pay structure, or a problem of workforce morale.

(1)   Has the number of grievances increased significantly?
(2)   Has there been a tendency for grievances to be settled at higher levels than in the past?
(3)   Is there a frequent failure to observe existing procedures?
(4)   Is there resort to industrial action before the procedure is exhausted?
(5)   Have there been complaints from workers, union representatives or junior management about the length of time taken to obtain decisions on grievances?
(6)   Have workers or union representatives complained that those making decisions, especially in the later stages of procedure, do not know enough about the issue being considered or that better qualified people are left out of key discussions?
(7)   Are there problems of morale within management as a result of inadequate authority, of being by-passed in grievance handling or of not being consulted when they have a potentially useful contribution to make?
(8)   Are there feelings amongst managers that there is not sufficient consistency in the settlement of grievances, and that undesirable precedents are being created which might have repercussions elsewhere?
(9)   Are workers, union representatives, or junior managers concerned at an apparent lack of flexibility in the way grievances are handled?
(10) Are there any other facets of industrial relations in the plant which may have a bearing on the grievance procedure?
(11) Has consideration been given to the use of a questionnaire for diagnostic purposes?

II   The procedural review and formulation process
(1)   In the course of the decision making process has every effort been

187

made to gather all available quantitative and qualititative data which is relevant to the operation of the procedure and to ascertain the possible reasons for difficulties?

(2) Has a wide spread of policy options been examined, or has the review consisted merely of potential amendments to what currently exists?

(3) Have the options been related to the overall industrial relations policy of the plant?

(4) In preparing new or revised procedures has adequate consultation taken place with union representatives and junior management?

(5) Has adequate consideration been given to the nature and amount of joint decision making that will take place?

(6) Have the discussions taken into account other industrial relations problems which may be affecting the overall labour–management relationship?

(7) Has consultation taken place with outside bodies, such as the parent company, the full-time union official, and the employers' association?

III The context of new procedures

(1) Have procedures been provided for all employees in the plant, irrespective of position or level, in accordance with the Contracts of Employment Act 1972?

(2) Has thought been given to the possible need for different procedures to meet special cases, e.g., different types of grievances, or to deal with employees whose position may require different treatment, e.g., shift-workers, non-unionised employees?

(3) Do the procedures reflect the reality of the authority structure as it exists in both union and management organisations? Put another way, if new procedures are developed, should there be concomitant changes in the authority and responsibilities assigned to various positions on both management and union sides?

(4) Do the stages of the procedure correspond with real and significant points at which knowledge and authority exist? Have 'ritual' stages been avoided?

(5) Has careful thought been given to the role of key managers in staff positions, especially personnel management?

(6) Are the procedures clear as to where a grievant should go with a complaint and who should be involved at each stage?

(7) Do the procedures help to clarify the issues, especially at the later stages, e.g., by requiring that a grievance be presented in writing or that the parties at the previous stage submit a written report on the outcome of their discussions?

(8) Do the procedures ensure that unnecessary delays will not occur, e.g., by specifying time limits, or that if delays do occur, that all relevant parties will be adequately informed as to the reasons?

(9) Has an attempt been made to differentiate between (a) the grievance procedure; (b) the negotiating procedure for the collective agreement; (c) the procedure for joint consultation? Given that some overlap between these procedures is inevitable, has this been recognised and provided for?

(10) Is it clear what actions should follow the terminal stage of the plant procedure, e.g., referral to industry procedure, conciliation, arbitration; and what actions are not condoned?

IV Implementation and dissemination of new procedures

(1) Has the procedure been distributed to every person at all levels who might be affected by it?

(2) Has an explicit programme of publicity been undertaken to communicate the letter and the spirit of the procedures?

(3) Have management and unions jointly or separately trained those who handle grievances in the operation of this particular procedure?

(4) Has provision been made for keeping records of grievance decisions and agreements arising out of the procedure, and for their use as a diagnostic device for evaluating the industrial relations situation?

(5) Has provision been made for regular reviews of the operation of the procedures?

Index

The authors

Dr Andrew Thomson took his first degree at Oxford and then undertook research for further degrees at Cornell University. In 1968 he joined the Department of Social and Economic Research at Glasgow University, where he is Senior Lecturer in Applied Economics.

Professor Victor Murray has studied for various degrees at the Universities of Manitoba, Minnesota and Cornell. From 1962 to 1966 he was Assistant Professor in the Faculty of Commerce at the University of British Columbia, and in 1966 he took up his present position as Associate Professor in the Faculty of Administrative Studies at York University, Toronto.

Other SAXON HOUSE Publications